# CHOICE MENUS

QUICK AND EASY MEALS AND MENUS TO
HELP YOU PREVENT OR MANAGE DIABETES

MARJORIE ANDERSON HOLLANDS, M.Sc., RD

MARGARET HOWARD, B.Sc., RD, P.H.Ec.

**Collins**

*An Imprint of* HarperCollins*Publishers*

*Choice Menus*
© 1993, 2007 by Marjorie Hollands and Margaret Howard.
All rights reserved.

Published by Collins, an imprint of HarperCollins Publishers Ltd.

Originally published in Canada by Macmillan Canada, an imprint of CDG Books
Canada: 1993
This Collins edition: 2007

HarperCollins books may be purchased for educational, business,
or sales promotional use through our Special Markets Department.

HarperCollins Publishers Ltd
2 Bloor Street East, 20th Floor
Toronto, Ontario, Canada
M4W 1A8

*www.harpercollins.ca*

Library and Archives Canada Cataloguing in Publication information
is available upon request.

Hollands, Marjorie and Margaret Howard
Choice Menus: Quick and easy meals and menus to help you
prevent or manage diabetes

ISBN-10: 0-00-200843-2
ISBN-13: 978-0-00-200843-3

RRD 9 8 7 6 5 4 3 2 1

Printed and bound in China

Photography by Hal Roth/Assisted by Paolo Christante
Food styling by Julie Zambonelli/Prop styling by Maggie Jones
Design by Sharon Kish
Photograph on page 144 by Emilia Stasiak/iStockphoto
Photograph on page 158 by Alex Shebanov/iStockphoto

# CONTENTS

........................................................................................

# FOREWORD

Diabetes is a serious condition, and although we know a lot about the complexities of the disease, the number of people who have been diagnosed with it continues to escalate. In Canada today, over 2 million people have some form of diabetes, and it is estimated that over 3 million people will have it by the year 2010.

Eating well and getting enough physical activity are central to both the prevention of type 2 diabetes and the management of all forms of diabetes. People who have diabetes or who are at risk for the development of diabetes, and even those who are simply interested in the benefits of healthier eating, may find it challenging to figure out what to eat, when to eat, how much to eat and how to prepare meals that meet all their nutritional requirements—not to mention offering interesting and appealing choices to family members.

Marjorie Hollands and Margaret Howard have readily accepted this challenge, and the Canadian Diabetes Association is pleased to have this revised and updated version of their highly successful *Choice Menus* as a resource. We hope you enjoy not only their delicious recipes, but also their innovative and supportive ideas toward a healthier lifestyle.

Donna Lillie
Vice President, Research and Professional Education
Canadian Diabetes Association

# INTRODUCTION

Maybe you've just learned you have diabetes or that your blood glucose is a bit too high. Maybe you've been told to lose some weight because there's a good chance you'll develop type 2 diabetes if you don't. Maybe you have a family member or friend who has diabetes and you don't know what foods to serve them. Maybe you want to be healthier and need to change your eating habits. Whatever the case, the revised *Choice Menus* comes to your rescue.

*Choice Menus* is not just another cookbook. It offers 94 healthy and tasty menus that you can "mix and match" to take the guesswork out of diabetes and meal planning. It contains more than 100 delicious, easy-to-prepare recipes to use with the menus. We believe that *Choice Menus* will find a place on your kitchen counter, not just on your bookshelf. It will be a ready source of inspiration when you ask yourself, "What will I eat today?"

Making food choices and planning menus can sometimes seem like a lot of work. *Choice Menus* will make this much easier. It is written for all those searching for a healthier eating style who may have said to their dietitian, "Couldn't you just write out a month of menus for me?" That was why we wrote the original *Choice Menus* back in 1993.

Many of the menus are quick and easy to prepare. Others are more elaborate, to choose when you have more time or are entertaining. Many need no special recipes. Other menus include wonderful new recipes we know will become family favourites.

All the menus are based on the Canadian Diabetes Association's Food Choice System as described in the *Beyond the Basics* meal planning resource. They are planned especially for someone with type 2 diabetes (although many with gestational or type 1 diabetes will find them very helpful as well). All recipes include Carbohydrate Choices so you can use them in menus you plan yourself. *Choice Menus* is not intended to replace the meal plan prepared by a dietitian. It is meant to be used *with* a meal plan, providing variety and fresh ideas. Meal planning and the Food Choice System can be confusing at first. The goal of *Choice Menus* is to make meal planning simpler.

Our menus do not replace nutritional counselling by a registered dietitian who is a diabetes educator. You are an individual, with your own food preferences and lifestyle. A dietitian can help

you identify problem areas and set realistic goals, then work with you to prepare an individualized meal plan. You will also need ongoing support and encouragement and someone to answer questions as they arise. But our menus and recipes are always there to give variety and fresh ideas.

If you have type 1 diabetes (insulin-dependent), your insulin action may require a different meal pattern than is used in our menus. Consult your dietitian or diabetes health professional before making any change.

Achieving and maintaining a healthy weight is very important in preventing or managing type 2 diabetes. *Choice Menus* allows you to choose the calorie level that best meets your energy needs and weight goal. Any day's combination of breakfast, lunch and dinner menus provides about 1,300 calories. Adding one or more snacks from the snack menus will increase your daily intake to 1,500 or 1,800 calories a day or more. This is ideal for the person with type 2 diabetes, for the person who needs to lose weight and for the person who wishes to adopt a healthier way of eating. See page 15 for more on how to use this book.

## PREVENTION AND MANAGEMENT OF DIABETES

We believe *Choice Menus* has an important role to play in preventing and managing diabetes. Over 2 million Canadians have diabetes (although 3 out of 10 don't know it), with an estimated 60,000 new cases diagnosed every year. Of those diagnosed, 90 per cent have type 2 diabetes and 10 per cent have type 1. It is a condition to be taken seriously.

The good news is that the onset of type 2 diabetes can be delayed successfully and sometimes prevented, and a diagnosis of type 2 diabetes does not need to lead to complications. The key is to keep blood glucose and cholesterol levels controlled and near normal.

Many diabetes pills, or oral hypoglycemic drugs, have been developed to increase insulin production or decrease insulin resistance. Most people with type 2 diabetes will need either pills or insulin eventually to maintain near-normal blood glucose levels. But exercise, diet (meaning the food you eat) and glucose monitoring are still the cornerstones of diabetes management and are important whether or not medication is prescribed. We hope that with the help of *Choice Menus* you will find it a bit easier to manage your diabetes effectively.

## ARE YOU AT RISK FOR DIABETES?

- I'm age 40 or older.
- I'm of Aboriginal, Hispanic, Asian or South Asian or African descent.
- I'm overweight, especially around the middle.
- I have a parent, brother or sister with diabetes.
- I gave birth to a baby that weighed more than 4 kilograms (9 pounds).
- I had gestational diabetes during pregnancy.
- I have high cholesterol or triglycerides.
- I have high blood pressure.
- I have impaired glucose tolerance (IGT) or impaired fasting glucose (IFG).

## What is diabetes?

There are really three kinds of diabetes: type 1, type 2 and gestational.

*Type 1 diabetes* is usually, but not always, diagnosed in children and teenagers, and occurs when the pancreas is unable to produce insulin. Insulin is a hormone that allows muscle cells to get the glucose they need for energy, so those with type 1 diabetes must take insulin daily, either by injection or by insulin pump, in order to survive. Only about 10 per cent of diabetes is type 1.

*Type 2 diabetes,* which is the type most people have, occurs when the pancreas, over a period of time, does not produce enough insulin, or when the body cannot effectively use the insulin it does produce. It is usually diagnosed in adults, although increasing numbers of children are being diagnosed in high-risk populations.

*Gestational diabetes* is a temporary form of diabetes that can occur during the last part of a pregnancy, when hormonal changes increase the body's demand for insulin. It affects over 3 per cent of pregnancies and increases the chance that both mother and child may develop type 2 diabetes later in life.

## Prevention of type 2 diabetes

Before people develop type 2 diabetes, they often have higher-than-normal blood glucose levels, but not high enough for a diagnosis of diabetes (7 mmol/L fasting). Studies show that people with *pre-diabetes* can cut in half their risk of progressing to full-blown diabetes by making changes in exercise and eating habits. Even mild to moderate weight loss can make a big difference. Losing just 5 to 10 per cent of your body weight has been shown to improve blood glucose and cholesterol levels as well as lower high blood pressure. If you weigh 68 kilograms (150 pounds), that would be 3.5 to 7 kilograms (8 to 15 pounds).

Maybe you don't have diabetes, but there is a history of diabetes in your family, and you've been thinking that you really should lose some weight and improve your eating habits. Maybe none of the above describes you, but you've been thinking it's time to eat in a healthier way and are looking for some direction. Whatever your goal, planning healthy meals is very important. A healthier lifestyle

**SYMPTOMS OF DIABETES**
- Unusual thirst
- Frequent urination
- Weight change (gain or loss)
- Extreme fatigue or lack of energy
- Blurred vision
- Frequent or recurring infections
- Cuts or bruises that are slow to heal
- Tingling or numbness in hands or feet
- Sexual difficulties

helps you feel better, have more energy and decreases your risk for chronic diseases such as diabetes, heart disease and cancer.

## THE IMPORTANCE OF MEAL PLANNING

Our goal in *Choice Menus* is to take the guesswork out of meal planning. For the person who has diabetes or is trying to avoid diabetes, careful meal planning has never been more important. Research makes it clear that keeping blood glucose levels as close to normal as possible can delay and, possibly, prevent the complications of diabetes.

The person with type 1 diabetes needs to balance carbohydrate intake with insulin and exercise to achieve good control. Someone with gestational diabetes is usually treated with a meal plan and careful blood glucose monitoring, and sometimes insulin, to make sure both mother and baby get the nutrients they need for the duration of the pregnancy. For those who are overweight and have type 2 diabetes or pre-diabetes, a combination of healthy eating and daily exercise, such as walking, is the key. As the British Diabetic Association says so well, "Eat less, walk more!"

If you are a lean person with type 2 diabetes, weight maintenance is likely your goal. You need to carefully balance food intake and exercise with your available insulin supply. Planning five or six meals over the day is one strategy.

In every case, we're talking *what* to eat, *how much* to eat and even *when* to eat—in other words, meal planning.

### Why is meal planning so important in type 2 diabetes?

Since this is the most common kind, let's talk more about it. Normally, before you developed diabetes, you ate food, you digested it, and nutrients (including glucose) were absorbed into your bloodstream and either used or stored for future use. As the blood glucose level rose after a meal, the beta cells in your pancreas immediately released a gush of insulin (called first phase), then continued to release insulin (second phase) until the glucose level was back to normal again. No problem—no matter what or how much you ate at a meal, your blood glucose never rose higher than 10 mmol/L and was always back to between 4 and 6 mmol/L a few hours later.

Then you developed type 2 diabetes. You still digest food in the same way, still absorb nutrients, but your first phase response may be sluggish or lacking, and you may not make as much second phase

### HOW IS DIABETES TREATED?

- Physical activity
- Healthy eating
- Weight management
- Medication
- Stress management
- Blood pressure control

insulin as before. In any case, your blood glucose rises faster and higher than it did before, resulting in too-high blood glucose levels two hours after a meal. This is perhaps when you discovered you had diabetes. Over the long term, too much blood glucose can lead to changes in the small blood vessels supplying the nerves and eyes and kidneys, and lead to the serious complications of diabetes.

These high blood glucose levels make the pancreas secrete more and more insulin. Your body's liver and muscle cells gradually become resistant to insulin, and your beta cells become exhausted. High after-meal insulin levels are also associated with an increased risk of developing heart disease, the most common cause of death in people with diabetes. So you need a strategy, the sooner the better, to slow the rise in blood glucose after a meal and to decrease your body's "insulin resistance" so that you can keep blood glucose in a healthy range (at or below 7 mmol/L).

## GUIDELINES FOR THE NUTRITIONAL MANAGEMENT OF DIABETES

The National Nutrition Committee of the Canadian Diabetes Association publishes guidelines for diabetes and healthy eating every few years, basing them on a review of current research on food and diabetes. The *Choice Menus* series has always followed these guidelines.

The current nutritional guidelines stress the importance of near-normal blood glucose and cholesterol levels, as well as the importance of healthy eating and a healthy weight. With the use of glucose monitors to measure blood glucose before and after meals, it is now possible to fine-tune meal plans and medication to preferences and lifestyle in a way that was not possible 10 or 15 years ago.

### Carbohydrate

When you have diabetes, the kind and amount of carbohydrate you eat in a meal is very important, since it has the most effect on the rise in blood glucose after a meal. Digestion releases starch and sugar from carbohydrate-rich foods and breaks them down into glucose, the simplest form of sugar and our main source of energy. Glucose passes into the bloodstream after meals, resulting in a rise in blood glucose (or "blood sugar") and a release of insulin hormone by the pancreas. So the total amount of carbohydrate you eat at a meal is very important (see Appendix I, page 180).

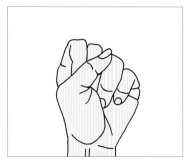

Figure 1

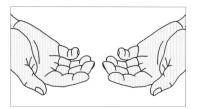

Figure 2

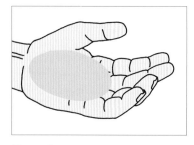

Figure 3

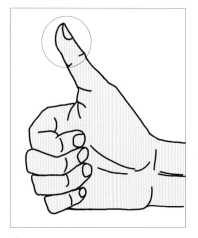

Figure 4

The Handy Portion Guide © Canadian Diabetes Association (2005) Reprinted with permission.

### Carbohydrate counting

Carbohydrate counting is one of several meal planning tools developed to help you manage your blood glucose levels. For most people with diabetes, carbohydrate counting is more flexible and simpler to use than an exchange system of meal planning. With "carb counting" you keep track of the amount of carbohydrate eaten at each meal with the goal of staying within a planned amount. In this way, carbohydrate intake is consistent throughout the day, and from one day to the next, making it easier to adjust your medication or insulin to match your activity and eating patterns.

So how do you count carbs? One way is the Plate Method, a simple visual guide to meal planning. Picture your plate half filled with vegetables and the other half filled with equal portions of starchy food and meat or alternatives. Add a glass of milk and a fruit to complete your meal.

Another visual method is The Handy Portion Guide, which promotes healthier portion sizes and teaches you to eat a consistent amount of carbohydrate at each meal. In this method you choose an amount of Grains & Starches to match the size of your closed fist (see fig. 1), as much Vegetable as you can hold in both hands (see fig. 2), an amount of Meat & Alternatives the size of the palm of your hand (and the thickness of your little finger—see fig. 3) and an amount of fat no bigger than the end of your thumb (see fig. 4). The Handy Portion Guide is a good method to use when eating away from home.

Some people use food tables (such as *Nutrient Content of Common Foods*) and label information to keep track of carbohydrate. When reading a food label, keep in mind that the amount of carbohydrate listed is for the serving size indicated. Does it match the portion you're having? Note, too, that the total carbohydrate amount listed includes starch, sugar and dietary fibre. However, fibre does not raise blood glucose levels and therefore must be subtracted from the total carbohydrate. The result will give you the amount of carbohydrate "available" to raise blood glucose.

*Beyond the Basics*, published by the Canadian Diabetes Association, is another meal planning tool that can be used to keep carbohydrate consistent from meal to meal. A serving of carbohydrate, or a Carb Choice, is defined as a portion of food containing 15 grams of available carbohydrate with so many Carb Choices planned for each meal (see Appendix 1, page 180).

You may find that using a combination of all of the above methods works best for you. Carbohydrate counting is an option for anyone with diabetes. However, for it to be effective, you must be willing to work closely with your dietitian and/or diabetes educator and test your blood glucose levels several times a day, before and after meals, on a regular basis. By keeping a precise record of your results, you can track what is happening and look for patterns. Understanding how meals, activity and medication affect your blood glucose levels means you will be able to lead a more flexible lifestyle.

We have tried to take the guesswork out of "carb counting," making it easier for you to get started. In our menu sections, each meal contains a consistent planned amount of carbohydrate, less at breakfast and more at lunch and dinner. Snacks vary in carbohydrate content according to size (see page 18 for details). Menus for special occasions (page 156) have the same amount of carbohydrate but a few extra calories. We have included weights and measures in both menus and recipes wherever we thought they would be useful, especially for high-carbohydrate foods. This should help those of you "counting carbs" to keep your carbohydrate intake planned and consistent (for further information, see Appendix I, *Beyond the Basics*, page 180). All recipes and menus were planned with *Canada's Food Guide* in mind.

Perhaps you have different carbohydrate goals than we have used in our menus. You may want to discuss this with your dietitian. Since each recipe shows Carbohydrate Choices as well as other nutrition information, you can plan your own menus, but let ours provide inspiration for variety and healthy eating.

## Fibre

*Canada's Food Guide* advises Canadians to eat 25 grams of dietary fibre a day, about twice as much as is eaten by most people now. Increasing fibre intake can reduce your risk of coronary heart disease by lowering the "bad" cholesterol in your blood, especially if it is high, and may also reduce your risk of type 2 diabetes and certain cancers.

There are two kinds of fibre in foods: insoluble and soluble. Both types have a special role to play. Foods that contain insoluble fibre are full of "roughage," so they are great laxatives that help keep bowels healthy and regular and may help prevent certain kinds of cancer. Insoluble fibre also acts as a barrier to digestive enzymes, thus slowing the digestion of a meal. Key sources of insoluble fibre are wheat

**FRUITS WITH THE MOST FIBRE:**

- apples
- blueberries
- cherries
- peaches
- pears
- plums
- raspberries
- strawberries

**VEGETABLES WITH THE MOST FIBRE:**

- broccoli
- carrots
- cauliflower
- corn
- green beans
- green peas
- rutabaga
- tomato

- Compare labels for fibre content.
- Choose high-fibre vegetables more often.
- Eat, don't drink, your fruit choices.
- Eat edible skin on fruits and vegetables.
- Have lentils, beans and split peas often.

bran and foods made with whole wheat, whole grains and seeds, and the skins of fruits and vegetables.

Soluble fibre is a bit different. After it is eaten, soluble fibre forms a sticky gel. This also slows the digestion of the starch in food, thus slowing the rise in blood glucose after the meal. Key sources are oat bran and barley, legumes such as lentils, dried beans and dried peas, and pectin-rich fruits such as apples, peaches, pears, strawberries and citrus fruits.

Getting 25 to 35 grams of fibre a day may seem a challenge (especially when the average Canadian gets no more than 15 grams a day). However, we paid special attention to fibre in our recipes and menus. The average amount of fibre in our breakfast, lunch and dinner menus is about 8 grams. Choose three and that adds up to 24 grams a day. Of course, some menus are higher in fibre than others, but all recipes list their fibre content.

### What about sugars and diabetes?

Sugar appears in many different forms in the foods we eat: glucose and fructose in honey and corn syrup; glucose, fructose and sucrose in fruits and vegetables; lactose in milk; maltose in beer. The sugar in the sugar bowl is pure sucrose, a sugar that occurs naturally in all living plants, and especially in sugar beets and cane sugar. When the juice from these plants is extracted and crystallized, the result is table sugar, which has been the sweetener of choice for generations.

Sugar has been seen as a forbidden food and a guilty pleasure for those with a sweet tooth and diabetes. Persons with diabetes have traditionally been told to avoid anything sweet because of the popular belief that it worsens diabetes control. This is not true and is just one of the myths about sugar and diabetes. Here are two others.

**MYTH:** Eating too much sugar causes diabetes.
**FACT:** There is no scientific evidence that links sugar intake with the development of diabetes. However, overweight people have an increased risk of developing type 2 diabetes whether they eat sugar or not, especially when there is diabetes in the family.

**MYTH:** Sweet foods are fattening because sugar is high in calories.
**FACT:** Any food eaten in excess of your energy needs can be fattening and cause weight gain.

Sugar itself is not fattening, nor are other carbohydrate-rich foods. The villain in high-calorie foods is usually fat, not sugar. Carbohydrate has less than half the calories of fat: 4 calories per gram versus 9 calories per gram. Anyone who needs to lose weight to avoid diabetes or to bring diabetes under better control would be wise to limit fat and increase exercise rather than act as if only sugar mattered.

At one time, the use of sugar from all sources was restricted. Today, the position of the Canadian Diabetes Association is that sugar need not be completely avoided but should be used carefully. The secret is to work it in, not add it on. Research shows that sugar can take the place of other carbohydrate in a slowly digested mixed meal without upsetting diabetes control (see the section "Other Choices" in Appendix I, page 180). And current guidelines recommend making naturally occurring sugars from vegetables, fruits and milk products part of every meal. *Beyond the Basics* encourages this and so do we. The *total amount of carbohydrate* eaten in a meal is more important than whether or not a food contains some sugar.

Our recipes call for a variety of nutritive and non-nutritive sweeteners (see Appendix I, page 180). Sugar is used in some recipes but in small amounts—for flavour or texture—and counts as part of the carbohydrate in that meal.

## GLYCEMIC INDEX

At one time, it was believed that all starchy carbohydrate foods digested slowly and all sweet foods containing sugar digested more rapidly. We understand much more about food and diabetes now, thanks to glycemic index (GI) research. Recognizing that carbohydrate has a major impact on blood glucose, and that we were being encouraged to eat less fat and more carbohydrate, Dr. David Jenkins and Dr. Tom Wolever, in their Toronto laboratory, addressed this question: Are all carbohydrate foods created equal? Their research studied the effect that various carbohydrate-rich foods had on after-meal blood glucose in an individual, then compared it to how that same individual responded to a standard meal of glucose or white bread.

In other words, glycemic index, or GI, measures how quickly or slowly a carbohydrate food is digested—and

## Go for
## Lower-Gi Foods

- Choose at least one low-GI food at each meal.
- Eat fresh fruits and vegetables.
- Choose parboiled brown rice more often than instant rice.
- Cook pasta just until al dente (tender but firm).
- Choose baked potatoes more often than mashed, boiled or instant.
- Eat whole grain, pumpernickel and oat bran bread more often than white.

carbohydrate foods are definitely not all the same! GI rates foods from 0 to 100, with glucose rated at 100 and white bread at 71. High-GI foods score 70 and above, medium-GI foods between 56 and 69, and low-GI foods 55 and below.

Foods with a high-GI value contain carbohydrate that is quickly digested and absorbed, resulting in a fast and high rise in blood glucose after a meal, followed by a rapid fall. Foods with a low-GI value contain carbohydrate that is digested and absorbed more slowly, resulting in a lower, slower rise in blood glucose followed by a more gradual decline.

Many factors decide what the glycemic index of a food will be. Here are some of them.

- *Food form.* Drinking a glass of fruit juice will raise blood glucose more quickly than eating a solid whole fruit.
- *Degree of processing.* The starch in a highly processed breakfast cereal, such as cornflakes, digests faster than the starch in a whole grain cereal, such as oatmeal. Parboiled or converted rice digests more slowly than quick-cooking rice.
- *Cooking method.* Starch in a mashed potato digests more rapidly than starch in a boiled or new potato.
- *Cooking time.* Overcooked pasta and vegetables digest more quickly than al dente (tender but firm).

Choosing low-GI foods along with a heart-healthy diet has obvious benefits for people with diabetes whose goal is a slower rise in blood glucose after a meal. Another benefit is that low-GI foods are bulkier, take longer to eat and are digested more slowly. This can increase your feeling of satiety, or fullness, so that you eat less—a plus whether your goal is weight loss or weight maintenance. With obesity on the rise and a major risk factor for heart disease and diabetes, it makes sense to include more low-GI foods in meals and snacks. When you look at foods in the low-GI group—split pea soup, baked beans, oatmeal porridge—it looks like good old-fashioned healthy eating!

The following table illustrates how different foods with the same carbohydrate content are rated.

| LOW-GI FOODS 55 OR LESS CHOOSE MOST OFTEN | MEDIUM-GI FOODS 56 TO 69 CHOOSE MORE OFTEN | HIGH-GI FOODS 70 OR MORE CHOOSE LESS OFTEN |
|---|---|---|
| skim milk | banana | watermelon |
| plain yogurt | pineapple | dried dates |
| soy beverage | raisins | instant mashed potatoes |
| apple, plum, orange | whole new potatoes | baked white potato |
| sweet potato | popcorn | parsnips |
| oat bran bread | split pea or green pea | rutabaga |
| rolled oats (large flake) | soup | instant rice |
| All-Bran | brown rice | cornflakes |
| converted or parboiled rice | couscous | Rice Krispies |
| cooked firm (al dente) pasta | basmati rice | Cheerios |
| lentils | shredded wheat cereal | bagel, white |
| kidney beans | whole wheat bread | soda crackers |
| navy beans | rye bread | jelly beans |
| chickpeas | pita bread | ice cream |
| | | french fries |
| | | digestive cookies |
| | | table sugar |

*Glycemic Index: A New Way of Looking at Carbs*, published by the Canadian Diabetes Association (2005). Reprinted with permission.

## "Surge" protection

This valuable research into how various foods affect blood glucose has helped us learn more about how to plan meals that will raise blood glucose more gradually, avoiding rapid surges in blood glucose. We have written *Choice Menus* with this in mind, and have based menus and recipes on the following principles.

- *Eat carbohydrate foods as part of a mixed meal*, one that contains protein and fat as well as fibre. Most carbohydrate-based foods already contain some protein or fat. Animal or vegetable protein and fats or oils digest very slowly, and also slow the digestion of the starches and sugars eaten with them. However, too much fat or oil in a meal can make it difficult for insulin to work effectively. So can too much carbohydrate at one meal. Moderation and balance are the secret.

- *Choose carbohydrate-containing foods that digest slowly.* Fruits and vegetables rich in fibre take longer to digest than their juices; foods containing soluble sticky fibre (oats, barley, legumes, pectin), as well as insoluble bran fibre, digest even more slowly.
- *Avoid cooking methods that speed up digestion of foods.* Choose whole grains and whole fruits, and don't overcook vegetables and pasta. Let your body do the processing.
- *Space meals at regular intervals throughout the day* so as to make better use of a limited insulin supply. Skipping meals then over-eating at the next meal is not a good idea. Research has shown that spreading food over several small meals a day can result in better blood glucose and cholesterol values after meals (see the Snacks chapter, page 145).
- *Limit the amount of starch and sugar you eat at each meal.* This is the most important factor if you are to achieve improved blood glucose control. You need a certain amount of carbohydrate in each meal to encourage your pancreas to produce insulin. And the brain requires a steady supply of glucose fuel to think clearly. But too much starch or sugar at one time may be too much for your insulin supply to handle. Balance and moderation are the key.

## Other concerns

### Protein

People with diabetes do not need any more (or less) protein than those without diabetes, but the guidelines do suggest that excessive intake should be avoided. However, anyone following a weight loss plan must be sure to get enough protein, as must vegetarians (see pages 86–87). Vegetarian recipes are listed in the recipe index at the back of the book under the heading "Vegetarian."

### Fats and oils

Many studies indicate that high-fat diets can impair glucose toler-ance and promote obesity, high cholesterol levels and heart disease. When saturated fat is reduced, all these problems reverse or improve. Thus the emphasis continues to be on reducing intake of *saturated fat* in meat, poultry and dairy products by choosing lower-fat foods more often.

And there is new emphasis in the current guidelines on avoid-ing processed foods, such as fast foods, packaged snacks and baked goods, that contain *trans fatty acids.* This fat is even more harmful than saturated fat since it not only raises the "bad" LDL cholesterol but also lowers the "good" HDL cholesterol. That's another good reason to read labels carefully when shopping.

Some fats are better for diabetes than others. *Omega-3 fatty acids*, found in fatty fish (see pages 190–191), are linked to heart health and may reduce serum triglyceride, a type of blood fat often elevated in diabetes. For that reason, guidelines recommend eating fish such as salmon or sardines at least once or twice a week.

Research indicates that *monounsaturated fats* (such as canola and olive oils) may have a beneficial effect on both triglycerides and glycemic control. Current guidelines recommend that these oils, and the soft non-hydrogenated margarines containing them, be used in amounts that avoid weight gain. Our recipes and menus do this.

### Sodium and hypertension (high blood pressure)

It is important to keep hypertension (high blood pressure) under control, especially if you have type 2 diabetes. The body uses sodium to regulate blood pressure and keep muscles and nerves operating properly, but too much sodium can lead to high blood pressure in some individuals. The recommendation is to limit sodium to 2,400 mg per day (about the amount in a teaspoon of salt). However, the salt shaker is probably not your main source of sodium. Most of the sodium in our diet is hidden in packaged and processed foods, another reason to read labels and compare or avoid. Attaining a healthier weight through balanced eating and regular physical activity is often enough to bring high blood pressure back to normal. Guidelines also advise avoiding or limiting alcohol and smoking as ways to reduce blood pressure. Our recipes give the sodium content per serving as well as many tips on how to reduce salt intake.

### Variety, moderation and balance

While it's important to understand diabetes and meal planning and to be able to use carb counting and low-GI strategies, one must always remember that healthy eating is still of utmost importance.

*Canada's Food Guide* has three key healthy messages: *variety, moderation* and *balance.*

- Enjoy a variety of foods from each food group each day.
- Choose lower-fat foods more often.
- Choose whole grain and enriched products more often.

## WAYS TO CUT DOWN ON SALT

- Choose fresh or frozen vegetables rather than canned.
- Look for canned foods with less sodium or rinse canned food to remove some of the salt.
- Choose hard brick cheeses rather than cheese slices and spreads.
- Choose unsalted popcorn and fruits and vegetables rather than salty snacks.
- Flavour food with herbs, spices, garlic, onion, lemon and lime rather than salt.
- Limit bologna, wieners, bacon, ham, salami, pepperoni and luncheon meats.

- Choose dark green and orange vegetables and orange fruit more often.
- Choose lower-fat milk products more often.
- Choose leaner meats, poultry and fish, as well as dried peas, beans and lentils more often.

These nutrition guidelines apply to people with diabetes as much as to other Canadians and are the basis of the *Beyond the Basics* resource, as well as our recipes and menus in *Choice Menus*. When you choose daily menus like the ones in *Choice Menus*, you know you are getting a variety of healthy foods in moderate portions, enjoyed in balanced meals spaced over the day. And that's eating well. We believe that eating a variety of healthy foods is a more effective and enjoyable route to good health than the regular use of nutritional supplements.

# HOW TO USE THIS BOOK

In the split-pages section that follows, you will find 30 healthy breakfast menus, 30 appetizing lunches, 30 delectable dinner menus and a variety of snacks in different shapes and sizes to fill the gap between meals. Any breakfast menu you choose plus any lunch menu plus your choice of dinner menu will add up to about 1,300 calories. Then add in one or more snacks during the day to fit your lifestyle and energy needs (see below). Simply separate the tabs where perforated to mix and match the menus

First, decide *how many calories* you want your meals to provide each day. Are you trying to trim away a few extra pounds? Or do you simply want to maintain your present healthy weight? Your age, sex, body metabolism and active or inactive lifestyle determine how many calories of food energy you use each day. No two people are alike, so it is difficult to say exactly how much you need. Ask your dietitian if you're not sure.

The table below shows average energy needs at different stages in life (based on Canada's Nutrition Recommendations, 1990).

### Calories Needed Per Day

| Age | Sex | To Maintain Weight | To Lose Weight |
|---|---|---|---|
| 25 to 49 years | M | 2700 | 2200 to 2400 |
| | F | 1900 | 1400 to 1600 |
| 50 to 74 years | M | 2300 | 1800 to 2000 |
| | F | 1800 | 1300 to 1500 |
| 75 and over | M | 2000 | 1500 to 1700 |
| | F | 1700 | 1200 to 1500 |

**For 1,300 to 1,500 calories:**
- Choose three meals (any breakfast, lunch and dinner)
  = 1,300 calories (and 11 CARB CHOICES)
- Choose three meals plus one 75-calorie snack
  = 1,375 calories (and 12 CARB CHOICES)

OR

- Choose three meals plus one 150-calorie snack
  = 1,450 calories (and 13 to 15 CARB CHOICES)

## Blood Glucose Testing

- Blood glucose is measured in millimoles of glucose per litre of blood and can be determined with a glucose meter. Blood glucose is usually tested just before and after meals. The recommended blood glucose level for all kinds of diabetes is 4 to 7 mmol/L before meals and 5 to 10 mmol/L two hours after meals.
- Your diabetes health professional will help you decide what pattern of blood glucose testing works best for you. What's important is not how many tests you do, but how you use the information they provide. The goal is to make changes to your lifestyle or treatment that keep your diabetes well controlled.

**For 1,600 to 1,800 calories:**

- Choose three meals plus two 150-calorie snacks OR three meals plus two 75-calorie snacks and one 150-calorie snack
  = 1,600 calories (and 13 to 15 CARB CHOICES)
- Choose three meals plus snacks worth 450 calories
  = 1,750 calories (and 16 to 18 CARB CHOICES). You get the idea.

The snack menus come in three different sizes:

- 75 calories when you just want a bite
- 150 calories to fit in mid-morning, afternoon or as a bedtime snack
- 300-calorie ones that are really small meals, great for snacks on active days

If you are a carbohydrate counter, you may want to consider how many carbs a snack contains as well. Look on the coloured tab of each snack menu.

*When* you eat is up to you and what's convenient. Most people find that spacing meals at intervals over the day helps keep energy levels high—and hunger pangs low. This pattern of eating also helps you avoid hypoglycemia, or low blood sugar, often a concern if you are on medication for diabetes. When meals are more than four or five hours apart, snacks come in handy. A planned snack is better than an unplanned snack! Ask a dietitian to help you map out a meal plan based on your usual day's routine. If weekends are a lot different than weekdays, you may want to have another plan in mind for them. Many people who work different shifts find it's simpler to have a plan in mind for each shift worked, as well as one for days off.

Everyone's different! Blood glucose monitoring may suggest that the amount of carbohydrate in the breakfast menus is a little too much for you and your insulin supply. No problem—just save part of breakfast and eat it a couple of hours later.

## A Month of Menus

The book's mix-and-match format allows you to plan meals to suit each particular day, at the same time keeping carbohydrate content of meals consistent. You probably won't use the menus in sequence, although we tried to plan them to avoid repeating the same foods—except when we knew you'd have leftovers on hand. You will, no doubt, find favourite menus to repeat over and over, or you may have the same breakfast two or three days in a row. It's your choice!

We have worked hard to streamline each recipe so you can minimize time spent in the kitchen but still make meals from scratch. The recipes in this book are simple. Most take no longer than 30 minutes to prepare. We have tried to use ingredients that are readily available. Those who are familiar with the format of our other books will remember that menus are the basis of these books. Each menu describes one serving. Sometimes you will be cooking for several people, other times for just one or two. To help you in your choice of menu, the majority of the recipes show the serving size as a fraction of the recipe (⅙ means one serving of a 6-person recipe).

**Food is one of life's great pleasures**

We believe that mealtimes should be high points in your day. To prove this, *Choice Menus*, first issued in 1993 and now revised, still aims to bring you a month of nutritious but delicious meal ideas, including more than 100 well-tested recipes. As before, some meals are simpler and easier to prepare; others take longer. Some menus need recipes; others do not. Many dishes can be prepared ahead; others are last minute. The first menus you come to need no special recipes or only simple ones described in the menus themselves. Other menus call for the more detailed recipes that follow.

Rather than group recipes as in a traditional cookbook, we have organized them according to the meals in which they are used. So you'll find a Breakfast chapter, Lunch chapter, Dinner chapter and Snacks chapter, each with information about the importance of that meal and tips for healthy meal planning. That way, all the recipes you need in a menu are there in the same chapter for easy use. When you're planning a meal for company, remember the Special Occasions chapter (page 157); it contains wonderful menus and recipes for entertaining, and each menu still fits into the diabetes dinner plan, with the same amount of carbohydrate (although a few more calories).

We hope this edition makes life a little simpler for you, by taking some of the guesswork out of meal planning and by helping you plan varied, delicious and healthy meals that are both good for you and good tasting. We firmly believe that eating well results in better total health. Enjoy!

# FOOD CHOICE VALUES OF MENUS

**Each breakfast menu provides about 350 calories\* and is based on:**
- 3 Carbohydrate choices (45 grams carbohydrate)
  2 Grains & Starches choices
  ½ Fruits choice
  ½ Milk & Alternatives choice
- 1 Meat & Alternatives choice
- 1 Fats choice

**Each lunch menu provides about 450 calories\* and is based on:**
- 4 Carbohydrate choices (60 grams carbohydrate)
  2 Grains & Starches choices
  1 Fruits choice
  1 Milk & Alternatives choice
- 2 Meat & Alternatives choices
- 1 Fats choice

**Each dinner menu provides about 500 calories\* and is based on:**
- 4 Carbohydrate choices (60 grams carbohydrate)
  2 Grains & Starches choices
  1 Fruits choice
  1 Milk & Alternatives choice
- 3 Meat & Alternatives choices
- 1 Fats choice

**Snack menus provide:**
- 75 calories (and 1 carbohydrate choice)
- 150 calories (and 1 or 2 carbohydrate choices)
- 300 calories (and 2 or 3 carbohydrate choices)

*\*with skim milk*

*For more about Food Choice Values, see Appendix I (page 180).*

½ small banana, sliced

1 shredded wheat biscuit OR cereal of your choice (page 187) with
½ cup (125 mL) low-fat milk

1 poached egg on 1 slice unbuttered whole wheat toast

coffee or tea (with or without milk)

½ can (10 oz/284 mL) half-fat mushroom soup and (5 oz/150 mL) low-fat milk

½ whole wheat bagel (30 g), toasted, topped with
⅓ cup (75 mL) salmon
lettuce and sliced cucumber

1 medium apple (or fruit of your choice, page 188)

½ cup (125 mL) low-fat milk

1 boneless loin pork chop (115 g raw), baked with Dijon mustard

1 medium baked sweet potato (150 g raw)

½ cup (125 mL) each steamed sliced zucchini and snow peas with
1 tsp (5 mL) soft margarine or butter

2 slices fresh pineapple (120 g) OR ½ cup (125 mL) canned pineapple chunks with juice,
    sprinkled with 1 tsp (5 mL) unsweetened coconut

1 cup (250 mL) low-fat milk

2 medium kiwi fruit
OR
1 small banana (with peel, 125 g)
OR
3 cups (750 mL) air-popped light popcorn
OR
⅔ cup (150 mL) black cherries

½ grapefruit

½ whole wheat bagel (30 g), toasted with 2 tbsp (25 mL) light cream cheese

coffee or tea (with or without milk)

**Ham on Rye:**
  2 slices rye bread
  sliced lean ham (60 g)
  2 tsp (10 mL) light mayonnaise
  mustard
  lettuce

celery and cucumber sticks

1 small banana (or fruit of your choice, page 188)

1 cup (250 mL) low-fat milk

1 chicken breast (125 g raw), skin removed, baked with 2 tbsp (25 mL) crumb coating

½ medium baked potato (85 g) with 1 tsp (5 mL) soft margarine or butter

½ cup (125 mL) cooked carrots

1 cup (250 mL) steamed cauliflower with ¼ cup (50 mL) *Light Parmesan Hollandaise* (page 92)

1 cup (250 mL) cut-up watermelon (or fruit of your choice, page 188)

1 cup (250 mL) low-fat milk

1 cup (250 mL) melon balls drizzled with lime juice

OR · · · · · · · · · · · · · · · · · · · · · · · · · · · · · · · · · · · · · · · · · · · · · · · · · · · · · · · · · · · · · · · · · · · · · · · · · · · · · ·

1 large peach (with skin and pit, 175 g)

OR · · · · · · · · · · · · · · · · · · · · · · · · · · · · · · · · · · · · · · · · · · · · · · · · · · · · · · · · · · · · · · · · · · · · · · · · · · · · · ·

1 medium pear (170 g)

OR · · · · · · · · · · · · · · · · · · · · · · · · · · · · · · · · · · · · · · · · · · · · · · · · · · · · · · · · · · · · · · · · · · · · · · · · · · · · · ·

½ cup (125 mL) unsweetened or *Microwave Applesauce* (page 75) with cinnamon and
2 tbsp (25 mL) plain low-fat yogurt

½ cup (125 mL) blueberries

½ cup (125 mL) wheat bran flakes OR cereal of your choice (page 187) with
½ cup (125 mL) low-fat milk

1 egg, scrambled in non-stick pan with ½ tsp (2 mL) soft margarine or butter

1 slice whole wheat toast

coffee or tea (with or without milk)

**Fruit and Cottage Cheese Salad Plate:**
  ½ cup (125 mL) low-fat cottage cheese
  ¼ pink grapefruit, sectioned
  4 strawberries, 1 kiwi fruit, ½ small banana, sliced
Arrange on leaf lettuce and top with ¼ cup (50 mL) fruit-flavoured low-fat yogurt with
  aspartame. Garnish with 1 tsp (5 mL) toasted sesame seeds.

1 whole wheat roll (30 g) with 1 tsp (5 mL) soft margarine or butter

1 cup (250 mL) low-fat milk

**Backyard Burger:**
  1 whole wheat hamburger bun (50 g)
  1 grilled hamburger patty (90 g) (½ cup/125 mL raw), topped with
  hot pepper rings, mustard, tomato slices, sliced onion, shredded lettuce

½ cob of corn

sweet red and green pepper sticks, cucumber slices, baby carrots with
1 tbsp (15 mL) *Handy Mayo Dip* (page 52)

½ cup (125 mL) cubed honeydew melon (or melon of your choice)

coffee or tea (with or without milk) OR diet soft drink

**Strawberry Smoothie:**
  5 strawberries with ½ cup (125 mL) low-fat plain yogurt, sweetener to taste and several ice
    cubes. Blend until smooth.
OR · · · · · · · · · · · · · · · · · · · · · · · · · · · · · · · · · · · · · · · · · · · · · · · · · · · · · · · · · · · · · · · · · · · · · · ·
¾ cup (175 mL) *Spring Rhubarb Sauce* (page 74) with 2 tbsp (25 mL) low-fat plain yogurt
OR · · · · · · · · · · · · · · · · · · · · · · · · · · · · · · · · · · · · · · · · · · · · · · · · · · · · · · · · · · · · · · · · · · · · · · ·
1 cup (250 mL) *Chilled Tomato Quencher* (page 51)
OR · · · · · · · · · · · · · · · · · · · · · · · · · · · · · · · · · · · · · · · · · · · · · · · · · · · · · · · · · · · · · · · · · · · · · · ·
**Pudding Sundae:**
  ½ cup (125 mL) light vanilla pudding, made with low-fat milk, topped with
  ¼ cup (50 mL) canned crushed unsweetened pineapple

## BREAKFAST · 4

1 cup (250 mL) cut-up honeydew melon

**Toasted Cheese Sandwich:**
    2 slices unbuttered whole wheat bread
    ⅓ cup (75 mL) shredded light Cheddar cheese

**Café au Lait:**
    ½ cup (125 mL) each strong hot coffee and hot low-fat milk

## LUNCH · 4

1 cup (250 mL) chunky vegetable soup

sliced turkey (45 g)
lettuce, tomato slices
2 tsp (10 mL) light mayonnaise, wrapped in
1 (8-inch/20 cm) whole wheat tortilla

½ cup (125 mL) canned peaches in light syrup (or fruit of your choice, page 188)

1 cup (250 mL) low-fat milk

## DINNER · 4

**Barbecued Chicken Vegetable Kebab:**
    boneless cubed chicken breast (100 g raw) marinated in
    2 tbsp (25 mL) *Herb Vinaigrette* (page 91)
Thread onto skewer with 4 mushrooms, 4 pineapple chunks and 4 chunks green pepper.

⅔ cup (150 mL) cooked parboiled brown or white rice

tossed green salad with 1 tbsp (15 mL) *Herb Vinaigrette* (page 91)

**Strawberries and Cream:**
    1 cup (250 mL) whole strawberries dipped in 3 tbsp (45 mL) *Honey Almond Dip* (page 141)

coffee or tea (with or without milk)

## SNACKS · 4
½ CARB CHOICE
75 CALORIES

6 low-fat tortilla chips (10 g) with ¼ cup (50 mL) salsa

OR

assorted raw vegetables with
⅓ cup (75 mL) *Yogurt Feta Dip* (page 100) OR 2 tbsp (25 mL) low-calorie Ranch dressing

OR

⅔ cup (150 mL) *Popcorn Munch* (page 152)

**Chilled Lemonade:**
    Stir together juice of ½ lemon, ¾ cup (175 mL) water, sweetener to taste and ice cubes.

OR

3 whole wheat crackers with 1 tbsp (15 mL) light cream cheese

2 stewed prunes with 1 tbsp (15 mL) juice

½ cup (125 mL) high-fibre wheat bran cereal OR cereal of your choice (page 187) with
½ cup (125 mL) low-fat milk

1 boiled egg

1 slice whole wheat toast with
½ tsp (2 mL) soft margarine or butter and 1 tbsp (15 mL) reduced sugar fruit spread

coffee or tea (with or without milk)

---

**Restaurant Toasted Western/Denver Sandwich:**
Ask for your sandwich with 1 egg, cooked with as little fat as possible, on
2 slices whole wheat toast, hold the mayo and butter.

assorted green salad with 1 tbsp (15 mL) low-calorie dressing (on the side)

1 carton (250 mL) low-fat milk

1 fruit of your choice (page 188)

---

3 thin slices lean roast pork loin (90 g) with
¼ cup (50 mL) unsweetened applesauce

1 medium baked potato (170 g) with 1 tsp (5 mL) soft margarine or butter

½ cup (125 mL) mashed turnip

1 cup (250 mL) cooked spinach or kale with lemon

1 serving (⅙) *Springtime Rhubarb Jelly Dessert* (page 138) with
¼ cup (50 mL) *Light Custard Sauce* (page 139)

coffee or tea (with or without milk)

---

1 small apple

1 cube (30 g) light Cheddar cheese

OR · · · · · · · · · · · · · · · · · · · · · · · · · · · · · · · · · · · · · · · · · · · · · · ·

**Cinnamon Toast:**
1 slice whole wheat toast
1 tsp (5 mL) soft margarine or butter, cinnamon and sweetener mixed together

1 serving light hot chocolate made with water (see package directions)

½ small banana, sliced

⅔ cup (150 mL) O-shaped toasted oat cereal OR cereal of your choice (page 187) with ½ cup (125 mL) low-fat milk

1 slice whole wheat bread with 1 tbsp (15 mL) peanut butter

coffee or tea (with or without milk)

½ cup (125 mL) each tomato soup and low-fat milk

**Grilled Apple Cheese Sandwich:**
    ½ medium apple, sliced
    25 g light Cheddar cheese, sliced
    2 slices whole wheat bread
Grill until cheese melts.

5 baby carrots

coffee or tea (with or without milk)

poached salmon (100 g raw) with lemon wedge

⅔ cup (150 mL) cooked parboiled brown or white rice

1 cup (250 mL) steamed green beans

½ cup (125 mL) strawberries and ½ kiwi fruit, sliced

1 whole meal digestive cookie

1 cup (250 mL) low-fat milk

½ small cantaloupe with
½ cup (125 mL) cottage cheese

OR

2 tbsp (25 mL) *Ham 'n' Cheddar Cheese Spread* (page 147) on 6 whole wheat soda crackers

1 medium apple

1 cube (30 g) light Cheddar cheese

2 oblong rye crispbreads

1 cup (250 mL) low-fat milk

**Chili in a Pita:**
  2 whole wheat pita bread halves (65 g)
  ½ cup (125 mL) *Chili con Carne* (page 103)
  shredded lettuce, chopped tomato and green onions
  ¼ cup (50 mL) shredded light Cheddar cheese

1 cup (250 mL) low-fat milk

1 serving (¼) *Chicken and Vegetable Bundles* (page 95)

⅔ cup (150 mL) *Minted Couscous* (page 120)

¼ cup (50 mL) *Chocolate Fondue* (page 169) with 10 strawberries

coffee or tea (with or without milk)

1 scoop (½ cup/125 mL) light ice cream in plain ice cream cone

OR

1 *Lemon Blueberry Flax Muffin* (page 35)

coffee or tea (with or without milk)

1 orange, sliced

½ whole wheat bagel (30 g) topped with
2 tbsp (25 mL) light cream cheese
1 slice (20 g) smoked salmon
sliced cucumber and tomato

coffee or tea (with or without milk)

1 cup (250 mL) French Canadian pea soup

1 cube (25 g) light Cheddar cheese
4 whole wheat soda crackers

1 nectarine (or fruit of your choice, page 188)

1 cup (250 mL) low-fat milk

1 serving (¼) *Skewered Beef* (page 99)
⅓ cup (75 mL) *Yogurt Feta Dip* (page 100)

⅔ cup (150 mL) cooked parboiled brown rice

1 cup (250 mL) sliced mushrooms sautéed in ½ tsp (2 mL) olive oil in non-stick skillet

1 cup (250 mL) steamed green beans

1 serving (¼) *Frozen Mango Dessert* (page 137)

coffee or tea (with or without milk)

¼ cup (50 mL) *Zesty Sardine Spread* (page 148) on
4 whole wheat Melba toasts

coffee or tea (with or without milk)

OR · · · · · · · · · · · · · · · · · · · · · · · · · · · · · · · · · · · · · · · · · · · · ·

2 *Peanut Butter Cookies* (page 154)

½ cup (125 mL) low-fat milk

1 peach, sliced

½ cup (125 mL) high-fibre wheat bran cereal with psyllium
   OR cereal of your choice (page 187) with
½ cup (125 mL) low-fat milk

1 slice unbuttered raisin bread, toasted, with 1 tbsp (15 mL) crunchy peanut butter

coffee or tea (with or without milk)

**Brown-Bag Peanut Butter and Banana Sandwich:**
   2 slices whole wheat bread
   1 tbsp (15 mL) crunchy peanut butter
   1 tsp (5 mL) light mayonnaise
   ½ small banana, sliced

celery sticks

1 kiwi fruit

1 cup (250 mL) low-fat milk

1 serving (¼) *Broiled Rainbow Trout with Fresh Tomato* (page 114)

2 small new potatoes with skin (85 g)

steamed asparagus with lemon wedge

1 serving (⅛) *Apple Bavarian Torte* (page 132)

coffee or tea (with or without milk)

**Blueberry Smoothie:**
   ½ cup (125 mL) blueberries
   1 cup (250 mL) low-fat vanilla yogurt with aspartame
   ice cubes
Blend until smooth.

OR · · · · · · · · · · · · · · · · · · · · · · · · · · · · · · · · · · · · · · · · · · · · · ·

1 medium pear (165 g)

7 dry-roasted almonds (10 g)

1 cup (250 mL) sliced strawberries

½ cup (125 mL) multi-grain flaked cereal OR cereal of your choice (page 187) with ½ cup (125 mL) low-fat milk

1 egg, scrambled with ½ tsp (2 mL) soft margarine or butter in non-stick pan

1 slice unbuttered whole wheat toast

coffee or tea (with or without milk)

2 whole wheat pita bread halves (65 g) topped with
2 tbsp (25 mL) salsa
½ cup (125 mL) shredded light Monterey Jack cheese
Broil until cheese melts.

1 cup (250 mL) cut-up papaya with lime juice (or fruit of your choice, page 188)

1 cup (250 mL) low-fat milk

2 slices (60 g) cooked lean cold roast beef

1 cup (250 mL) *Kathryn's Tabbouleh Salad* (page 89)

1 small whole wheat dinner roll (30 g) with 1 tsp (5 mL) soft margarine or butter

celery sticks, cherry tomatoes and zucchini slices

1 cup (250 mL) sweet black cherries (or fruit of your choice, page 188)

1 cup (250 mL) low-fat milk

1 slice toasted raisin bread with 1 tbsp (15 mL) light cream cheese

**Café au Lait:**
  ½ cup (125 mL) each strong hot coffee and hot low-fat milk

OR · · · · · · · · · · · · · · · · · · · · · · · · · · · · · · · · · · · · · · · · · · · · · · · · · · · · ·

**Fresh Fruit Sundae:**
  ½ cup (125 mL) light ice cream
  ½ peach, sliced, OR ½ cup (125 mL) blueberries

1 pear

1 whole wheat bun (50 g), split and toasted
1 slice Canadian back bacon (25 g)
sliced tomato and lettuce

1 serving light hot chocolate made with ½ cup (125 mL) low-fat milk (see package directions)

2 slices thin-crust whole wheat vegetarian cheese pizza (¼ 10-inch/25 cm pizza) with olives, mushrooms, green peppers and chopped fresh tomato

1 cup (250 mL) low-fat milk

1⅓ cups (325 mL) *Hearty Lamb Scotch Broth* (page 107)

1 small crusty whole wheat roll (30 g) with 1 tsp (5 mL) soft margarine or butter

1 cup (250 mL) cubed honeydew melon with lime (or fruit of your choice, page 188)

1 cup (250 mL) low-fat milk

1 cup (250 mL) sliced strawberries, layered with
½ cup (125 mL) low-fat vanilla yogurt with aspartame
2 tbsp (25 mL) *Multi-Grain Morning Granola* (page 26)

OR · · · · · · · · · · · · · · · · · · · · · · · · · · · · · · · · · · · · · · · · · · · · · · · · · · · · · · · · · · · · · · · · · · · · · · · · · · · · · · · · · · · · · · · · · · · · ·

1 *Cornmeal Cheddar Muffin* (page 153) with
1 tbsp (15 mL) reduced sugar fruit spread

coffee or tea (with or without milk)

2 slices fresh pineapple (120 g)

1 whole wheat English muffin (65 g), split and toasted
1 slice (30 g) part-skim mozzarella cheese, halved
1 tbsp (15 mL) reduced sugar fruit spread

coffee or tea (with or without milk)

*Microwave Mushroom Scrambled Egg* (page 72) on
1 slice whole wheat toast

sliced tomatoes and cucumber on lettuce
1 tbsp (15 mL) low-calorie dressing

1 medium apple (or fruit of your choice, page 188)

2 graham wafers with 1 tbsp (15 mL) light cheese spread

1 cup (250 mL) low-fat milk

1 serving (⅙) *Baked Chicken 'n' Mushroom Loaf* (page 93)

½ cup (125 mL) *Baked Orange Squash* (page 125)

1 cup (250 mL) steamed snow peas

½ cup (125 mL) light ice cream
½ cup (125 mL) raspberries

1 cup (250 mL) low-fat milk

⅓ cup (75 mL) *Hummus Dip* (page 151)
6 *Tortilla Crisps* (page 151)

OR · · · · · · · · · · · · · · · · · · · · · · · · · · · · · · · · · · · · · · ·

¼ cup (50 mL) *Veggie 'n' Hummus Layered Spread* (page 149)
½ whole wheat pita bread (30 g), warmed and torn into pieces

1 cup (250 mL) cut-up cantaloupe with lime wedge

**One-Egg Omelette:**
    1 egg, beaten with 1 tbsp (15 mL) water
    cooked in ½ tsp (2 mL) melted soft margarine or butter in non-stick pan

1 hot cross bun (50 g), split, toasted, unbuttered
1 tbsp (15 mL) *Light Citrus Strawberry Spread* (page 37) OR reduced sugar fruit spread

coffee or tea (with or without milk)

---

**Chicken Sandwich:**
    2 slices whole wheat bread topped with
    sliced chicken (60 g)
    2 tsp (10 mL) light mayonnaise, sliced tomato, shredded lettuce

**Fruit Cup:**
    ½ cup (125 mL) orange or grapefruit sections
    ¼ cup (50 mL) green grapes
    ¼ cup (50 mL) sliced banana, topped with
    1 tsp (5 mL) sunflower seeds

1 cup (250 mL) *Chilled Tomato Quencher* (page 51) OR 1 cup (250 mL) low-fat milk

---

1 cup (250 mL) (⅛) *Lentil Vegetable Spaghetti Sauce* (page 118)
1 cup (250 mL) cooked whole wheat pasta, topped with
3 tbsp (45 mL) freshly grated Parmesan cheese

1 serving (⅙) *Favourite Caesar Salad* (page 88)

**Café au Lait:**
    ½ cup (125 mL) each strong hot coffee and hot low-fat milk

---

2 *Cranberry Raisin Oatmeal Cookies* (page 155)

½ cup (125 mL) low-fat milk

OR · · · · · · · · · · · · · · · · · · · · · · · · · · · · · · · · · · · · · · · · · · · · · · · · · · · · · · · · · · · · · · · · · · · · · · · · · · · · · · · · · · · · · · · · · · · · · · ·

1 slice *Bruschetta Appetizer* (page 150)

**Café au Lait:**
    ½ cup (125 mL) each strong hot coffee and hot low-fat milk

¾ cup (175 mL) chilled fresh pineapple cubes
¼ cup (50 mL) cottage cheese

½ cup (125 mL) *Multi-Grain Morning Granola* (page 26)

**Café au Lait:**
   ½ cup (125 mL) each strong hot coffee and hot low-fat milk

1 serving (⅕) *Microwave Soup 'n' Sandwich in a Bowl* (page 59)

1 large peach (or fruit of your choice, page 188)

1 whole meal digestive cookie

1 cup (250 mL) low-fat milk

1 serving (¼) *Oriental Salmon with Onions* (page 113)

⅔ cup (150 mL) cooked broad egg noodles

1 serving (¼) *Snow Peas with Ginger* (page 126)

**Pear with Strawberry Sauce:**
   ½ medium pear, topped with
   ½ cup (125 mL) mashed fresh or frozen unsweetened strawberries
   1 tsp (5 mL) sweetener

½ cup (125 mL) low-fat milk

1 shredded wheat biscuit or cereal of your choice (page 187) with
½ small banana, sliced
½ cup (125 mL) low-fat milk

OR · · · · · · · · · · · · · · · · · · · · · · · · · · · · · · · · · · · · · · · · · · · · · · · · · · · · · · · · · · · ·

1 cup (250 mL) *Chilled Tomato Quencher* (page 51)

2 tbsp (25 mL) cottage cheese on
2 oblong rye crispbreads

double serving (1 cup/250 mL) *Microwave Autumn Oatmeal Porridge* (page 27), topped with
½ medium apple, chopped
dash cinnamon
granulated brown low-calorie sweetener
½ cup (125 mL) low-fat milk

coffee or tea (with or without milk)

⅔ cup (150 mL) *Pack-to-Go Chickpea Salad* (page 65)

1 *Raisin Bran Buttermilk Muffin* (page 36)

2 medium plums (or fruit of your choice, page 188)

1 cup (250 mL) low-fat milk

1¼ cups (300 mL) *Chili con Carne* (page 103)

⅓ cup (75 mL) cooked parboiled brown rice

1 serving (¼) *Waldorf Salad* (page 67)

1 small whole wheat dinner roll (30 g) with 1 tsp (5 mL) soft margarine or butter

½ cup (125 mL) low-fat milk

1 cup (250 mL) *Popcorn Munch* (page 152)

½ cup (125 mL) low-fat milk

OR · · · · · · · · · · · · · · · · · · · · · · · · · · · · · · · · · · · · · · · · · · · · · · · · · · · · · · · · · · · · · · · · · · · · · · · ·

1 *Raisin Bran Buttermilk Muffin* (page 36)

½ cup (125 mL) low-fat milk

1 cup (250 mL) citrus fruit sections

**BLT Muffin:**
  1 whole wheat English muffin (65 g), split and toasted, topped with
  2 slices crisp cooked side bacon
  lettuce, sliced tomato
  1 tsp (5 mL) light mayonnaise

**Café au Lait:**
  ½ cup (125 mL) each strong hot coffee and hot low-fat milk

1 serving (¼) *Open-Face Tuna Apple Melt* (page 63)

**Blender Smoothie:**
  ½ small banana and ½ cup (125 mL) fresh or frozen blueberries
  ½ cup (125 mL) low-fat plain yogurt or silken tofu
  ice cubes
  Blend until smooth.

1 serving (¼) *Herbed Citrus Pork Chop* (page 112)

1 microwave-baked sweet potato (150 g raw) with 1 tsp (5 mL) soft margarine or butter

1 cup (250 mL) steamed Brussels sprouts with lemon wedge

1 serving (¼) *Granola Apple Crisp* (page 133)

coffee or tea (with or without milk)

1 medium apple

¼ cup (50 mL) dry roasted peanuts

1 mandarin orange

1 serving *Hot Seven-Grain Cereal* (page 28), topped with
granulated brown low-calorie sweetener
½ cup (125 mL) low-fat milk

1 slice whole wheat toast with 1 tbsp (15 mL) crunchy peanut butter

coffee or tea (with or without milk)

1 cup (250 mL) *Black Bean, Macaroni and Vegetable Soup* (page 53), sprinkled with
1 tbsp (15 mL) freshly grated Parmesan cheese

1 *Cornmeal Cheddar Muffin* (page 153) OR 1 slice whole wheat bread
1 tsp (5 mL) soft margarine or butter

1 orange, sectioned and topped with
½ cup (125 mL) low-fat plain yogurt and
dash cinnamon

coffee or tea (with or without milk)

½ cup (125 mL) low-sodium vegetable juice cocktail

1 serving (¼) *Chicken and Asparagus Stir-Fry* (page 96)

½ cup (125 mL) cooked parboiled brown or white rice

1 serving (⅛) *Mochaccino Dessert Cake* (page 135)

½ cup (125 mL) low-fat milk

1 medium pear (170 g)

12 walnut halves (or 6 whole walnuts)

sliced cantaloupe or honeydew melon (80 g) with lime

2 frozen oat bran waffles, toasted,
⅓ cup (75 mL) low-fat plain yogurt
¼ cup (50 mL) *Spiced Blueberry Sauce* (page 31)

coffee or tea (with or without milk)

1 serving (⅙) *Warm Tortellini, Asparagus and Tomato Salad* (page 66)

4 rye Melba toasts

½ cup (125 mL) *Spring Rhubarb Sauce* (page 74) OR 1 cup (250 mL) whole strawberries

1 cup (250 mL) low-fat milk

2 lean loin lamb chops (240 g with bone, trimmed), broiled, OR 2 lamb medallions (130 g raw)

**Mint Sauce:**
    Mint leaves and vinegar, with sweetener if desired

½ cup (125 mL) *Barley Pilaf* (page 122)

1 cup (250 mL) cooked carrots

asparagus spears with lemon wedge

1 serving (⅙) *Rhubarb Fool* (page 138)

coffee or tea (with or without milk)

½ cup (125 mL) *Multi-Grain Morning Granola* (page 26) with
½ cup (125 mL) low-fat milk OR ½ cup (125 mL) *Homemade Vanilla Yogurt* (page 43)

1 nectarine or 1 peach, sliced

½ cup (125 mL) *Multi-Grain Morning Granola* (page 26) with
½ cup (125 mL) low-fat milk

coffee or tea (with or without milk)

1 serving (¼) *Southwestern Grilled Cheese Sandwich* (page 61)

celery and cherry tomatoes

1 nectarine (or fruit of your choice, page 188)

1 serving light hot chocolate made with ¾ cup (175 mL) low-fat milk (see package directions)

1 serving (¼) *Italian Beef and Vegetables* (page 104) served over
1 cup (250 mL) cooked fettuccine, sprinkled with
1 tbsp (15 mL) freshly grated Parmesan cheese

mixed green salad with 1 tbsp (15 mL) *Herb Vinaigrette* (page 91)

1 cup (250 mL) cubed honeydew melon with
¼ cup (50 mL) *Light Custard Sauce* (page 139)

coffee or tea (with or without milk)

*Microwave Ham 'n' Cheese Egg* (page 42)

1 serving light hot chocolate made with ¾ cup (175 mL) low-fat milk (see package directions)

½ cup (125 mL) unsweetened applesauce with cinnamon

1 serving *Hot Seven-Grain Cereal* (page 28) with
granulated brown low-calorie sweetener
½ cup (125 mL) low-fat milk

1 poached egg on 1 slice whole wheat toast

coffee or tea (with or without milk)

1 cup (250 mL) *Salmon Vegetable Chowder* (page 54)

1 small whole wheat roll (30 g) with 1 tsp (5 mL) soft margarine or butter

½ cup (125 mL) seedless green grapes

½ cup (125 mL) low-fat milk

1 serving (⅙) *Vegetarian Lasagna* (page 119)

1 serving (⅙) *Favourite Caesar Salad* (page 88)

**Chilled Cantaloupe and Blueberry Cup:**
   ½ cup (125 mL) cantaloupe balls
   ½ cup (125 mL) blueberries
   1 tsp (5 mL) lime juice
   ¼ tsp (1 mL) rum extract

1 cup (250 mL) low-fat milk

**Ham 'n' Cheese Sandwich:**
   2 slices whole wheat bread
   ¼ cup (50 mL) *Ham 'n' Cheddar Cheese Spread* (page 147)

1 cup (250 mL) low-fat milk

3 *Oat Cinnamon Pancakes* (page 30) with
¼ cup (50 mL) *Spiced Blueberry Sauce* (page 31)

1 slice (25 g) Canadian peameal bacon cooked in non-stick skillet

coffee or tea (with or without milk)

---

1¼ cups (300 mL) *Stove-Top Macaroni and Cheese with Roasted Tomato* (page 73)

1 serving (¼) *Waldorf Salad* (page 67)

herbal tea

---

1 serving (¼) *Curried Shrimp and Mushrooms* (page 117)

⅔ cup (125 mL) cooked parboiled brown or basmati rice

1 serving (¼) *Baby Greens with Oranges and Strawberries* (page 90)

**Café au Lait:**
    ½ cup (125 mL) each strong hot coffee and hot low-fat milk

---

2 cups (500 mL) *Popcorn Munch* (page 152)

**Frosty Mocha Shake:**
    ½ cup (125 mL) low-fat milk
    1 tsp (5 mL) each unsweetened cocoa powder and instant coffee granules
    dash vanilla, sweetener to taste and 2 ice cubes
Blend until smooth.

½ grapefruit

1 serving *Microwave Porridge for One* (page 27) with
granulated brown low-calorie sweetener
½ cup (125 mL) low-fat milk

1 slice raisin bread, toasted, topped with
3 tbsp (45 mL) cottage cheese
1 tbsp (15 mL) *Light Spiced Raspberry Spread* (page 38) OR reduced sugar fruit spread

coffee or tea (with or without milk)

1 cup (250 mL) *Lentil, Vegetable and Kasha Salad* (page 68)

1 slice rye bread with 1 tsp (5 mL) soft margarine or butter

**Pudding Sundae:**
    ½ cup (125 mL) light vanilla pudding made with low-fat milk, topped with
    ¼ cup (50 mL) *Spiced Blueberry Sauce* (page 31) OR ¼ cup (50 mL) canned crushed pineapple

1 cup (250 mL) low-fat milk

3 slices (90 g) *Garlic Lovers' Pot Roast* (page 101) with
½ medium potato (84 g), 1 small onion and 5 mini carrots, cooked

¼ cup (50 mL) *Light Beef Gravy* (page 173)

1 cup (250 mL) steamed broccoli

1 serving (¼) *Granola Apple Crisp* (page 133) with
¼ cup (50 mL) frozen vanilla yogurt

coffee or tea (with or without milk)

1 *Cornmeal Cheddar Muffin* (page 153) with 1 tsp (5 mL) soft margarine or butter

1 medium apple

1 cup (250 mL) low-fat milk

1 kiwi fruit

⅓ cup (75 mL) dry oat bran cereal, made with 1 cup (250 mL) water
granulated brown low-calorie sweetener
½ cup (125 mL) low-fat milk

1 *Lemon Blueberry Flax Muffin* (page 35) with ½ tsp (2 mL) soft margarine or butter

coffee or tea (with or without milk)

1 cup (250 mL) Italian-style minestrone soup

**Toasted Egg Sandwich:**
    2 slices unbuttered whole wheat toast with
    ⅓ cup (75 mL) *Crunchy Egg Sandwich Filling* (page 60)
    leaf lettuce

1 cup (250 mL) low-fat milk

1 serving (¼) *Salmon Loaf* (page 116) with 2 tbsp (25 mL) *Tartar Sauce* (page 116)

¾ cup (175 mL) *Light Scalloped Potatoes* (page 128)

1 cup (250 mL) steamed bok choy OR kale OR broccoli with lemon slice

1 serving (⅙) *Apple Cranberry Clafouti Dessert* (page 131)

1 cup (250 mL) low-fat milk

2 slices whole wheat bread with
⅓ cup (75 mL) *Crunchy Egg Sandwich Filling* (page 60)

1 cup (250 mL) low-fat milk

½ cup (125 mL) each orange and grapefruit sections and ½ small banana, sliced

1 serving (⅙) *Polenta, Cheddar Cheese and Spinach Bake* (page 39)

coffee or tea (with or without milk)

1 serving (¼) *Extra-Easy Pizza* (page 64)

1 medium apple, microwaved or baked with cinnamon

½ cup (125 mL) low-fat plain yogurt OR ½ cup (125 mL) low-fat milk

1 serving (⅙) *Oven Beef Stew* (page 105)

1 serving (⅙) *Spinach Orange Salad with Raspberry Vinaigrette* (page 163)

½ cup (125 mL) *Microwave Applesauce* (page 75)

2 gingersnaps (20 g)

1 cup (250 mL) low-fat milk

**Mango Milkshake:**
   ½ cup (125 mL) mashed mango
   1 cup (250 mL) low-fat milk
   ½ cup (125 mL) light vanilla ice cream
Blend until smooth.

3 *Buttermilk Pancakes* with
⅓ cup (75 mL) *Maple Syrup Apples* (page 33)

**Café au Lait:**
    ½ cup (125 mL) each strong hot coffee and hot low-fat milk

---

1 cup (250 mL) *Mushroom Barley Lentil Soup* (page 55) with
2 tbsp (25 mL) low-fat plain yogurt and chopped green onion

4 whole wheat soda crackers with 1 tbsp (15 mL) peanut butter

¾ cup (175 mL) fresh pineapple cubes OR 2 canned pineapple slices with 2 tbsp (25 mL) juice

1 cup (250 mL) low-fat milk

---

1 serving (⅕) *Mediterranean Chicken* (page 97)

½ cup (125 mL) cooked sliced beets with beet greens, if desired, with
1 tsp (5 mL) soft margarine or butter

½ cup (125 mL) *Spring Rhubarb Sauce* (page 74)

1 cup (250 mL) low-fat milk

---

2 *Raisin Bran Buttermilk Muffins* (page 36)

1 cup (250 mL) low-fat milk

1 cup (250 mL) sliced strawberries and kiwi fruit

1 serving (⅛) *Baked Asparagus Cheese Frittata* (page 40)

1 whole wheat English muffin (65 g), split and toasted, with
1 tbsp (15 mL) reduced sugar fruit spread

coffee or tea (with or without milk)

1 serving (¼) *Fruit and Feta Salad with Basil Buttermilk Dressing* (page 69)

1 whole wheat English muffin (65 g) with 1 tsp (5 mL) soft margarine or butter

3 low-fat spice cookies (20 g)

**Café au Lait:**
    ½ cup (125 mL) each strong hot coffee and hot low-fat milk

1 serving (¼) *Salmon with Roasted Cherry Tomatoes* (page 115)

3 slices (¼) *Grilled Polenta* (page 121) OR ½ cup (125 mL) cooked parboiled brown or white rice

1 cup (250 mL) green peas

mixed green salad with 1 tbsp (15 mL) light Italian dressing

1 cup (250 mL) sliced strawberries (or fruit of your choice, page 188)

coffee or tea (with or without milk)

**Grilled Mozzarella and Apple Sandwich:**
    2 slices raisin bread
    1 slice (30 g) part-skim mozzarella cheese
    ½ medium apple, sliced
Grill in non-stick skillet until bread is toasted and cheese is melted.

½ cup (125 mL) low-fat milk

½ cup (125 mL) chilled melon balls with lime

1 serving (¼) *Apple Cheese Breakfast Quesadilla* (page 41)

**Café au Lait:**
    ½ cup (125 mL) each strong hot coffee and hot low-fat milk

1 cup (250 mL) *East Indian Peanut Tomato Soup* (page 56)
7 whole wheat soda crackers

**Mango Smoothie:**
    ½ mango and ½ small banana
    ½ cup (125 mL) low-fat plain yogurt or silken tofu
    several strawberries
    ice cubes
Blend until smooth.

3 slices (90 g) *Butterflied Leg of Lamb* (page 108) with
3 tbsp (45 mL) *Red Wine Sauce* (page 109)

1 serving (¼) *Oven-Roasted Winter Vegetables* (page 123)

½ cup (125 mL) steamed leeks

1 serving (⅛) *Coffee Flan* (page 136)

coffee or tea (with or without milk)

1 whole wheat English muffin (65 g), split and toasted, with
1 tbsp (15 mL) crunchy peanut butter

1 cup (250 mL) low-fat milk

**Fruit Yogurt Parfait:**
    1 cup (250 mL) sliced strawberries, layered with
    ½ cup (125 mL) *Homemade Vanilla Yogurt* (page 43) and
    ½ cup (125 mL) high-fibre wheat bran cereal OR cereal of your choice (page 187)

1 *Raisin Bran Buttermilk Muffin* (page 36) with 1 tsp (5 mL) soft margarine or butter

coffee or tea (with or without milk)

3 *Ham Melt Mini Pita Pockets* (page 62)

assorted raw vegetables with
2 tbsp (25 mL) *Handy Mayo Dip* (page 52)

1 pear (or fruit of your choice, page 188)

1 cup (250 mL) low-fat milk

1 serving (⅙) *Rosemary Lemon Chicken* (page 98)

1 cup (250 mL) whole grain couscous (¼ cup/50 mL dry)

⅓ each sweet red, yellow and green pepper, cut into strips and sautéed in non-stick skillet
    OR 1 cup (250 mL) steamed spinach

1 serving (⅙) *Lemon Curd* with
⅓ cup (75 mL) *Strawberry Sauce* (page 140)

coffee or tea (with or without milk)

2 whole grain oats granola bars (23 g each)

1 cup (250 mL) low-fat milk

2 slices *Overnight Spicy French Toast* (page 29) with
⅓ cup (75 mL) *Orange Yogurt Sauce* (page 29)

coffee or tea (with or without milk)

1 serving (⅕) *Curried Chicken, Peach and Pecan Salad* (page 70)

4 rye Melba toasts

½ cup (125 mL) *Microwave Applesauce* (page 75)

2 gingersnaps (20 g)

1 cup (250 mL) low-fat milk

2 slices (90 g) *Stuffed Pork Tenderloin* (page 111)

1 cup (250 mL) steamed green beans with thyme

½ cup (125 mL) *Butternut Squash Casserole* (page 124)

½ cup (125 mL) light vanilla ice cream topped with
½ cup (125 mL) sliced strawberries

1 cup (250 mL) low-fat milk

1 hot cross bun (50 g), split and toasted, with
2 tbsp (25 mL) fruit-flavoured soft cream cheese

1 cup (250 mL) low-fat milk

½ cup (125 mL) sliced mango with lime

*Microwave Ham 'n' Cheese Egg* (page 42)

½ whole wheat English muffin (30 g), toasted
1 tbsp (15 mL) reduced sugar fruit spread

coffee or tea (with or without milk)

1 serving (⅙) *Garden-Fresh Tomato Cheese Pie* (page 71)

**Green Salad:**
    torn spinach, romaine and radicchio
    1 tbsp (15 mL) *Basil Buttermilk Dressing* (page 69)

4 whole wheat Melba toasts OR 6 *Tortilla Crisps* (page 151)

**Fruit and Dip:**
    1 cup (250 mL) whole strawberries
    1 slice (120 g) fresh pineapple, cut into wedges
    ¼ cup *Homemade Vanilla Yogurt* (page 43)

1 slice *Bruschetta Appetizer* (page 151)

1 serving (¼) *Balsamic Strip Loin Steak* (page 106)

1 serving (¼) *Sweet Potato Frites* (page 129) OR 1 small baked potato (84 g) with
2 tbsp (25 mL) light sour cream

1 serving (¼) *Minted Carrots and Snow Peas* (page 127)

½ slice watermelon (230 g with rind)

**Café au Lait:**
½ cup (125 mL) each strong hot coffee and hot low-fat milk

2 whole wheat pita bread halves (65 g) filled with
¼ cup (50 mL) *Zesty Sardine Spread* (page 148)
shredded lettuce and chopped tomatoes

1 cup (250 mL) low-fat milk

## Grill Time & the Cookin' Is Easy

6 large shrimp with 2 tbsp (25 mL) *Seafood Cocktail Dip* (page 160)
1 serving (⅙) *Herb-Rubbed Grilled Chicken* (page 161)
½ cup (125 mL) *Summertime Potato Salad* (page 162)
1 serving (⅙) *Spinach Orange Salad with Raspberry Vinaigrette* (page 163)
1 whole wheat dinner roll (30 g) with 1 tsp (5 mL) soft margarine or butter

½ cup (125 mL) *Watermelon Ice* (page 164)
coffee or tea (with or without milk)

## The Crowning Moment

1 cup (250 mL) *Spicy Tomato Wine Bouillon* (page 165)
1 chop from *Crown Roast of Pork* (page 166) with
½ cup (125 mL) *Wild Rice Almond Dressing* (page 166)
¾ cup (175 mL) *Balsamic Baked Mushrooms* (page 168)
steamed asparagus tips

Dip ⅔ cup (150 mL) assorted melon balls and 8 strawberries into
     ¼ cup (50 mL) *Chocolate Fondue* (page 169).
coffee or tea (with or without milk)

## A Festive Holiday Classic

Assorted crudités with 2 tbsp (25 mL) *Handy Mayo Dip* (page 52)
3 slices (90 g) *Roast Turkey* with ⅔ cup (150 mL) *Savoury Dressing* (page 170)
¼ cup (50 mL) *Light Turkey Gravy* (page 173) and 2 tbsp (25 mL) *Light Cranberry Sauce* (page 172)
½ cup (125 mL) mashed potatoes
½ cup (125 mL) French-style green beans with diced sweet red pepper
½ cup (125 mL) *Braised Red Cabbage with Cranberries* (page 174)

**Festive Raspberry Parfait:**
     ¼ cup (50 mL) *Raspberry Sauce* (page 140) with ⅓ cup (75 mL) light vanilla ice cream
coffee or tea (with or without milk)

## A Greek Taverna Dinner

¼ cup (50 mL) *Tzatziki* (page 175)
½ whole wheat pita bread (30 g)
⅙ *Moussaka* (page 176)
⅙ *Marouli Salata* (page 178)

1 orange, sliced and sprinkled with cinnamon
coffee or tea (with or without milk)

# BREAKFAST

Did you know the word breakfast comes from *break* (meaning "to stop or interrupt") and *fast* (meaning "to go without food")? How apt! By morning, after you've fasted for 8 to 12 hours, your brain and muscles need a fresh supply of glucose energy. Eating a balanced breakfast helps your body refuel. You'll concentrate better, solve problems more effectively, have the energy you need to get through your morning without yielding to mid-morning hunger pangs, and have better control of your weight. Furthermore, studies show that breakfast eaters consume less fat and more nutrients each day than breakfast skippers. A healthy breakfast is truly a healthy start to the day.

Those who have diabetes should not even think of skipping breakfast! If you have type 2 diabetes, you may have noticed your blood glucose is often higher before breakfast than before other meals—and eating breakfast helps bring blood glucose back to more normal levels. This first meal of the day can also be an experience rich in flavours and variety. Our recipes and menus will help you achieve a great breakfast cuisine that is both enjoyable and healthy. So yes, it is important to eat breakfast.

## BREAKFAST STRATEGIES

Plan breakfasts for the time available. Weekends are a perfect time for leisurely breakfasts. Family members can make and eat a meal at a relaxed pace. But weekdays are another matter—time is often short as family members go off in all directions. Night-before organization reduces the morning breakfast panic. Any or all of the following can be done the night before:

- Set the table along with any non-perishable breakfast items.
- Plan coffee preparation, maybe with an automatic timer.
- Have ready-to-eat whole grain cold cereals handy.
- Organize hot cereals for microwaving (see **Hot Seven-Grain Cereal**, page 28).

Make breakfast so exciting that you could never think of missing it.

*Opposite:* Overnight Spicy French Toast with Orange Yogurt Sauce (page 29)

## THE IMPORTANCE OF FRUIT

Fruits are packed with vitamins, minerals and fibre. They are also low in fat, low in calories and most have a low glycemic index (pages 9–11). New research suggests those eating more fruit have a lower risk of heart disease, stroke, diabetes and some types of cancer. So our menus include lots of fruit ideas to encourage more fruit in meals, starting with breakfast. We have a marvellous variety of healthy choices to choose from year-round, although fruits in season are usually more economical choices. The best vitamin C selections include oranges, grapefruit, tangerines, kiwifruit, pineapple, honeydew melon, mangoes, apricots, cantaloupe and papaya. Fibre-rich, low-GI fruits include blueberries, strawberries, raspberries, apples, bananas, pears and cherries. All are found in our menus. Realizing that you won't always have on hand the fruit specified in a menu, we've included a list of alternate fruit portions in Appendix III (page 188), each equal to 1 FRUITS or 1 CARB CHOICE.

### Fruit or juice?

"Eat your fruit, don't drink it." While fruit juices do contain vitamins and minerals, valuable fibre is lost during processing. Adding it back later isn't the same thing. Whole raw fruits contain both soluble and insoluble fibre. Since it takes more time to digest the fibre in raw fruit, the fruit's natural sugar is released more slowly and gradually than when you drink juice. This, in turn, results in a slower and more gradual increase in blood glucose levels. And there is an additional dividend: you'll feel more satisfied after eating a piece of fruit than after drinking a glass of juice. However, if fresh fruit is unavailable, frozen orange juice is better than no fruit at all. If you do happen to drink a small glass of juice, sip it slowly.

## WHOLE GRAIN CEREALS

Cereals are the foundation of a healthy breakfast. The whole grains found in cereals can be thought of as the "great regulators" because of their action on blood glucose, blood cholesterol, regularity and appetite. If ever there were a "magic bullet" food, cereals may be it!

Breakfast cereals containing whole grains, such as wheat, oats and barley, digest more slowly than refined rice or corn cereals. This results in a more gradual rise in blood glucose, giving you a more satisfied feeling. Wheat and oat bran (the outer layer of the whole kernel) add extra fibre to keep the digestive system healthy and to promote regularity. Eating oat bran as part of a low-fat diet helps lower cholesterol levels. Flaxseeds not only give cereals a pleasant nutty flavour but they also add a nutritional boost.

Being refined may be fine in some circles, but not if you're a breakfast cereal! Refining removes the fibre-rich bran coating of the grain, as well as the nutrient-packed germ, so the health benefits of whole grains are largely lost. Check labels; look for the words "whole grain" or "high source of fibre" when choosing a packaged ready-to-eat cereal. The first ingredient listed (the one that weighs the most) should be the whole grain component, not the sugar. The amount of fibre per serving is found on the nutrition facts panel. Compare when you shop.

Our breakfast menus use a variety of packaged ready-to-eat whole grain and high-fibre cereals. Since everyone has a favourite, when you see the words *"or cereal of your choice"* in a menu, refer to Appendix II, page 187, for a listing of cereals with serving sizes equal to 1 GRAINS & STARCHES or 1 CARB CHOICE. This is the amount of cereal containing 15 grams of available carbohydrate (total grams carbohydrate minus grams fibre). Use our recipes for **Multi-Grain Morning Granola** (page 26) and **Hot Seven-Grain Cereal** (page 28) to create your own "bulk mixes" rich in whole grain and bran. They are easy to prepare in single servings. And all the ingredients can be found in bulk and health food stores, so you can buy just the amounts you need.

## BREADS AND ALL THAT STUFF

Today there is an endless variety of breads, buns, bagels, muffins and the like available. When shopping for these bakery products, the words "whole wheat" and "high fibre" on the label suggest a wise choice. Those labelled "multi-grain," "100% wheat" or "seven grain" are often not whole grains but have white flour as their base. Colour is not an indication of whole grain content either, since molasses or caramel may have been added for colour. Enriched wheat flour is white flour with added nutrients. Check the ingredient list on labels and choose products listing whole grain flour first.

Having a small scale on your kitchen counter lets you judge serving sizes. 1 GRAINS & STARCHES CHOICE (or 1 CARB CHOICE) is equal to 1 ounce (30 grams) of bread containing 15 grams of carbohydrate (total minus fibre*). Some bagels, both whole wheat and white, weigh 2 ounces (60 grams), so they count as 2 CARB CHOICES. Many weigh up to 4 ounces (120 grams), so they would count as 4 CARB CHOICES! Since bagels tend not to be sold in labelled packages, it's best they be weighed.

| **Nutrition Facts** | |
|---|---|
| Per 90 g serving (2 slices) | |
| **Amount** | **% Daily Value** |
| **Calories** 170 | |
| **Fat** 2.7 g | 4 % |
| Saturated 0.5 g + Trans 0 g | 5 % |
| **Cholesterol** 0 mg | |
| **Sodium** 200 mg | 8 % |
| **Carbohydrate** 36 g | 13 % |
| Fibre 6 g | 24 % |
| Sugars 3 g | |
| **Protein** 8 g | |
| Vitamin A 1 % Vitamin C | 0 % |
| Calcium 2 % Iron | 16 % |

*Since fibre does not raise blood glucose (although it's classed as carbohydrate), always subtract grams of fibre from grams total carbohydrate, as shown on the food label, to determine the grams of available carbohydrate that do increase blood glucose.*

### Margarine or butter?

Our breakfast menus don't use much of either! A good-tasting bread or warm muffin needs little if any margarine or butter for flavour—thus reducing both fat and calories. The same can be said for a non-stick pan. Each breakfast menu contains 1 FATS CHOICE, but often it's hidden in other foods.

Non-hydrogenated soft tub margarine appears to be a better choice than butter because it contains much less saturated fat. And whenever a recipe calls for melted margarine, use a healthy oil like canola or olive oil instead. But remember, even oils and margarine are fats that should be used only in small amounts. Still want more flavour? Use a small amount of a reduced sugar fruit spread.

### Fruit spreads with less sugar

A fruit spread labelled "lower in sugar" or "sugar reduced" must contain 25 per cent less sugar than a regular jam. You may find more than one kind at the grocery store. All will contain fruit sweetened with a combination of concentrated fruit juice (usually white grape juice) and a non-nutritive sweetener such as sucralose, aspartame or sorbitol. Check the Nutrition Facts panel for the *amount of carbohydrate per tablespoon (15 mL)*. To qualify as an EXTRA, a serving should not contain more than 5 grams of sugar and 20 calories. So read labels carefully. Remember that EXTRA doesn't mean "free."

Making your own fruit spreads can be rewarding, both for the taste and savings. Try **Light Citrus Strawberry Spread** (page 37) and **Light Spiced Raspberry Spread** (page 38).

## Milk and Yogurt

The six nutrients necessary for healthy adult bones—calcium, vitamin D, protein, phosphorus, vitamin A and magnesium—are all contained in milk in a form easily absorbed by our bodies. So all our breakfast menus include milk. We have milk as a beverage, milk on cereal, milk as a recipe ingredient, as well as milk in tea or coffee. In all instances, milk is no-fat skim or 1%, your choice. Or you may prefer a soy beverage, unflavoured and fortified with calcium and vitamin D. Either way, 1 cup (250 mL) is 1 MILK & ALTERNATIVES or 1 CARB CHOICE.

Along with its satisfying creamy texture and subtly tart flavour, yogurt offers an impressive nutritional profile of calcium, B vitamins and minerals. Many who cannot tolerate milk find they can eat yogurt. Low-fat yogurt appears in many of our menus. Try **Homemade Vanilla Yogurt** (page 43) layered with fresh fruit and high-fibre cereal (Breakfast Menu 28).

## The Best Nutritional Bang

Since breakfast is such an important meal, make it a healthy start to your day. For carbohydrate and fibre, include servings of fresh fruit along with whole grains, such as cereals, whole wheat toast or healthy muffins. Spread peanut butter on whole wheat toast for protein. Use a reduced sugar fruit spread instead of margarine or butter to reduce fat intake. Add milk to cereal for calcium. This kind of breakfast gives us nutrition while limiting total fat, saturated fat and sodium consumption. Breakfast already has you on the road to healthy eating!

## HIGH FIBRE

**Breakfast Menus 14, 19**
**Dinner Menus 16, 22**
**Snack Menus 11, 18**

**Prep** · 10 minutes
**Cook** · 8 to 10 minutes
**Yield** · about 7 servings
3½ cups (875 mL)

........................................

**Each Serving** · ½ cup (125 mL)
Carb choices                          1½
Meat & Alternatives choice  ½
Fats choices                            2

........................................

**Carbohydrate** 30 g
   Fibre 5 g
**Protein** 7 g
**Fat** 9 g
   Saturated 1 g
**Sodium** 56 mg
**Calories** 213

Fat and sugar are reduced in this version of fibre-rich granola. As a cereal it makes a great start to anybody's day. It also makes a great "crisp" for fruit desserts. See page 133 in our Dinner chapter for *Granola Apple Crisp* and *Granola Blueberry Crisp*.

| | | |
|---|---|---|
| 1½ cups | large flake rolled oats | 375 mL |
| ½ cup | natural bran | 125 mL |
| ¼ cup | wheat germ | 50 mL |
| 3 tbsp | chopped almonds | 45 mL |
| 2 tbsp | liquid honey | 25 mL |
| 2 tbsp | soft margarine or butter | 25 mL |
| 2 tbsp | water | 25 mL |
| ¼ cup | skim milk powder | 50 mL |
| ⅓ cup | raisins | 75 mL |
| ¼ cup | sunflower seeds | 50 mL |
| 1 tsp | cinnamon | 5 mL |

In large bowl, combine oats, bran, wheat germ and almonds.

In saucepan, heat honey, margarine and water until hot. Stir into oat mixture. Spread on baking pan.

Bake in 350°F (180°C) oven for 8 to 10 minutes or until lightly toasted; stir once. Let cool completely.

Stir in skim milk powder, raisins, sunflower seeds and cinnamon. Store in tightly sealed container.

# MICROWAVE PORRIDGE FOR ONE

Kick-start your day with this rich-in-soluble-fibre hot cereal. Oatmeal lovers will appreciate the taste and consistency of this porridge as much as its fast preparation time. Be sure to check out the variations.

| ½ cup | water | 125 mL |
| ¼ cup | quick-cooking rolled oats | 50 mL |
| ¼ tsp | vanilla or maple extract | 1 mL |

In microwave-safe serving bowl, combine water, rolled oats and vanilla. Microwave, uncovered and stirring once, on High (100%) for 1½ minutes or until bubbly. Let stand for 2 minutes or until desired consistency. Stir and serve.

For a thinner porridge, add 1 to 2 tbsp (15 to 25 mL) more water.

## VARIATIONS

*Microwave Autumn Oatmeal Porridge:* Replace vanilla extract with 1 tbsp (15 mL) sunflower, pumpkin or sesame seeds. Cook as above.

*Stove-Top Porridge for Four:* In saucepan, combine 1 cup (250 mL) rolled oats and 2 cups (500 mL) water; cook over medium heat, stirring occasionally, for 5 minutes or until thickened. Cover and remove from heat. Stir in 1 tsp (5 mL) vanilla extract. Let stand for a few minutes before serving. Yields 4 servings, 2 cups (500 mL).

**Breakfast Menu 22**

. . . . . . . . . . . . . . . . . . . . . . . . . . . . . . . .

**MICROWAVE PORRIDGE FOR ONE:**
**Prep** • under 5 minutes
**Cook** • about 2 minutes
**Yield** • 1 serving

**Each Serving** • ½ cup (125 mL)
Carb choice                              1

**Carbohydrate** 14 g
  Fibre 2 g
**Protein** 3 g
**Fat** 1 g
  Saturated 0 g
**Sodium** 4 mg
**Calories** 79

**Breakfast Menu 15**

. . . . . . . . . . . . . . . . . . . . . . . . . . . . . . . .

**MICROWAVE AUTUMN OATMEAL PORRIDGE:**
**Each Serving** • ½ cup (125 mL)
Carb choice                              1
Fats choice                              1

**Carbohydrate** 19 g
  Fibre 3 g
**Protein** 5 g
**Fat** 6 g
  Saturated 1 g
**Sodium** 5 mg
**Calories** 144

A superb way to start the day! Cook in the microwave or on the stove top in single or family-size servings.

### DRY CEREAL MIX:

| | | |
|---|---|---|
| 1 cup | large-flake rolled oats | 250 mL |
| 1 cup | three-grain cereal (see Tip) | 250 mL |
| 1 cup | whole wheat flakes | 250 mL |
| ½ cup | each oat bran and cream of wheat | 125 mL |

Combine rolled oats, three-grain cereal, whole wheat flakes, oat bran and cream of wheat. Store in tightly sealed container.

### For Single Serving:

*Microwave:* In microwave-safe serving bowl, combine ¼ cup (50 mL) **Dry Cereal Mix** and ¾ cup (175 mL) water. Microwave, uncovered, on High (100%) for 2 minutes; stir. Microwave on Low (30%) for 3 minutes. Let stand for 2 minutes. Stir and serve.

*Stove top:* In saucepan, combine ingredients as above. Bring to a boil; reduce heat to medium-low and cook, stirring occasionally, for 5 minutes or until desired consistency. Cover and remove from heat. Let stand for a few minutes, then stir and serve.

- ◉ *Look for a combination of cracked wheat, cracked rye and whole flax when choosing a three-grain cereal.*
- ◉ *Wheat flakes are whole wheat berries that have been flattened between rollers. They resemble rolled oats and can be used in much the same way.*

---

**Breakfast Menus 17, 20**

..................................

**Prep** · 5 minutes for dry mix
**Cook** · 5 minutes for 1 serving
**Yield** · 16 servings, 4 cups (1 L)

..................................

**Each Serving**
Dry mix (¼ cup/50 mL)
Cooked (¾ cup/175 mL)
Carb choice                    1
Meat & Alternatives choice   ½

..................................

**Carbohydrate** 22 g
  Fibre 3 g
**Protein** 4 g
**Fat** 1 g
  Saturated 0 g
**Sodium** 8 mg
**Calories** 112

# Overnight Spicy French Toast with Orange Yogurt Sauce

Does making French toast on a busy morning seem like too much work? Our version allows you to prepare it the night before. Plus, it gets a perk-up with this tangy *Orange Yogurt Sauce*.

| | | |
|---|---|---|
| 2 | eggs | 2 |
| ½ cup | low-fat milk | 125 mL |
| 2 tsp | granular low-calorie sweetener with sucralose | 10 mL |
| 1 tsp | grated orange rind | 5 mL |
| ½ tsp | vanilla extract | 2 mL |
| ¼ tsp | ground nutmeg | 1 mL |
| 4 | slices whole wheat bread (120 g total) | 4 |
| 1 tsp | soft margarine or butter | 5 mL |
| Pinch | cinnamon | Pinch |

In small bowl, whisk together eggs, milk, sweetener, orange rind, vanilla and nutmeg until blended.

Place bread slices in large shallow baking dish; pour egg mixture evenly over each slice, turning to coat. Sprinkle with cinnamon. Cover and refrigerate overnight.

In large non-stick skillet, heat margarine over medium-high heat; add bread slices and cook for 2 minutes per side or until golden.

## Orange Yogurt Sauce:

| | | |
|---|---|---|
| ⅔ cup | low-fat plain yogurt | 150 mL |
| 4 tsp | frozen orange juice concentrate | 20 mL |
| Pinch | ground nutmeg | Pinch |
| | sweetener to taste | |

In small bowl, whisk together yogurt, orange juice concentrate and nutmeg. Flavour with sweetener as desired.

---

**Breakfast Menu 29**

### French Toast:
**Prep** · 10 minutes
**Refrigerate** · overnight
**Cook** · about 4 minutes
**Yield** · 2 servings, 4 slices

**Each Serving** · ½ recipe (2 slices)
Carb choices 2
Meat & Alternatives choice 1
Fats choices 1½

**Carbohydrate** 32 g
  Fibre 4 g
**Protein** 14 g
**Fat** 10 g
  Saturated 3 g
**Sodium** 414 mg
**Calories** 268

### Sauce:
**Prep** · 5 minutes
**Yield** · 2 servings,
       ⅔ cup (150 mL) sauce

**Each Serving** · ⅓ cup (75 mL)
Carb choice ½

**Carbohydrate** 11 g
  Fibre 0 g
**Protein** 4 g
**Fat** 0 g
**Sodium** 58 mg
**Calories** 300

...........................................

**Prep** · 10 minutes
**Cook** · about 5 minutes
            per pancake
**Yield** · 5 servings, 15 pancakes

...........................................

**Each Serving** · 3 pancakes
Carb choices                     2½
Meat & Alternatives choice    1
Fats choice                         1

...........................................

**Carbohydrate** 47 g
    Fibre 6 g
**Protein** 11 g
**Fat** 9 g
    Saturated 1 g
**Sodium** 375 mg
**Calories** 300

## OAT CINNAMON PANCAKES

Making pancakes from scratch lets you control the ingredients. Whole wheat flour and rolled oats make these pancakes an excellent source of fibre. The pancake mix recipe can be doubled or tripled and stored for additional batches.

| | | |
|---|---|---:|
| 1½ cups | low-fat milk | 375 mL |
| 1 | egg | 1 |
| 2 tbsp | canola oil | 25 mL |
| 1 tsp | vanilla extract | 5 mL |
| 2½ cups | *Oat Cinnamon Pancake Mix* | 625 mL |

To make pancakes: In glass measure, whisk together milk, egg, oil and vanilla. Place pancake mix in bowl; pour egg mixture into dry mixture and stir just until dry ingredients are moistened (don't worry about lumps).

Heat large non-stick skillet over medium heat until hot (a drop of water will sizzle). Spray with non-stick cooking spray. Drop batter by ¼-cup (50 mL) measure onto pan. Cook pancakes for 3 minutes or until bubbles break on top and underside is golden brown; turn and cook other side until golden.

### OAT CINNAMON PANCAKE MIX:

| | | |
|---|---|---:|
| 2⅔ cups | whole wheat flour | 650 mL |
| 1½ cups | large-flake rolled oats | 375 mL |
| ¼ cup | brown sugar | 50 mL |
| ¼ cup | granular low-calorie sweetener with sucralose | 50 mL |
| 2 tbsp | baking powder | 25 mL |
| 2 tsp | cinnamon | 10 mL |
| ½ tsp | salt | 2 mL |

In bowl, combine flour, oats, sugar, sweetener, baking powder, cinnamon and salt. Store in tightly sealed container for up to 1 month. Yields 4 servings, 5 cups (1.25 L).

⊕ *Be sure to cook all the batter. Batter refrigerated for a day or two will yield thin, tough pancakes. Instead, freeze leftover cooked pancakes.*

# Spiced Blueberry Sauce

Use this sauce as a flavourful, high-energy replacement for syrup. We've paired it with **Oat Cinnamon Pancakes** (page 30) and frozen oat bran waffles, as well as with milk pudding in Lunch Menu 22.

| | | |
|---|---|---|
| ⅔ cup | water | 150 mL |
| 1–2 tbsp | granular low-calorie sweetener with sucralose | 15 to 25 mL |
| 1 tbsp | cornstarch | 15 mL |
| 1¼ cups | fresh or frozen blueberries | 300 mL |
| Pinch | each ground nutmeg and cinnamon | Pinch |

In 2-cup (500 mL) glass measure, combine water, sweetener and cornstarch. Stir in blueberries.

Microwave on High (100%), stirring once, for 3 minutes or until slightly thickened and blueberries have softened. Stir in nutmeg and cinnamon.

### Variation

*Citrus Blueberry Sauce:* Substitute grated lemon or orange rind for cinnamon and nutmeg.

---

**Breakfast Menus 18, 21**
**Lunch Menu 22**

**Prep ·** 5 minutes
**Cook ·** about 3 minutes
**Yield ·** 1 cup (250 mL)

**Each Serving ·** ¼ cup (50 mL)
Carb choice ½

**Carbohydrate** 9 g
Fibre 1 g
**Protein** 0 g
**Fat** 0 g
Saturated 0 g
**Sodium** 4 mg
**Calories** 35

## BUTTERMILK PANCAKES WITH MAPLE SYRUP APPLES

Buttermilk makes these light, moist pancakes particularly tender, and combining them with yogurt gives a real calcium boost to the recipe. Yes, the maple syrup apples can fit into a food plan for those with diabetes.

**Prep** • 20 minutes
**Cook** • about 5 minutes per pancake
**Yield** • 5 servings, 15 pancakes

| | | |
|---|---|---|
| ¾ cup | whole wheat flour | 175 mL |
| ½ cup | all-purpose flour | 125 mL |
| ¼ cup | ground flax | 50 mL |
| 2 tbsp | granular low-calorie sweetener with sucralose | 25 mL |
| 2 tsp | baking powder | 10 mL |
| ½ tsp | baking soda | 2 mL |
| ¼ tsp | salt | 1 mL |
| ¾ cup | low-fat plain yogurt | 175 mL |
| ½ cup | buttermilk (see Tip) | 125 mL |
| 2 | eggs | 2 |
| 1 tbsp | canola oil | 15 mL |

**Each Serving** • 3 pancakes

| | |
|---|---|
| Carb choices | 1½ |
| Meat & Alternatives choice | 1 |
| Fats choice | 1 |

**Carbohydrate** 30 g
  Fibre 4 g
**Protein** 10 g
**Fat** 7 g
  Saturated 1 g
**Sodium** 426 mg
**Calories** 219

In bowl, combine whole wheat and all-purpose flours, flax, sweetener, baking powder, baking soda and salt.

In small bowl, whisk together yogurt, buttermilk, eggs and oil. Pour into dry mixture; stir just until dry ingredients are moistened (don't worry about lumps; see Tip below).

Heat large non-stick skillet over medium heat until hot (a drop of water will sizzle). Spray with non-stick cooking spray. Drop batter by ¼-cup (50 mL) measure onto pan. Cook pancakes for 3 minutes or until bubbles break on top and underside is golden brown; turn and cook other side until golden.

⊕ *For best pancakes, don't overmix—they'll become tough. Allow batter to sit for a few minutes before cooking.*

⊕ *Be sure to cook all the batter. Batter refrigerated for a day or two will yield thin, tough pancakes. Freeze leftover cooked pancakes instead.*

⊕ *If you don't have buttermilk, simply add 1 tsp (5 mL) vinegar or lemon juice to ½ cup (125 mL) low-fat milk.*

### Maple Syrup Apples:

| | | |
|---|---|---:|
| 2 tbsp | soft margarine or butter | 25 mL |
| 2 | large apples, peeled, cored and thinly sliced | 2 |
| ¼ cup | maple syrup, divided (see Tip) | 50 mL |
| ½ tsp | cinnamon | 2 mL |

In large non-stick skillet, melt margarine over medium-high heat. Add apples and 2 tbsp (25 mL) of the syrup; sauté, uncovered and stirring occasionally, for about 5 minutes or until apples are tender but still remain in slices.

Stir in remaining syrup and cinnamon.

◉ *If you use sucralose-sweetened syrup in place of pure maple syrup, add ½ tsp (2 mL) maple extract for flavour. A ⅓ cup (75 mL) serving then equals ½ Carb choice.*

**Prep** · 10 minutes
**Cook** · about 5 minutes
**Yield** · about 2 cups (500 mL),
⅓ cup (75 mL) per serving

.......................................

**Each Serving** · ⅓ cup (75 mL),
enough for 3 pancakes
Carb choice                          1
Fats choice                          1

.......................................

**Carbohydrate** 18 g
Fibre 1 g
**Protein** 0 g
**Fat** 4 g
Saturated 1 g
**Sodium** 50 mg

**Calories** 104

# LEMON BLUEBERRY FLAX MUFFINS

Blueberries and flax boost the nutrition and flavour in this tasty, wholesome muffin, with low-glycemic carbohydrate and healthy fibre.

| ½ cup | fresh or frozen blueberries | 125 mL |
|---|---|---|
| 1½ cups | whole wheat flour | 375 mL |
| ⅓ cup | ground flax (see Tips) | 75 mL |
| 3 tbsp | granulated sugar | 45 mL |
| 3 tbsp | granular low-calorie sweetener with sucralose | 45 mL |
| 1 tsp | each baking powder and baking soda | 5 mL |
| ¼ tsp | salt | 1 mL |
| ⅔ cup | low-fat plain yogurt | 150 mL |
| ¼ cup | canola oil | 50 mL |
| 2 tsp | grated lemon rind | 10 mL |
| 2 tbsp | fresh lemon juice | 25 mL |
| 1 | egg | 1 |

In small bowl, toss blueberries with 1 tsp (5 mL) of the flour. Set aside.

In separate bowl, stir together remaining flour, flax, sugar, sweetener, baking powder, baking soda and salt.

In glass measure, whisk together yogurt, oil, lemon rind, lemon juice and egg. Pour into dry ingredients; stir just until moistened. Stir in reserved blueberries.

Divide batter evenly among 12 non-stick or paper-lined medium muffin cups, filling two-thirds full. Bake in 400°F (200°C) oven for 18 minutes or until muffins are lightly browned and firm to the touch.

- ⊚ *Flaxseeds contain several essential nutrients, including calcium, iron, phosphorus and vitamin E, and are a rich source of omega-3 fatty acids and both soluble and insoluble fibre.*
- ⊚ *To reap the benefits of flaxseed, you'll need to grind it. Left whole, the seeds pass through the body undigested. Although you can find ground flaxseed, it will last longer if left whole and ground just before using. Use a spice or coffee grinder and grind until it reaches an almost flour-like consistency. One-quarter cup whole flaxseeds yields about 6 tbsp (⅓ cup/75 mL) ground flaxseed.*
- ⊚ *Because flaxseed is high in fat, store it in the refrigerator or freezer to prevent spoilage. Whole seeds will keep for up to one year, while ground flaxseed will keep for three to four months.*

**Breakfast Menu 23**
**Snack Menu 7**

**Prep** · 10 minutes
**Cook** · about 18 minutes
**Yield** · 12 medium muffins

**Each Serving** · 1 muffin

| | |
|---|---|
| Carb choice | 1 |
| Fats choice | 1 |

**Carbohydrate** 18 g
  Fibre 3 g
**Protein** 4 g
**Fat** 6 g
  Saturated 1 g
**Sodium** 183 mg
**Calories** 137

**Breakfast Menu 28**
**Lunch Menu 15**
**Snack Menus 15, 25**

...............................................

**Prep** · 15 minutes
**Cook** · 18 minutes
**Yield** · 12 medium muffins

...............................................

**Each Serving** · 1 muffin
Carb choice                1
Fats choice                1

...............................................

**Carbohydrate** 19 g
   Fibre 4 g
**Protein** 4 g
**Fat** 5 g
   Saturated 1 g
**Sodium** 215 mg
**Calories** 118

Raisin bran muffins bring back childhood memories of your mother's warm-from-the-oven bran muffins after school. This is an extremely reliable recipe with several variations. Mom would like them, too.

| | | |
|---|---|---:|
| 1½ cups | buttermilk (see Tip) | 375 mL |
| 1½ cups | high-fibre wheat bran cereal (see Tip) | 375 mL |
| 1 | egg, beaten | 1 |
| 3 tbsp | canola oil | 45 mL |
| 1 tsp | vanilla extract | 5 mL |
| 1 cup | whole wheat flour | 250 mL |
| 2 tbsp | granulated sugar | 25 mL |
| 2 tsp | baking powder | 10 mL |
| ½ tsp | baking soda | 2 mL |
| 2 tbsp | chopped raisins | 25 mL |

In bowl, stir buttermilk into cereal; let stand for 5 minutes or until cereal is softened. Stir in egg, oil and vanilla.

In large bowl, combine flour, sugar, baking powder and baking soda; sprinkle in raisins. Stir in buttermilk mixture just until moistened.

Divide batter evenly among 12 non-stick or paper-lined medium muffin cups, filling two-thirds full. Bake in 400°F (200°C) oven for 18 minutes or until muffins are lightly browned and firm to the touch.

**VARIATIONS**
Replace raisins with:
   2 tbsp (25 mL) chopped dried apricots (4 halves); OR
   ½ cup (125 mL) fresh or frozen blueberries and ½ tsp (2 mL) cinnamon; OR
   ½ cup (125 mL) chopped apple (½ medium apple) and ½ tsp (2 mL) ground nutmeg.

⊕ *If you don't have buttermilk, stir 4 tsp (20 mL) vinegar or lemon juice into 1½ cups (375 mL) milk; let stand for 5 minutes.*
⊕ *Examples of high-fibre wheat bran cereals are Kellogg's All-Bran and Post's 100% Bran.*

# Light Citrus Strawberry Spread

Diced orange extends the strawberries, particularly helpful if you are using more expensive out-of-season berries. The tangy spread is quite refreshing. If you find it too tart, a low-calorie liquid sweetener may be added to taste.

| | | |
|---|---|---|
| 1 | large orange | 1 |
| 4 cups | strawberries, hulled | 1 L |
| 2 tbsp | granulated sugar | 25 mL |
| 1 tbsp | fresh lemon juice | 15 mL |
| 1 box | light fruit pectin crystals (49 g) | 1 box |
| 1 cup | granular low-calorie sweetener with sucralose | 250 mL |

Partially fill a boiling water canner with hot water. Place 3 clean 1-cup (250 mL) jars in the canner. Bring water to a boil over high heat. Cover and boil for at least 10 minutes to sterilize jars.

Grate 2 tsp (10 mL) rind from orange; place in large stainless steel saucepan. Remove and discard white rind from orange. Chop pulp and place in 4-cup (1 L) measure.

Mash strawberries; add to orange pulp. (You should have 3 cups/750 mL fruit).

Add fruit, sugar, lemon juice and pectin to saucepan; mix well. Bring to a boil over high heat, stirring frequently. Stir in sweetener and return to boil; boil for 1 minute, stirring constantly. Meanwhile, place snap lids in boiling water to soften seal.

Remove jars from canner. Ladle spread into jars to within ½ inch (1 cm) of top; wipe rims. Centre snap lids on jars; apply screw band just until fingertip tight. Place jars in canner so that water level covers jars by 1 inch (2.5 cm). Cover canner; return water to a boil. Process for 5 minutes.

Remove jars from canner; cool for 24 hours. Check seals (sealed lids curve downward). Wipe jars, label and store in cool, dark place. Once opened, these are best kept in the refrigerator and used within 3 weeks.

**Breakfast Menu 13**

**Prep** · 20 minutes
**Cook** · about 6 minutes
**Yield** · 3 cups (750 mL)

**Each Serving** · 1 tbsp (15 mL)
Extra

**Carbohydrate** 3 g
  Fibre 1 g
**Protein** 0 g
**Fat** 0 g
**Sodium** 0 mg
**Calories** 11

# Light Spiced Raspberry Spread

**Prep** • 20 minutes
**Cook** • about 20 minutes
**Yield** • 2 cups (500 mL)

**Each Serving** • 1 tbsp (15 mL)
Extra

**Carbohydrate** 5 g
    Fibre 1 g
**Protein** 0 g
**Fat** 0 g
**Sodium** 1 mg
**Calories** 21

This fresh-tasting spread uses little sugar and no sweetener. Most of its sweetness comes from apple juice concentrate and fruit.

| | | |
|---|---|---:|
| 3 cups | frozen raspberries | 750 mL |
| 1 | tart apple, peeled, cored and chopped | 1 |
| ½ cup | frozen apple juice concentrate, thawed | 125 mL |
| 2 tbsp | granulated sugar | 25 mL |
| 1 tsp | grated lemon rind | 5 mL |
| 2 tsp | fresh lemon juice | 10 mL |
| Pinch | each ground nutmeg, ginger and cinnamon | Pinch |
| ½ tsp | almond extract | 2 mL |

Partially fill boiling water canner with hot water. Place 2 clean 1-cup (250 mL) Mason jars in the canner. Bring water to a boil over high heat. Cover and boil for at least 10 minutes to sterilize jars.

In stainless steel bowl, mash raspberries and measure; you should have 2 cups (500 mL). Add apple, apple juice, sugar, lemon rind and lemon juice; bring to a boil over high heat. Reduce heat and boil gently, uncovered and stirring frequently, for 20 minutes or until mixture is thickened.

Stir in nutmeg, ginger and cinnamon; simmer for 3 minutes. Remove from heat and stir in almond extract. Meanwhile, place snap lids in boiling water to soften rubber seal.

Remove jars from canner. Ladle spread into jars to within ½ inch (1 cm) of top; wipe rims. Centre snap lid on jar; apply screw band just until fingertip tight. Place jars in canner so that water level covers jars by 1 inch (2.5 cm). Cover canner; return water to a boil. Process for 5 minutes.

Remove jars from canner; cool for 24 hours. Check seals (sealed lids curve downward). Wipe jars, label and store in a cool, dark place. Once opened, these are best kept in the refrigerator and used within 3 weeks.

## Polenta, Cheddar Cheese and Spinach Bake

Enjoy this satisfying vegetarian dish for lunch or a special brunch. Make ahead and serve with a crisp salad. For those wondering about polenta, it is a staple of northern Italy referred to as "cornmeal mush." In this recipe, it becomes the crust for this quiche-like vegetable recipe.

| 4 cups | water | 1 L |
|---|---|---|
| 1 | chicken or vegetable bouillon sachet | 1 |
| | (4.5 g, with 25% less salt) | |
| 1 cup | cornmeal | 250 mL |
| ½ tsp | freshly ground pepper | 2 mL |
| 4 cups | tightly packed spinach leaves | 1 L |
| 6 | small mushrooms, thinly sliced | 6 |
| 6 | eggs | 6 |
| ½ cup | low-fat milk | 125 mL |
| 1 cup | shredded light Cheddar cheese | 250 mL |

In large saucepan, bring water and bouillon to a boil over high heat; reduce heat to low. Gradually whisk in cornmeal and pepper; cook, whisking frequently, for about 5 minutes or until cornmeal is thick enough to mound on a spoon. Spread in greased 9-inch (2.5 L) springform pan. Place spinach leaves and mushroom slices over cornmeal.

In small bowl, whisk eggs with milk; pour over mushrooms. Sprinkle with cheese.

Bake on rimmed baking sheet in 400°F (200°C) oven for 40 minutes or until cheese is golden and eggs are set. Remove from oven; let stand for 10 minutes. Cut into 6 wedges to serve.

◉ *You can prepare the polenta, spinach and mushroom base, then refrigerate for several hours or overnight; add egg mixture and cheese when ready to bake.*

**Breakfast Menu 24**

........................................

**Prep** · 20 minutes
**Cooking:** · 40 minutes
**Yield** · 6 servings

........................................

**Each Serving** · ⅙ of recipe
Carb choice                                  1
Meat & Alternatives choices 1½
Fats choice                                   1

........................................

**Carbohydrate** 19 g
  Fibre 3 g
**Protein** 14 g
**Fat** 9 g
  Saturated 4 g
**Sodium** 272 mg
**Calories** 210

# BAKED ASPARAGUS CHEESE FRITTATA

**Breakfast Menu 26**

....................................

**Prep** • 20 minutes
**Cook** • about 30 minutes
**Yield** • 8 servings

....................................

**Each Serving** • ⅛ of recipe
Meat & Alternatives choices 1½
Fats choice                    ½

....................................

**Carbohydrate** 3 g
   Fibre 1 g
**Protein** 11 g
**Fat** 7 g
   Saturated 3 g
**Sodium** 193 mg
**Calories** 122

A frittata is an Italian omelette. Typically, the ingredients are mixed with the eggs rather than folded inside as with the French omelette. Delicious warm or at room temperature, this frittata is served as a special breakfast with a whole wheat English muffin. Perfect for the "bed-and-breakfast" hostess!

| | | |
|---|---|---|
| 8 | eggs | 8 |
| 1 cup | coarsely shredded light Cheddar cheese, divided | 250 mL |
| ½ cup | low-fat milk | 125 mL |
| 2 | green onions, sliced | 2 |
| ¼ tsp | each salt and freshly ground pepper | 1 mL |
| ½ lb | asparagus | 250 g |

In bowl, whisk together eggs, half of the cheese, milk, onions, salt and pepper.

Wash asparagus and cut into small pieces. Cook until al dente (tender but still firm). Reserve tips.

Add cooked asparagus to egg mixture. Pour into greased 11- x 7-inch (2 L) baking dish. Arrange cooked asparagus tips over surface of frittata. Sprinkle with remaining cheese.

Bake in 350ºF (180ºC) oven for 30 minutes or until golden and knife inserted in centre comes out clean. Cut into 8 squares.

⊕ *This recipe can easily be halved but it may cook faster; reduce baking time to about 20 minutes.*

# Apple Cheese Breakfast Quesadillas

Quesadillas are flour tortillas filled with a savoury mixture, then folded in half to form a turnover. This easy-to-assemble sandwich is a perfect way to "bone" up on your calcium. Prepare the night before and refrigerate.

| | | |
|---|---|---|
| 1 tbsp | Dijon mustard | 15 mL |
| 1 tbsp | mango chutney (see Tip) | 15 mL |
| 4 | 8-inch (20 cm) whole wheat flour tortillas | 4 |
| 1¼ cups | coarsely shredded light Cheddar cheese | 300 mL |
| 2 | small apples, cut into quarters, peeled and sliced | 2 |

In small bowl, combine mustard and chutney. Lightly spray one side of each tortilla with non-stick cooking spray. Spread mustard mixture evenly over other side.

For each tortilla, layer ¼ cup (50 mL) cheese and one quarter of the sliced apples over half of the tortilla. Top with 1 tbsp (15 mL) of the remaining cheese. Fold tortilla over, pressing firmly.

In large non-stick skillet over medium-high heat, cook filled tortillas for 3 minutes or until golden. Carefully turn and cook for another 2 minutes or until golden brown and cheese is melted. Cut each into quarters and serve.

◉ *If chutney is not available, use either 2 tbsp (25 mL) mustard or a reduced sugar spread.*

**Breakfast Menu 27**

........................................

**Prep** · 15 minutes
**Cook** · about 5 minutes
**Yield** · 4 servings, 4 quesadillas

........................................

**Each Serving** · 1 quesadilla
Carb choices                            2
Meat & Alternatives choice     1
Fats choice                             1

........................................

**Carbohydrate** 32 g
   Fibre 3 g
**Protein** 11 g
**Fat** 9 g
   Saturated 3 g
**Sodium** 386 mg
**Calories** 247

# Microwave Ham 'n' Cheese Egg

......................................

**Prep** · 5 minutes
**Cook** · about 3 minutes
**Yield** · 1 serving

......................................

**Each Serving** · 1 egg on
½ English muffin
Carb choice                                    1
Meat & Alternatives choices 1½
Fats choices                                   1½

......................................

**Carbohydrate** 17 g
  Fibre 3 g
**Protein** 14 g
**Fat** 12 g
  Saturated 4 g
**Sodium** 504 mg
**Calories** 227

This approach to traditional ham 'n' eggs serves up maximum satisfaction from a small amount of ham and one egg.

| | | |
|---|---|---|
| 1 tbsp | finely chopped ham | 15 mL |
| 1 tbsp | each chopped sweet green pepper and onion | 15 mL |
| ½ tsp | soft margarine or butter | 2 mL |
| 1 | egg, beaten | 1 |
| Pinch | each freshly ground pepper and paprika | Pinch |
| 1 tbsp | shredded part-skim mozzarella cheese | 15 mL |
| ½ | whole wheat English muffin (65 g), toasted | ½ |
| OR | | |
| 1 | slice whole wheat toast (30 g) | 1 |

In small custard cup, combine ham, green pepper, onion and margarine. Microwave, uncovered, on High (100%) for 2 minutes.

Stir in egg, pepper and paprika. Microwave on Medium-High (70%), stirring once, for 45 seconds.

Sprinkle with cheese; let stand for about 1 minute to allow cheese to melt.

Serve on toasted English muffin half or whole wheat toast.

# HOMEMADE VANILLA YOGURT

Want a change from plain yogurt but don't want to buy another large container of flavoured? Try replacing it with our Homemade Vanilla or one of our suggested variations.

| | | |
|---|---|---|
| 1 cup | plain low-fat yogurt | 250 mL |
| ½–1 tsp | vanilla extract | 2–5 mL |
| | low-calorie sweetener, if desired (see Tip) | |

In small bowl, stir together yogurt, vanilla and sweetener (if using). Cover and refrigerate for about 1 hour to allow flavours to develop.

◉ *Taste after adding the extract and before adding sweetener. The flavour may be sweet enough. If still too tart, add sweetener to taste.*

## VARIATIONS

***Maple or Rum Nutmeg:*** Add maple or rum extract and ground nutmeg.
***Lemon, Orange or Almond:*** Add lemon, orange or almond extract.

---

**Breakfast Menu 28**
**Lunch Menu 30**
**Snack Menu 18**

..................................................

**Prep** · 2 minutes
**Refrigerate** · up to 1 week (see expiry date on container)
**Yield** · 1 cup (250 mL)

..................................................

**Each Serving** · ½ cup (125 mL)
Carb choice                                    ½

..................................................

**Carbohydrate** 9 g
  Fibre 0 g
**Protein** 6 g
**Fat** 0 g
**Sodium** 87 mg
**Calories** 68

# LUNCH

Soup, a sandwich and a salad are old standbys. And rightly so. Each makes an easily prepared nutritious meal to satisfy midday hunger pangs. Soups and sandwiches can be served hot in the winter and cold in the summer. But the same old selections day after day become oh so dull. Our lunch recipes and menus offer new twists on old favourites, as well as some nifty new ideas.

Lunch is a marvellous time to stock up on nutrition. Soups, depending on the variety, can have fibre and protein from barley, lentils and beans, protein from meat, and vitamins and minerals from vegetables. Sandwiches made from whole wheat breads are full of fibre, to say nothing of the fibre, protein, vitamins and minerals in the fillings. And a low-fat salad is really just a tasty medley of fibre, vitamins and minerals finished off with protein from any added meat or cheese.

## POT OF SOUP

We think soup is one of the most perfect foods. It's economical, easy to make, gets better with each reheating and tends to be low in fat. A pot of soup simmering on the stove gives warmth and comfort to a cold, blustery winter day. And a lively, refreshing cold soup just makes a summer lunch sing. A nourishing lunch is not far away when you have a freezer full of assorted frozen soups. All our soups in this section freeze well for up to two months.

Soup is best made with homemade broth, and we think our recipes are pretty good ones (see pages 57 and 58). Whenever you see a reference to broth in a recipe, think homemade! Your soup will taste better, plus you control the salt level, an important consideration if you are to limit sodium intake (see page 13). If you should decide to use a commercial broth instead, look for a lower-sodium choice. Read the labels before you buy. All commercial broths tend to be high in sodium content, even those claiming sodium reduction. Dehydrated broths tend to be even higher. See pages 57 and 58 for comparisons.

Many flavourful (though expensive) ready-to-serve soups are available in grocery stores and taste almost homemade. Check the Nutrition Facts on the label for serving size, then subtract the fibre from the carbohydrate to see how it fits your meal.

*Opposite:* Warm Tortellini, Asparagus and Tomato Salad (page 66)

This chapter offers several new and quite unusual hot soups: *Mushroom Barley Lentil Soup* (page 55) and *Black Bean, Macaroni and Vegetable Soup* (page 53) are filled with plain old-fashioned goodness—as well as slowly digested low-glycemic carbohydrate. When time is limited, *Microwave Soup 'n' Sandwich in a Bowl* (page 59) makes a fast, simple and nutritious lunch. And if you want something more exotic, try the spicy *East Indian Peanut Tomato Soup* (page 56).

## SANDWICHES

Bread in a sandwich does more than just hold the filling; it adds flavour, texture and variety to the total package. Breads come in all shapes and sizes, as do buns, bagels, baguettes, pita breads and wraps (flour tortillas). And they all come in whole wheat and multi-grain versions. Each gives the filling a different taste. And do we have fillings! How about our slant on the traditional *Open-Face Tuna Apple Melt* (page 63) or *Ham Melt Mini Pita Pockets* (page 62) or *Southwestern Grilled Cheese Sandwiches* (page 61)?

But the variety of sizes in bread products can create a problem for those with diabetes. Since bagels and breads come in so many sizes, how do you know what's intended in a certain menu? To deal with this, we have assigned weights to bread products in our menus and recipes. Remember that a 30 gram roll or slice of bread contains 15 grams of available carbohydrate and is equal to 1 GRAINS & STARCHES CHOICE or 1 CARB CHOICE (see pages 23–24 and 181).

## THE JOY OF SALADS

The profusion of ready-to-use salad greens now available gives us a riot of exciting choices with few calories and little carbohydrate. They can all be used generously in a diabetes meal plan. But a crisp, well-dressed salad doesn't happen by chance. Here are some ideas to make a salad work.

- Wash leafy greens and use a salad spinner to dry. They keep fresher if wrapped in paper or cloth towelling and stored in a tightly sealed plastic container in the refrigerator. Or use one of the new ventilated plastic storage bags. Lettuce and spinach purchased in airtight packaging should be refrigerated "as is."
- Tear greens, don't chop; that way, you'll have crisper salads.
- Darker greens have more nutrients.

- Keep some raw vegetables on hand to use in a green salad. Small broccoli and cauliflower florets, shredded carrots and chopped bok choy are all ideal candidates.
- Add fresh herbs, such as basil, dill, oregano or tarragon.
- Toss greens with the dressing at the last minute.

## Main-course salad

A salad may be an addition to a meal, or it may be the meal itself. We have both kinds in our lunch menus. A lunchtime vegetarian salad is a great way to add more vegetables to your day, as well as an opportunity to include high-fibre, low-glycemic foods. See **Pack-to-Go Chickpea Salad** (page 65) and **Lentil, Vegetable and Kasha Salad** (page 68).

Some of our recipes add fresh fruit to a salad for a refreshing change. See **Fruit and Cottage Cheese Salad Plate** (recipe in Lunch Menu 3), **Fruit and Feta Salad** (page 69) and easy-to-prepare **Warm Tortellini, Asparagus and Tomato Salad** (page 66). All make the perfect lunch!

## Dressing light

A salad dressing can make or break a salad. When it comes to dressing, less is best. Like perfume, the purpose of dressing is to enhance, not overpower. Our recipes provide a given amount, enough to lightly coat the greens. Be sure the greens are dry so the dressing will cling to the leaves and not slide off. A too-heavy or mundane dressing insults fresh greens. Of course, the dressing should be low in fat. While canola oil and olive oil are both healthy oils to use in dressings, surveys show that salad dressings are one of the chief sources of added fat in the Canadian diet. So use high-fat dressings in moderation. Here are some tips for lowering fat in dressings.

- Choose light, reduced-fat mayonnaise and salad dressings.
- Use measuring spoons to measure even light dressings.
- Lighten mayonnaise with lemon juice, vinegar, low-fat plain yogurt or milk.
- Mix salsa into yogurt for a super-light and tasty dressing.
- When eating out, ask for a lower-fat dressing on the side and add just what you need.
- Make your own so you know what's in it. Try one of our home-made low-fat dressings, like **Curried Dressing** (page 70) or **Basil Buttermilk Dressing** (page 69).

## Midday Desserts

This chapter's lunchtime desserts consist mainly of fruit, sometimes with pudding or cookies. Fruit delivers the sweetness we expect from a dessert but with relatively few calories and lots of fibre, minerals and vitamins. Fruits are served either raw or in fruit-based recipes, such as **Microwave Applesauce** (page 75) and **Spring Rhubarb Sauce** (page 74). And if you don't have on hand the fruit suggested in a given menu, check Appendix III (page 188) for other choices. And what do you think of a **Mango Smoothie** (Lunch Menu 27) for dessert?

## Lunch in the Fast Lane

A lunch away from home can still be a healthy lunch. Here are some tips to keep in mind, especially if you eat out frequently.

- The best option of all is to brown bag it. Take along your own healthy lunch. See Lunch Menus 9 and 15 for ideas.
- Downsize it. Consider sharing a large portion with someone else, or ask for a doggy bag to take home.
- Pick one of the healthy options offered at many fast food restaurants.
- Survey all the choices a cafeteria offers before making your selection.
- Opt for the salad bar's fresh fruit, vegetable, bean, lentil or mixed greens salads.
- Make your pizza choice a healthy one. Choose one with a thin, whole grain crust, topped with feta cheese and roasted vegetables. Steer away from higher-fat toppings such as pepperoni, sausage and bacon.
- Find a vending machine with offerings of raw fruit, water, milk and sandwiches.

# Chilled Tomato Quencher

Yogurt's tart tang and tomato's intense freshness make this a zesty and flavourful beverage that's also good for you. Even one yogurt-hating husband we know enjoyed it when he tried some! A good friend who has diabetes offers this tip: "I use a large can of low-sodium vegetable juice cocktail and adjust the other ingredients to make up a supply to keep in the refrigerator."

| 2¼ cups | low-sodium vegetable juice cocktail | 550 mL |
| ¾ cup | low-fat plain yogurt or low-fat silken tofu | 175 mL |
| 1½ tsp | Worcestershire sauce | 7 mL |
| 1½ tsp | fresh lemon juice | 7 mL |
| ¼ tsp | hot pepper sauce | 1 mL |
| ¼ tsp | freshly ground pepper | 1 mL |
| | ice cubes | |
| 3 | lemon slices | 3 |

In blender, blend vegetable cocktail, yogurt, Worcestershire sauce, lemon juice, hot pepper sauce and pepper with several ice cubes until smooth.

Pour into 3 tall glasses. Garnish each with lemon slice.

⊕ *Refrigerate any remaining quencher for a snack later; stir before serving.*

⊕ *To make a single serving, use ¾ cup (175 mL) vegetable juice cocktail with ¼ cup (50 mL) yogurt and one-third of each seasoning.*

⊕ *Silken tofu is delicate and custard-like, perfect for smoothies and quenchers.*

Lunch Menu 13

Snack Menus 3, 14

..................................................

**Prep** · 5 minutes

**Yield** · 3 servings

..................................................

**Each Serving** · 1 cup (250 mL)

Carb choice                      1

..................................................

**Carbohydrate** 14 g

  Fibre 3 g

**Protein** 5 g

**Fat** 0 g

**Sodium** 164 mg

**Calories** 73

# HANDY MAYO DIP

.............................................

**Prep** · 10 minutes
**Refrigerate** · up to 2 weeks
**Yield** · 2 cups (500 mL)

.............................................

**Each Serving** · 2 tbsp (25 mL)

Fats choice                               1

.............................................

**Carbohydrate** 3 g
  Fibre 0 g
**Protein** 1 g
**Fat** 5 g
  Saturated 0 g
**Sodium** 106 mg

**Calories** 54

Our good friend Judy gives us this recipe with the comment "We love mayonnaise, but not the fat that comes with it." This mayo dip has a lovely fresh, authentic taste—with a fraction of the usual fat.

| | | |
|---|---|---|
| 1 cup | each light mayonnaise & low-fat plain yogurt | 250 mL |
| 1 tbsp | Dijon mustard | 15 mL |
| | juice of half a lemon | |

In small bowl, whisk mayonnaise, yogurt, mustard and lemon juice until smooth. Cover and store in the refrigerator.

◉ *Handy Mayo Dip can be used in place of mayonnaise and is also a great substitute for sour cream on baked potatoes and a dip for raw veggies. Or spoon some over chicken breasts before baking; add a pinch of dried thyme, a dash of Tabasco or Worcestershire sauce, and some chopped green onions.*

## Black Bean, Macaroni and Vegetable Soup

Allow one hour to make this low-fat hearty soup. The comfort-food quality of macaroni and the flavours of beans, leeks, onions and tomatoes make it all worth the effort. As well, the recipe yields sufficient amounts for leftovers to freeze for future meals.

| | | |
|---|---|---|
| 1 | can (19 oz/540 mL) black beans, drained and rinsed | 1 |
| 6 cups | vegetable or beef broth (see Tip) | 1.5 L |
| 2 cups | chopped leeks (see Tip) | 500 mL |
| 2 | medium carrots, chopped (1 cup/250 mL) | 2 |
| 1 | large onion, chopped (1 cup/250 mL) | 1 |
| 1 cup | canned diced tomatoes | 250 mL |
| 2 tbsp | chopped fresh parsley | 25 mL |
| 1 tsp | dried thyme | 5 mL |
| 2 | bay leaves | 1 |
| 1½ cups | diced zucchini (about 2) | 375 mL |
| ¾ cup | uncooked whole wheat elbow macaroni | 175 mL |
| | salt and freshly ground pepper | |

Place beans in large saucepan. Add broth, leeks, carrots, onion, tomatoes, parsley, thyme and bay leaves; bring to a boil. Reduce heat, cover and cook for 20 minutes or until vegetables are tender.

Add zucchini and macaroni; cook for 15 minutes or until macaroni is tender. Discard bay leaves. Season lightly with salt and pepper.

- ◉ *Washing leeks can be a hassle. Slice or chop them first, then rinse in a strainer.*
- ◉ *To make vegetable broth, use commercial vegetable bouillon cubes or saved vegetable cooking water. If using beef broth, see the recipe for **Homemade Light Beef Broth** (page 57).*

**HIGH FIBRE**

**Lunch Menu 17**

...........................................

**Prep** • 20 minutes
**Cook** • about 35 minutes
**Yield** • 10 servings, 10 cups (2.5 L)

...........................................

**Each Serving** • 1 cup (250 mL)
Carb choice     1

...........................................

**Carbohydrate** 22 g
   Fibre 6 g
**Protein** 5 g
**Fat** 1 g
   Saturated 0 g
**Sodium** 539 mg
**Calories** 112

# SALMON VEGETABLE CHOWDER

**Lunch Menu 20**

Salmon gives this easily made and satisfying soup a lot of heart-healthy, disease-fighting omega-3s.

**Prep** · 15 minutes
**Cook** · about 15 minutes
**Yield** · 5 servings, 5 cups (1.25 L)

| | | |
|---|---|---|
| 1 tbsp | soft margarine or butter | 15 mL |
| ½ cup | finely chopped onion | 125 mL |
| 1 | clove garlic, minced | 1 |
| ½ tsp | each dried thyme and basil | 2 mL |
| 1 cup | chicken broth or | 250 mL |
| | *Homemade Light Chicken Broth* (page 58) | |
| 1 cup | diced peeled potatoes (1 medium) | 250 mL |
| ½ cup | each frozen corn niblets, diced zucchini | |
| | and diced carrots | 125 mL |
| 1 | can (385 mL) low-fat evaporated milk | 1 |
| 1 | can (7.5 oz/213 g) salmon | 1 |
| | freshly ground pepper | |
| ½ cup | shredded light Cheddar cheese | 125 mL |

**Each Serving** · 1 cup (250 mL)

| | |
|---|---|
| Carb choice | 1 |
| Meat & Alternatives choices | 2 |
| Fats choice | ½ |

In saucepan, melt margarine over medium heat; sauté onion, garlic, thyme and basil for 5 minutes or until onions are soft. Add broth, potatoes, corn, zucchini and carrots; bring to a boil over high heat. Reduce heat and cook, covered, for 10 minutes or until vegetables are tender.

Add milk and salmon; simmer slowly until soup is hot (do not boil).

Season lightly with pepper. Divide among 5 bowls; sprinkle each evenly with cheese and serve.

**Carbohydrate** 21 g
Fibre 1 g
**Protein** 19 g
**Fat** 9 g
Saturated 3 g
**Sodium** 498 mg
**Calories** 237

## Mushroom Barley Lentil Soup

Make this robust soup as spicy as you like, depending on the kind of curry paste or powder used—mild, medium or hot. Or decide to make it without any—it will still have wonderful flavour. Lentils and barley make this a low-glycemic soup (pages 10–11). Barley is the latest grain to be added to the heart-healthy list of foods.

| | | |
|---|---|---:|
| 1 tbsp | canola oil | 15 mL |
| 2 | medium onions, chopped | 2 |
| 8 | cloves garlic, minced | 8 |
| 1 lb | mushrooms, sliced | 500 g |
| 1 cup | sliced celery | 250 mL |
| 2 tbsp | minced fresh gingerroot | 25 mL |
| 2 tbsp | curry powder or paste | 25 mL |
| ½ tsp | freshly ground pepper | 2 mL |
| 12 cups | salt-reduced beef broth (see Tip below) | 3 L |
| 1 cup | green lentils | 250 mL |
| 1 cup | pot or pearl barley | 250 mL |

In large pot, heat oil over medium-high heat; cook onions, garlic, mushrooms, celery, gingerroot, curry powder and pepper, stirring often, for 10 minutes or until liquid is evaporated.

Add broth, lentils and barley; return to a boil. Cover, reduce heat and simmer for about 1 hour or until lentils and barley are tender.

- ◉ *The soup can be made ahead, then cooled for 30 minutes and divided among serving-size containers. Refrigerate, uncovered, until cold. Cover and refrigerate for up to 3 days or freeze for longer storage.*
- ◉ *If you prefer to make your own broth, see page 57 for our **Homemade Light Beef Broth**, or for a vegetarian soup, use vegetable broth.*
- ◉ *If desired, top each bowl with 2 tbsp (25 mL) each low-fat plain yogurt and finely chopped green onion (see Lunch Menu 25).*

**Lunch Menu 25**

**Prep** · 25 minutes
**Cook** · about 1 hour
**Yield** · 14 servings, 14 cups (3.5 L)

**Each Serving** · 1 cup (250 mL)
Carb choices                1½
Meat & Alternatives choice   ½

**Carbohydrate** 23 g
  Fibre 4 g
**Protein** 7 g
**Fat** 2 g
  Saturated 0 g
**Sodium** 488 mg
**Calories** 128

# East Indian Peanut Tomato Soup

**Lunch Menu 27**

..............................

**Prep** • 10 minutes
**Cook** • about 15 minutes
**Yield** • 5 servings, 5 cups (1.25 L)

..............................

**Each Serving** • 1 cup (250 mL)
Carb choice                    ½
Meat & Alternatives choice    1
Fats choices                  1½

..............................

**Carbohydrate** 8 g
   Fibre 2 g
**Protein** 6 g
**Fat** 10 g
   Saturated 2 g
**Sodium** 308 mg
**Calories** 140

Curry, along with fresh coriander and peanut butter, gives this simple tomato-based soup a very special taste of India. Use vegetable broth instead of chicken broth to make the soup vegetarian.

| | | |
|---|---|---|
| 1 tbsp | canola oil | 15 mL |
| 1 | medium onion, chopped (1 cup/250 mL) | 1 |
| 2 tsp | curry powder | 10 mL |
| ¼ tsp | freshly ground pepper | 1 mL |
| ½ | can (28 oz/796 mL) diced tomatoes, undrained | ½ |
| 2 cups | salt-reduced chicken broth or | 500 mL |
| | *Homemade Light Chicken Broth* (page 58) | |
| 1 cup | hot water | 250 mL |
| ¼ cup | chunky peanut butter | 50 mL |
| 2 tbsp | chopped fresh coriander (optional) | 25 mL |

In heavy saucepan, heat oil over medium heat; sauté onion, stirring occasionally, for 5 minutes or until softened. Add curry powder and pepper; cook, stirring frequently, for 2 minutes.

Add tomatoes with their juice and broth. Cook, uncovered, for 5 minutes.

Stir hot water into peanut butter until smooth; add to soup. Simmer, uncovered and stirring occasionally, for 5 minutes or until hot. Stir in coriander (if using) just before serving

# Homemade Light Beef Broth

A bit more effort is required to make beef broth than chicken broth (see page 58) as the bones need to be browned, but it's well worth it.

| | | |
|---|---|---|
| 4 lb | beef bones | 2 kg |
| 2 | onions, coarsely chopped | 2 |
| 3 | carrots, coarsely chopped | 3 |
| 3 | celery stalks, chopped | 3 |
| 2 | parsley sprigs | |
| 2 | bay leaves | 2 |
| 1 tbsp | peppercorns | 15 mL |
| 3 | cloves of garlic | 3 |
| 1 tsp | dried thyme | 5 mL |

In roasting pan, combine beef bones, onions, carrots and celery. Bake in 450° F (230°C) oven for 1 hour or until well browned, stirring occasionally. Transfer bones and vegetables to large saucepan.

Drain and discard fat from roasting pan. Add 2 cups (500 mL) water; cook and stir to scrape up brown bits on bottom of pan. Add liquid to saucepan, along with parsley, bay leaves, peppercorns, garlic and thyme. Add enough cold water to cover the bones by 1 inch (2.5 cm); bring to a boil. Reduce heat and simmer, uncovered, for 2 hours or longer. Strain, discarding bones and vegetables. Chill. Refrigerate until cold. Remove congealed fat and discard. Measure stock and freeze in appropriate amounts to use as needed.

**Prep** • 15 minutes
**Cook** • about 3 hours
**Yield** • about 12 cups (3 L)

## Sodium Tip

How much sodium is in commercial beef broth? It's not easy to read labels and compare since some labels describe a serving of ⅔ cup (150 mL), others ¾ cup (175 mL) and still others 1 cup (250 mL). We have done the math for you and compared 1-cup (250 mL) servings below. The canned condensed beef broth with 25% less salt appears to have the least sodium—but that's still five times more than homemade.

*Beef Bouillon (cubes)*
1,300 mg sodium

*Beef Bouillon Regular (sachets)*
920 mg sodium

*Beef Bouillon 25% Less Salt (sachets)*
707 mg sodium

*Ready-to-Use Beef Broth (carton)*
920 mg sodium

*Condensed Consommé, Fat Free (water added)*
890 mg sodium

*Condensed Beef Broth, Fat Free (water added)*
800 mg sodium

*Condensed Beef Broth, Fat Free 25% Less Salt (water added)*
590 mg sodium

*Homemade Light Beef Broth*
105 mg sodium

## SODIUM TIP

How much sodium is in commercial chicken broth? It is not easy to read labels and compare since some labels describe a serving of ⅔ cup (150 mL), others ¾ cup (175 mL) and still others 1 cup (250 mL). We have done the math for you and compared 1-cup (250 mL) servings below. Again, the canned condensed chicken broth with 25% less salt appears to have the least sodium—but still much more than homemade.

*Chicken Bouillon (cubes)*
1,300 mg sodium

*Chicken Bouillon Regular (sachets)*
960 mg sodium

*Chicken Bouillon 25% Less Salt (sachets)*
720 mg sodium

*Ready-to-use Chicken Broth (carton)*
795 mg sodium

*Condensed Chicken Broth, Fat Free (water added)*
990 mg sodium

*Condensed Chicken Broth, Fat Free, 25% Less Salt (water added)*
610 mg sodium

*Homemade Light Chicken Broth*
about 115 mg sodium

Any recipe calling for chicken broth will only be as good as the broth you use. Our homemade broth will give your recipe maximum flavour with far less sodium than commercial varieties.

| 2–3 lbs | chicken bones | 2–2.25 kg |
|---|---|---|
| 1 | onion, coarsely chopped | 1 |
| 2 | celery stalks, coarsely chopped | 2 |
| 2 | sprigs parsley | 2 |
| 1 | bay leaf | 1 |

Store poultry bones in the freezer until you've saved enough to make a batch of broth. Then place the frozen bones, along with any fresh ones you may have on hand, in a large saucepan. Add onion, celery, parsley, bay leaf and enough cold water to cover the bones by 1 inch (2.5 cm); cover saucepan and bring to a boil. Reduce heat and simmer for 2 hours or longer. Strain, discarding the bones and vegetables. Refrigerate until cold.

Remove congealed fat and discard. Measure stock and freeze in appropriate amounts to use as needed. Freeze some in an ice cube tray too. Transfer frozen cubes to a resealable plastic bag so they're ready to use whenever you need only a small amount.

**Prep** · 15 minutes
**Cook** · about 2 hours
**Yield** · about 12 cups (3 L).

# Microwave Soup 'n' Sandwich in a Bowl

Here's a novel way to eat your soup and sandwich at the same time.

| | | |
|---|---|---|
| 1 | can (28 oz/798 mL) tomatoes, no salt added, undrained | 1 |
| 1 | can (10 oz/284 mL) condensed tomato soup | 1 |
| ⅔ cup | water | 150 mL |
| 1 tsp | dried basil | 5 mL |
| 2 | cloves garlic, chopped | 2 |
| ¼ tsp | freshly ground pepper | 1 mL |
| 5 | slices whole wheat bread (30 g each) | 5 |
| ½ cup | shredded light Cheddar cheese | 125 mL |
| 1 | green onion, chopped | 1 |

In 8-cup (2 L) microwave-safe casserole, combine tomatoes and their juice, tomato soup, water, basil, garlic and pepper. Cover and microwave on High (100%) for about 7 minutes or until soup is hot.

Toast bread; cut each slice into cubes.

Spoon 1 cup (250 mL) soup into each of 5 bowls. Top each with cubes from 1 slice of toast. Sprinkle each with cheese and some of the chopped green onion. Microwave for a few seconds until cheese melts.

**Lunch Menu 14**

**Prep** · 15 minutes
**Cook** · 7 minutes
**Yield** · 5 servings, 5 cups (1.25 L)

**Each serving** · 1 cup (250 mL)
Carb choices   2
Meat & Alternatives choice   ½

**Carbohydrate** 29 g
  Fibre 4 g
**Protein** 8 g
**Fat** 3 g
  Saturated 1 g
**Sodium** 538 mg
**Calories** 169

# Crunchy Egg Sandwich Filling

**Lunch Menu 23**
**Snack Menus 8, 23**

...............................................

**Prep** · 15 minutes
**Yield** · 2 cups (500 mL),
        6 servings

...............................................

**Each Serving** · ⅓ cup (75 mL)
Meat & Alternatives choice    1
Fats choice                   1

...............................................

**Carbohydrate** 2 g
  Fibre 0 g
**Protein** 5 g
**Fat** 8 g
  Saturated 3 g
**Sodium** 215 mg
_____
**Calories** 97

Adding mild, soft goat cheese (chèvre) to hard-cooked eggs gives a new twist to this old-favourite filling. Diced apple for crunch gives that final extra punch.

| | | |
|---|---|---|
| ¼ cup | light mayonnaise | 50 mL |
| ¼ cup | mild soft goat cheese | 50 mL |
| 1 tsp | Dijon mustard | 5 mL |
| ½ tsp | paprika | 2 mL |
| ¼ tsp | each salt and freshly ground pepper | 1 mL |
| 3 | hard-cooked eggs | 3 |
| ¾ cup | finely chopped apple with skin | 175 mL |
| 2 tbsp | chopped fresh parsley or chives | 25 mL |

In bowl, whisk together mayonnaise, goat cheese, mustard, paprika, salt and pepper.

Peel eggs and chop. Add eggs, apple and parsley to mayonnaise mixture; stir to combine.

# SOUTHWESTERN GRILLED CHEESE SANDWICHES

What makes this sandwich "southwestern"? It's the salsa and jalapeños added to a regular grilled cheese sandwich. Simple and flavourful! Choose your preferred heat level by using mild, medium or hot salsa.

| | | |
|---|---|---|
| 4 tsp | soft margarine or butter | 20 mL |
| 8 | slices whole wheat bread (30 g each) | 8 |
| ⅓ cup | mild salsa | 75 mL |
| 1 cup | shredded light Monterey Jack or Cheddar cheese, divided | 250 mL |
| 1 tbsp | minced drained pickled jalapeños (optional) | 15 mL |

Lightly spread margarine over one side of each bread slice (about ½ tsp/2 mL per slice). On plain side of 4 of the slices, spread salsa evenly. Top each with ¼ cup (50 mL) of the cheese. Sprinkle with jalapeños (if using).

Top with remaining bread slices, pressing down lightly.

Heat large non-stick skillet over medium heat; cook sandwiches (in batches if necessary) for 2 to 3 minutes per side or until golden and cheese has melted. Cut in half diagonally and serve.

**Lunch Menu 19**

..................................................

**Prep** • 15 minutes
**Cook** • about 5 minutes
**Yield** • 4 sandwiches

..................................................

**Each Serving** • ¼ of recipe,
    2 sandwich halves
Carb choices                1½
Meat & Alternatives choice    1
Fats choices                1½

..................................................

**Carbohydrate** 30 g
    Fibre 5 g
**Protein** 13 g
**Fat** 10 g
    Saturated 4 g
**Sodium** 572 mg
**Calories** 253

# Ham Melt Mini Pita Pockets

These miniature ham and cheese–filled pita rounds are just right for a lunch at home or a summer picnic. Heat them on a barbecue when the kitchen stove is not at hand.

| | | |
|---|---|---|
| 1 cup | finely chopped fat-reduced ham | 250 mL |
| 3 tbsp | light mayonnaise | 45 mL |
| ¼ cup | each finely chopped celery & sweet red pepper | 50 mL |
| 1 tbsp | Dijon mustard | 15 mL |
| Pinch | freshly ground pepper | Pinch |
| ½ cup | shredded light Cheddar cheese | 125 mL |
| 12 | whole wheat mini pita pockets | 12 |

In bowl, combine ham, mayonnaise, celery, red pepper, mustard and pepper. Stir in cheese. Set aside.

Slice pitas in half horizontally. Top each half with about 2 tbsp (25 mL) of the ham mixture; cover with other half. Wrap pitas in foil, 3 to a package. Refrigerate for up to 4 hours.

On baking sheet, heat foil packets in 400°F (200°C) oven for 10 minutes or until filling is hot and cheese has melted.

## Variation

***Spicy Tuna Filling:*** Replace ham with tuna. Stir 2 tbsp (25 mL) antipasto spread into 1 can (170 g) flaked tuna, drained, and continue with recipe above.

◉ *For a crunchy pita, do not wrap the pitas in foil. Instead place them on a baking sheet and toast them in a 350°F (180°C) oven for about 10 minutes.*

---

**Lunch Menu 28**

..........................................

**Prep** · 15 minutes
**Cook** · 10 minutes
**Yield** · 4 servings,
        12 mini pockets

..........................................

**Each Serving** · 3 filled mini
              pockets
Carb choice              1
Meat & Alternatives choices 1½
Fats choice              1

..........................................

**Carbohydrate** 18 g
   Fibre 2 g
**Protein** 13 g
**Fat** 9 g
   Saturated 2 g
**Sodium** 743 mg
**Calories** 198

# Open-Face Tuna Apple Melt

Served on a whole wheat English muffin, this sandwich filling combines all of the food groups.

| | | |
|---|---|---:|
| 1 | can (170 g) tuna, drained and rinsed | 1 |
| ¾ cup | finely diced unpeeled apple | 175 mL |
| ⅓ cup | diced celery | 75 mL |
| ½ cup | coarsely shredded light Cheddar cheese | 125 mL |
| ¼ cup | light mayonnaise | 50 mL |
| 2 tbsp | chopped walnuts | 25 mL |
| 2 tsp | fresh lemon juice | 10 mL |
| Pinch | freshly ground pepper | Pinch |
| 4 | whole wheat English muffins (65 g each), halved | 4 |

In bowl, flake tuna; add apple, celery, cheese, mayonnaise, walnuts and lemon juice. Season lightly with pepper to taste.

Place muffin halves on baking sheet, cut side up; toast under broiler. Remove pan from oven. Spread ¼ cup (50 mL) of the tuna mixture over each muffin half, covering entire surface. Return to oven and broil until cheese bubbles and filling is warm.

## HIGH FIBRE

**Lunch Menu 16**

........................................

**Prep** · 15 minutes
**Broil** · under 5 minutes
**Yield** · 2 cups (500 mL) filling, 8 open-face English muffin halves

........................................

**Each Serving** · 2 muffin halves, ½ cup (125 mL) filling
Carb choices                2
Meat & Alternatives choices   2
Fats choice                 1

........................................

**Carbohydrate** 33 g
  Fibre 5 g
**Protein** 20 g
**Fat** 11 g
  Saturated 2 g
**Sodium** 573 mg
**Calories** 295

## Lunch Menu 24

........................................

**Prep** · 15 minutes
**Cook** · 15 minutes
**Yield** · 4 servings

........................................

**Each Serving** · ¼ of recipe

| | |
|---|---|
| Carb choices | 2 |
| Meat & Alternatives choice | 1 |
| Fats choices | 2½ |

........................................

**Carbohydrate** 35 g
  Fibre 3 g
**Protein** 12 g
**Fat** 15 g
  Saturated 3 g
**Sodium** 517 mg

**Calories** 315

Pesto's intense basil flavour makes this simple cheese and tomato pizza sizzle. Using olive oil in the pesto sauce keeps this pizza low in saturated fat.

| | | |
|---|---|---|
| ¼ cup | bottled pesto sauce | 50 mL |
| 1 | unbaked (227 g) thin shell flatbread, 12 inches (30 cm) | 1 |
| ½ cup | shredded part-skim mozzarella or light Cheddar cheese | 125 mL |
| 2 tbsp | finely chopped onion | 25 mL |
| 1 cup | chopped tomatoes | 250 mL |

Spread pesto evenly over flatbread. Sprinkle with cheese and onion. Top with tomatoes.

Place on non-stick baking sheet or pizza pan. Bake in 425°F (220°C) oven for 15 minutes or until cheese has melted and tomatoes are slightly cooked.

Slice into 4 wedges to serve.

## Pack-to-Go Chickpea Salad

Fresh herbs brighten the flavour of chickpeas. If you decide to use dried herbs instead of fresh, reduce the amount.

| | | |
|---|---|---|
| 2 tbsp | red wine vinegar | 25 mL |
| 1 tbsp | olive or canola oil | 15 mL |
| 1 | clove garlic, minced | 1 |
| ¼ tsp | each salt and freshly ground pepper | 1 mL |
| 1 | can (19 oz/540 mL) chickpeas, drained and rinsed | 1 |
| ¼ cup | each diced sweet red pepper, cucumber and onion | 50 mL |
| ¼ cup | pitted black olives (see Tip) | 50 mL |
| 1 tbsp | chopped fresh parsley | 15 mL |
| 1 tsp | each chopped fresh oregano, rosemary and thyme (or ½ tsp/2 mL each dried) | 5 mL |

In bowl, whisk together vinegar, oil, garlic, salt and pepper. Set aside.

In large bowl, combine chickpeas, red pepper, cucumber, onion, olives, parsley, oregano, rosemary and thyme.

Pour vinegar mixture over salad, tossing gently. Cover and refrigerate for several hours or overnight to allow flavours to blend.

◉ *The easiest way to pit an olive is to smack it with the side of a chef's knife.*

◉ *Non-olive lovers may replace them with chopped sweet green pepper.*

**Lunch Menu 15**

..................................................

**Prep** · 15 minutes
**Refrigerate** · several hours or overnight
**Yield** · 4 servings, 3 cups (750 mL)

..................................................

**Each Serving** · about ⅔ cup (150 mL)

| | |
|---|---|
| Carb choice | 1 |
| Meat & Alternatives choice | ½ |
| Fats choice | 1 |

..................................................

| | |
|---|---|
| **Carbohydrate** 24 g | |
| Fibre 7 g | |
| **Protein** 7 g | |
| **Fat** 6 g | |
| Saturated 0 g | |
| **Sodium** 361 mg | |
| **Calories** 181 | |

## Warm Tortellini, Asparagus and Tomato Salad

**Lunch Menu 18**

......................................

**Prep** · 20 minutes
**Cook** · about 10 minutes
**Yield** · 6 servings, 8 cups
　　　　(2 L) pasta mixture

......................................

**Each Serving** · 1⅓ cups
　　　　(325 mL) pasta mixture
　　　　over salad greens
Carb choices　　　　　　　2
Meat & Alternatives choice　1
Fats choices　　　　　　　1½

......................................

**Carbohydrate** 35 g
　Fibre 3 g
**Protein** 11 g
**Fat** 10 g
　Saturated 3 g
**Sodium** 273 mg
**Calories** 264

A classic oil and vinegar dressing gives this pasta and vegetable salad lots of oomph. It makes a wonderful lunch when hosting friends. After enjoying this salad, our friend Mary said she had to have the recipe!

| | | |
|---|---|---|
| 3½ cups | frozen or fresh cheese-filled tortellini (350 g pkg) | 825 mL |
| 2 cups | sliced asparagus (about ½ lb/250 g) | 500 mL |
| ¼ cup | coarsely grated Parmesan cheese (see Tip) | 50 mL |
| ¼ cup | chopped fresh basil (or 1 tbsp/15 mL dried) | 50 mL |
| 2 tbsp | each red wine vinegar and balsamic vinegar | 25 mL |
| 1 tbsp | olive oil | 15 mL |
| 1 to 2 | cloves garlic, minced | 1 to 2 |
| | freshly ground pepper | |
| 4 cups | assorted greens | 1 L |
| 1 cup | halved cherry tomatoes (quartered if large) | 250 mL |
| 2 | green onions, sliced | 2 |

In large pot of boiling water, cook pasta according to package directions, adding asparagus during last 3 minutes of cooking. Drain and toss with cheese.

Meanwhile, in large bowl, combine basil, red wine and balsamic vinegars, oil, garlic, and pepper to taste. Add greens, tomatoes and onions; toss to combine.

To serve, place ¾ cup (175 mL) of the assorted greens on 6 individual plates and top each with 1⅓ cups (325 mL) of the pasta mixture.

⊕ *There are two kinds of grated Parmesan cheese available in stores. One is very fine, whereas the second is coarsely grated. We think the latter has a better flavour, but either is fine in this recipe. Remember that Parmesan is also available by the piece, to be freshly grated as you wish.*

## Waldorf Salad

The original salad developed at the Waldorf Astoria Hotel in New York City contained only apples, celery and mayonnaise. Chopped walnuts later became an integral part of the recipe—and here we add cabbage and raisins. Oh well, recipes are always evolving!

| | | |
|---|---|---|
| 2 cups | coarsely shredded cabbage (see Tip) | 500 mL |
| ½ cup | sliced celery | 125 mL |
| 2 tbsp | each finely chopped raisins and walnuts | 25 mL |
| ¼ cup | low-fat plain yogurt | 50 mL |
| 2 tbsp | light mayonnaise | 25 mL |
| ½ tsp | fresh lemon juice | 2 mL |
| 2 cups | chopped apples (2 medium) | 500 mL |
| | salt and freshly ground pepper | |

In bowl, combine cabbage, celery, raisins and walnuts.

In small bowl, whisk together yogurt, mayonnaise and lemon juice; stir into cabbage mixture. Season with salt and pepper to taste.

Cover and refrigerate for at least 30 minutes so flavours develop. Stir in apples just before serving.

⊛ *In a hurry? Use the packaged coleslaw mixtures available in the produce sections of supermarkets.*

**Lunch Menu 21**
**Dinner Menu 15**

..................................................

**Prep** · 15 minutes
**Refrigerate** · 30 minutes or longer
**Yield** · 4 servings, 5 cups (1.25 L)

..................................................

**Each Serving** · 1¼ cups (300 mL)
Carb choice — 1
Fats choice — 1

..................................................

**Carbohydrate** 20 g
   Fibre 3 g
**Protein** 2 g
**Fat** 5 g
   Saturated 0 g
**Sodium** 74 mg
**Calories** 122

## LENTIL, VEGETABLE AND KASHA SALAD

**Lunch Menu 22**

...............................................

**Prep** · 25 minutes
**Cook** · 10 minutes
**Refrigerate** · up to 4 days
**Yield** · 6 servings, 6 cups (1.5 L)

...............................................

**Each Serving** · 1 cup (250 mL)
Carb choices                          2
Fats choices                         1½

...............................................

**Carbohydrate** 30 g
    Fibre 3 g
**Protein** 7 g
**Fat** 7 g
    Saturated 1 g
**Sodium** 174 mg
**Calories** 196

Kasha is roasted hulled buckwheat kernels, cracked into granules—fine, medium and coarse. This recipe uses coarse, easily found in health food stores and some supermarkets. Like lentils, kasha alone is an incomplete protein, but when combined, they become a complete protein. We prefer using canned lentils to speed up preparation.

| | | |
|---|---|---|
| 1 cup | raw coarse kasha (see Tip) | 250 mL |
| 1 | can (19 oz/540 mL) lentils, drained and rinsed | 1 |
| 1 cup | grated carrot (1 large) | 250 mL |
| ½ cup | diced sweet red or green pepper | 125 mL |
| 2 | thinly sliced green onions | 2 |
| ¼ cup | chopped fresh coriander (see Tip) | 50 mL |
| ¼ cup | red wine vinegar | 50 mL |
| 2 tbsp | olive oil | 25 mL |
| 1 tbsp | dried tarragon | 15 mL |
| ¼ tsp | each salt and freshly ground pepper | 1 mL |
| 2 tbsp | chopped walnuts | 25 mL |

In saucepan over high heat, bring 2½ cups (625 mL) water to a boil; stir in kasha. Reduce heat, cover and cook for 12 minutes or until water is absorbed and kasha is tender. Cool.

In large bowl, combine lentils, carrot, red pepper, onions and coriander. Stir in vinegar, oil, tarragon, salt and pepper.

When kasha is cool, stir into lentil mixture. Serve salad at room temperature. Sprinkle each serving with 1 tsp (5 mL) chopped walnuts.

⊕ *Kasha and lentils are on the "use more often" list.*
⊕ *Coriander, also known as Chinese parsley or cilantro, is very commonly found in the salad section of stores. If you prefer, you can replace it with fresh parsley.*

## Fruit and Feta Salad with Basil Buttermilk Dressing

From berries to crumbled feta cheese, this salad is a kaleidoscope of bold flavours and compelling textures. Use pre-packaged assorted salad greens or any combination of lettuces. Add fresh berries, such as raspberries, blueberries and strawberries.

| 6 cups | assorted greens | 1.5 L |
| ¼ cup | *Basil Buttermilk Dressing* | 50 mL |
| 1 cup | each blueberries, raspberries and sliced strawberries | 250 mL |
| ¾ cup | crumbled feta cheese (110 g) | 175 mL |

Place greens in large bowl. Drizzle with dressing; toss gently to coat.

Divide salad evenly among 4 plates; top each serving with ¾ cup (175 mL) of the mixed berries and one-quarter of the cheese. Serve immediately.

### Basil Buttermilk Dressing:

| ⅔ cup | well-shaken buttermilk | 150 mL |
| ⅓ cup | light mayonnaise | 75 mL |
| 2 tbsp | finely chopped fresh basil or 2 tsp (10 mL) dried | 25 mL |
| 1 | small clove garlic, minced | 1 |
| Pinch | each salt and freshly ground pepper | Pinch |

In small bowl, whisk together buttermilk, mayonnaise, basil, garlic, salt and pepper.

Chill, covered, for 1 hour, to allow flavours to develop.

◉ *Save extra dressing for another salad or use as a dip for raw vegetables.*

**HIGH FIBRE**

**Lunch Menu 26**

..........................

**Salad:**
**Prep** · 20 minutes
**Yield** · 4 servings

**Each Serving** · ¼ of recipe
Carb choice                     ½
Meat & Alternatives choice    1
Fats choice                      1

**Carbohydrate** 16 g
  Fibre 5 g
**Protein** 7 g
**Fat** 8 g
  Saturated 4 g
**Sodium** 381 mg
**Calories** 160

..........................

**Dressing:**
**Prep** · 10 minutes
**Refrigerate** · 1 hour or longer
**Yield** · 1 cup (250 mL) (see Tip)

**Each Serving** · 1 tbsp (15 mL)
Extra

**Carbohydrate** 1 g
  Fibre 0 g
**Protein** 0 g
**Fat** 2 g
  Saturated 0 g
**Sodium** 53 mg
**Calories** 19

**Lunch Menu 29**

**SALAD:**

**Prep** · 30 minutes if chicken is cooked

**Yield** · 5 servings, 5 cups (1.25 L)

**Each Serving** · 1 cup (250 mL)

Carb choice ½

Meat & Alternatives choices 3½

**Carbohydrate** 12 g

Fibre 2 g

**Protein** 27 g

**Fat** 8 g

Saturated 1 g

**Sodium** 289 mg

**Calories** 227

**DRESSING:**

**Prep** · 10 minutes

**Refrigerate** · several days

**Yield** · 1 cup (250 mL) dressing

**Each Serving** · 1 tbsp (15 mL)

Extra

**Carbohydrate** 1 g

Fibre 0 g

**Protein** 1 g

**Fat** 1 g

Saturated 0 g

**Sodium** 99 mg

**Calories** 17

The sweetness of peaches complements the spiciness of curried chicken. Be sure to add the peaches just before serving. Make the dressing ahead of time to allow flavours to blend. You will have some left over; use it for a dip.

| | | |
|---|---|---|
| 3 cups | cooked bite-size pieces of chicken | 750 mL |
| 1 | can (14 oz/398 mL) peach halves, drained and cut into small pieces (see Tip) | 1 |
| ½ cup | sliced green onions | 125 mL |
| 1 cup | grated carrot | 250 mL |
| ¾ cup | *Curried Dressing* | 175 mL |
| ¼ cup | pecan halves, preferably toasted | 50 mL |

In large bowl, stir together chicken, peaches, green onions and carrot until combined; toss lightly with **Curried Dressing**.

Top with pecans. Serve immediately.

**CURRIED DRESSING:**

| | | |
|---|---|---|
| ½ cup | low-fat plain yogurt | 125 mL |
| ¼ cup | light mayonnaise | 50 mL |
| 2 tbsp | fresh lemon juice | 25 mL |
| 1 tbsp | minced fresh gingerroot | 15 mL |
| 2–3 tsp | curry powder | 10–15 mL |
| 2 | cloves garlic, minced | 2 |
| ½ tsp | salt | 2 mL |
| Pinch | each cayenne pepper & freshly ground pepper | Pinch |

In bowl, whisk yogurt, mayonnaise, lemon juice, gingerroot, curry powder, garlic, salt, cayenne and pepper until smooth.

Cover and refrigerate until ready to use (dressing will keep for a couple of days).

⊕ *Naturally, we like to use fresh peaches when they are in season, but peaches canned in juice work just fine.*

# GARDEN-FRESH TOMATO CHEESE PIE

Madame Velauney served us this great tomato pie at her *chambre d'hôte* in the Loire Valley, France. We don't think anything better could happen to a tomato. Serve this wonderful pie hot from the oven or at room temperature.

| | | |
|---|---|---|
| 1 | unbaked 9-inch (23 cm) frozen shallow pastry shell, thawed | 1 |
| 2–3 tbsp | Dijon mustard | 25–45 mL |
| 1½ cups | coarsely shredded part-skim mozzarella or Swiss cheese | 375 mL |
| 3 | medium tomatoes, sliced ½ inch (1 cm) thick | 3 |
| 2 tbsp | chopped fresh parsley | 25 mL |
| 1 to 2 | cloves garlic, minced | 1 to 2 |
| ½ tsp | dried thyme (or 2 tsp/10 mL chopped fresh) | 2 mL |
| Pinch | freshly ground pepper | Pinch |

Prick surface of pastry shell with fork in several places. Bake in 400°F (200°C) oven for 10 minutes.

Spread mustard over bottom of shell. Sprinkle with cheese. Top with tomato slices in single layer, overlapping slightly. Bake for 20 minutes longer or until cheese melts and tomatoes are slightly softened.

Meanwhile, in small bowl, stir together parsley, garlic, thyme and pepper. Sprinkle over pie just before serving. Cut into 6 wedges to serve.

**Lunch Menu 30**

..............................................

**Prep** · 15 minutes
**Cook** · about 30 minutes
**Yield** · 6 servings

..............................................

**Each Serving** · ⅙ of recipe

| | |
|---|---|
| Carb choice | 1 |
| Meat & Alternatives choice | 1 |
| Fats choices | 2 |

..............................................

**Carbohydrate** 15 g
  Fibre 1 g
**Protein** 10 g
**Fat** 12 g
  Saturated 5 g
**Sodium** 343 mg
**Calories** 206

# MICROWAVE MUSHROOM SCRAMBLED EGG

. . . . . . . . . . . . . . . . . . . . . . . . . . . . .

**Prep** · about 5 minutes
**Cook** · about 1½ minutes
**Yield** · 1 serving

. . . . . . . . . . . . . . . . . . . . . . . . . . . . .

**Each Serving** · 1 egg with
    mushrooms
Meat & Alternatives choice    1
Fats choice    1

. . . . . . . . . . . . . . . . . . . . . . . . . . . . .

**Carbohydrate** 3 g
    Fibre 1 g
**Protein** 7 g
**Fat** 7 g
    Saturated 2 g
**Sodium** 86 mg
**Calories** 102

This simple recipe is a fast approach to scrambled eggs for lunch. See below if you need more servings or would like additional seasoning suggestions.

| | | |
|---|---|---|
| ½ tsp | soft margarine or butter | 2 mL |
| ½ cup | sliced mushrooms | 125 mL |
| 1 | egg | 1 |
| 1 tbsp | water or milk | 15 mL |
| ¼ tsp | dried basil or oregano | 1 mL |

In large microwave-safe bowl, melt margarine on High (100%). Add mushrooms; cook on High (100%) for 30 seconds.

In small bowl, stir together egg, water and basil; add to mushrooms. Cover with plastic wrap. Microwave on Medium-High (70%), stirring once, for about 50 seconds. Let stand for about 30 seconds before serving.

**VARIATION**

***Seasoned Scrambled Egg:*** Vary flavours by adding seasonings such as a pinch of dry mustard or ground nutmeg, or sesame or celery seeds.

⊕ *For additional servings, increase cooking time according to how many eggs are being prepared. See chart below.*

*2 eggs* · 2 tbsp (25 mL) water or milk
    1 tsp (5 mL) soft margarine or butter
    Cook for 1½ to 1¾ minutes

*4 eggs* · ¼ cup (50 mL) water or milk
    2 tsp (10 mL) soft margarine or butter
    Cook for 2½ to 3 minutes

*6 eggs* · ⅓ cup (75 mL) water or milk
    1 tbsp (15 mL) soft margarine or butter
    Cook for 3 to 3½ minutes

## STOVE-TOP MACARONI AND CHEESE WITH ROASTED TOMATO

Busy days call for ready-to-serve lunches like the all-time favourite mac 'n' cheese. But we've given it a new twist—roasted tomatoes. Whole wheat pasta used in this recipe has twice as much fibre as regular pasta; however, regular pasta can also be used.

| | | |
|---|---|---|
| 4 cups | halved cherry tomatoes | 1 L |
| | freshly ground pepper | |
| 1 tsp | soft margarine or butter | 5 mL |
| 2 tbsp | finely chopped onion | 25 mL |
| 1 | small clove garlic, minced | 1 |
| 2 cups | low-fat milk | 500 mL |
| 2 tbsp | all-purpose flour | 25 mL |
| ½ tsp | Dijon mustard | 2 mL |
| ¼ tsp | salt | 1 mL |
| Dash | hot pepper sauce | Dash |
| 1½ cups | shredded light Cheddar cheese | 375 mL |
| 1¼ cups | whole wheat or regular elbow macaroni | 300 mL |

Place tomatoes in 13- x 9-inch (3.5 L) baking dish sprayed with non-stick cooking spray. Sprinkle with pepper. Bake in 375°F (190°C) oven, stirring occasionally, for 30 minutes or until lightly browned.

Meanwhile, melt margarine in saucepan over medium-low heat; cook onion and garlic for 5 minutes (do not brown).

Whisk together milk, flour, mustard, salt and hot pepper sauce; gradually stir into onion mixture. Cook, stirring constantly, until mixture is smooth and thickened. Add cheese; stir until melted.

In large pot of boiling water, cook macaroni for 7 minutes or until al dente (tender but firm); drain. Return to saucepan and add cheese sauce and roasted tomatoes; toss well to combine.

**Lunch Menu 21**

....................................

**Prep** · 20 minutes
**Cook** · 30 minutes,
        including roasting tomatoes
**Yield** · 4 servings, 5 cups (1.25 L)

....................................

**Each Serving** · 1¼ cups (300 mL)
Carb choices                    2½
Meat & Alternatives choices  2
Fats choice                         1

....................................

**Carbohydrate** 42 g
  Fibre 4 g
**Protein** 20 g
**Fat** 9 g
  Saturated 5 g
**Sodium** 415 mg
**Calories** 324

## Spring Rhubarb Sauce

**Lunch Menu 18**
**Dinner Menu 25**
**Snack Menu 3**

**Prep** · 10 minutes
**Cook** · about 5 minutes
**Yield** · 5 servings,
2½ cups (625 mL)

**Each Serving** · ½ cup (125 mL)
Carb choice ½

**Carbohydrate** 8 g
Fibre 2 g
**Protein** 1 g
**Fat** 0 g
**Sodium** 4 mg
**Calories** 34

Botanically speaking, rhubarb is a vegetable, a member of the buckwheat family, but is eaten as a fruit. (Be aware that the plant's leaves contain oxalic acid and can be quite toxic.) As rhubarb tends to be somewhat tart, a sweetener is often added. The first stalks pushing out of the ground are a welcome signal of spring's arrival.

| | | |
|---|---|---|
| 4 cups | sliced rhubarb (8 thin stalks) | 2 L |
| ½ cup | water | 125 mL |
| 2 tsp | grated orange rind | 10 mL |
| ¼ cup | granular low-calorie sweetener with sucralose | 50 mL |
| 1 tbsp | granulated sugar | 15 mL |

*Stove top*: In saucepan over medium heat, cook rhubarb, water and orange rind for 5 minutes or until rhubarb is tender. Remove from heat; stir in sweetener and sugar.
*Microwave:* Combine rhubarb, water and orange rind in microwave-safe casserole. Cover and microwave on High (100%), stirring once, for 3 minutes or until rhubarb is tender. Stir in sweetener and sugar.

⊕ *Since rhubarb freezes well, wash, chop and bag it in amounts suitable for this recipe.*

## Microwave Applesauce

Warm applesauce is one of life's great comfort foods. Using a microwave oven results in short cooking time and minimal cleanup!

| | | |
|---|---|---:|
| 3½ cups | peeled, cored and sliced cooking apples (about 3 large Spy, Spartan or McIntosh) | 875 mL |
| ¾ cup | water | 175 mL |
| ¼ tsp | cinnamon | 1 mL |

In 6-cup (1.5 L) microwave-safe dish, combine apple slices and water. Cover and microwave on High (100%), stirring once, for 8 minutes or until apples are tender. Stir in cinnamon. Serve warm or at room temperature.

**Lunch Menu 29**
**Dinner Menu 24**
**Snack Menu 2**

...................................................

**Prep** · 10 minutes
**Cook** · 8 minutes
**Yield** · 4 servings, 2 cups (500 mL)

...................................................

**Each Serving** · ½ cup (125 mL)
Carb choice                   1

...................................................

**Carbohydrate** 15 g
   Fibre 2 g
**Protein** 0 g
**Fat** 0 g
**Sodium** 1 mg
**Calories** 58

# DINNER

After the day's activities are done, it's time to relax and wind down with a satisfying meal. For most, it's the major meal of the day, and that's the way our menus treat it. Our recipes follow the healthiest, lowest-fat cooking methods: broiling, roasting, microwaving, steaming and stir-frying. Dinner is traditionally a meal made up of meat (the protein), potatoes or rice or pasta (the starch), vegetables and a dessert. When planning dinner, we tend to think of the protein portion of the meal first—will it be poultry, fish, meat or a meat alternative? But remember that protein is only a small part of a healthy meal. Better we question what vegetables and whole grains or starches we will eat, *then* fit in the protein choice. Think of filling your dinner plate this way: half covered by vegetables, one-quarter covered by whole grains or starches, and one-quarter covered by protein.

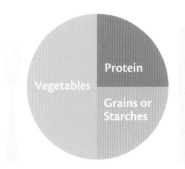

### How much?

Some of the prepared foods in the menus and recipes need to be measured so you know you have the right amount on your plate. We suggest you have a set of graduated "dry" measuring cups—the ones in ¼-cup, ⅓-cup, ½-cup and 1-cup (or 50 mL, 75 mL, 125 mL and 250 mL) sizes. Having these measures at hand speeds up serving. These are also useful for measuring dry ingredients in recipes, so they do double duty. Two or three glass "liquid" measuring cups in 1-cup, 2-cup and possibly 4-cup (or 250 mL, 500 mL and 1 L) sizes come in handy as well.

### VEGETABLES

Let's start with how we fill half the plate. What are vegetables and why are they so important?

*Opposite:* Italian Beef and Vegetables (page 104)

**VEGETABLES WITH THE MOST FIBRE:**

- broccoli
- carrots
- cauliflower
- corn
- green beans
- green peas
- rutabaga
- tomato

Vegetables are the cornerstone of any healthy meal, especially if you have diabetes. They help fill you up, have very little effect on blood glucose and supply nearly all the vitamins, minerals and fibre essential to good health—especially valuable disease-fighting anti-oxidants. From a diabetes point of view, potatoes and corn are not vegetables but rather are starches. However, tomatoes, eggplants, squashes and peppers, although considered fruits by botanists, are considered to be vegetables by the rest of us. Everything else we have always thought was a vegetable probably is a vegetable!

All living plants produce carbohydrate and store it in their roots or fruit in the form of starches and sugars. Vegetables that are the leaf, stem or flower of a plant, or that are very young, contain only small amounts of carbohydrate and thus can be eaten freely by someone with diabetes. Sweet-tasting root vegetables and other vegetables that take longer to ripen contain more carbohydrate, because they have more time to store it. They used to be grouped with fruit as FRUITS & VEGETABLES. However, we now know that some root vegetables, such as carrots and beets, have much less available carbohydrate than was once thought because of the large amount of fibre they contain. In the new meal planning system, all vegetables are classed as "free," with the exception of some of the sweeter vegetables (see Appendix I, page 180).

Vegetables are considered to be "nutrient dense," that is, they have a high amount of nutrients for the number of calories they supply. Considering the cost of most vegetables relative to meats, they are a magnificent nutrition bargain!

## EVERYTHING YOU ALWAYS WANTED TO KNOW ABOUT VEGETABLES!

*Asparagus:* Asparagus contains a good supply of vitamins and minerals. Microwave or cook, covered and upright in a small amount of boiling water, for 3 to 5 minutes. Or stir-fry as in **Chicken and Asparagus Stir-Fry** (page 96).

*Beets:* Notable for their sweet, earthy flavour, beets are a rich source of fibre and are very low in calories. The best way to cook beets is to microwave or roast them whole with their skins on and stem and root ends untrimmed.

**Bok choy:** No longer limited to Asian cooking, it is a mild versatile vegetable and a good source of vitamins A, C and calcium. Bok choy is very low in calories. Choose stalks with no sign of yellowing. Wash and chop as desired. Bok choy can be parboiled, steamed or fried.

**Broccoli and cauliflower:** Some call broccoli "green goodness." This high-fibre food certainly boasts more nutrients than almost any other vegetable, especially calcium and beta-carotene (vitamin A). Peel stalks if they are tough, but be sure to include the tender leaves. Cauliflower is rich in vitamin C and very low in calories. Steam both vegetables or microwave for about 5 minutes.

**Brussels sprouts and cabbage:** Along with vitamin C, both of these vegetables contain fibre. The best way to cook them is as quickly as possible and in the least amount of liquid possible—microwave, steam or stir-fry.

**Carrots:** They are one of the best sources of beta-carotene and fibre and one of the least expensive. 1 CARB CHOICE gets you 22 mini carrots—now that's a real bargain! Our **Minted Carrots and Snow Peas** recipe (page 127) is a great use for this humble vegetable.

**Green beans:** Beans contain good amounts of beta-carotene and vitamin C and are rich in fibre. Since they grow quickly and are picked young, they are low in carbohydrate. Trim stem ends only; cover and steam or microwave for 3 to 5 minutes.

**Leeks:** They are prized for their subtle onion flavour and rich folic acid content. Steam cut-up leeks for 3 to 5 minutes or steam whole for 10 to 15 minutes.

**Mushrooms:** Since mushrooms grow in the dark, they have little or no carbohydrate and few calories. Sauté mushrooms, uncovered, with a very small amount of broth or olive oil over medium-high heat for 3 to 5 minutes until all liquid is evaporated. Use as a great flavour addition to recipes or on their own. See **Curried Shrimp and Mushrooms** (page 117).

**Onions:** Sliced, chopped, grated or diced, onions add flavour to a dish. They are cooked in many ways, based on the recipe being

prepared. Since they are low in nutrients, the cooking method is not a concern.

*Rutabaga:* Some people still think of rutabagas as turnips, but they are two different vegetables. Rutabagas are larger, rounder and have a yellow flesh. Turnips are smaller and white fleshed. Cut rutabagas up and steam or boil for 7 to 10 minutes. They are the best source of vitamin C of all the root vegetables and contain beta-carotene.

*Sweet and hot peppers:* Like onions, peppers can be chopped, diced and sliced. Very rich in beta-carotene, they add flavour as well as colour. Peppers are great sautéed, stir-fried or stuffed.

*Snow peas:* Snow peas should be shiny and flat. The smallest ones are sweetest and most tender. Remove tips and strings from both ends of the pod. Cover and steam for 1 to 2 minutes to retain vitamin C. Try ***Snow Peas with Ginger*** (page 126).

*Spinach and Swiss chard:* Select small leaves with good green colour and thin stems. Wash but do not dry. Steam spinach for about 5 minutes. These greens are rich in vitamin A, folic acid and iron. You can increase iron absorption by serving with a source of vitamin C, such as a lemon or orange.

*Tomatoes:* Wonderful served raw with fresh basil, they can also be baked, broiled or sautéed. See ***Salmon with Roasted Cherry Tomatoes*** (page 115).

*Zucchini:* High in water content, zucchini is very low in calories. Eat raw or cut into slices and steam or sauté for 3 to 5 minutes.

### The sweeter vegetables

These are also packed with nutrients but have a significant amount of carbohydrate when eaten in larger portions. When you want to eat more than 1 cup (250 mL), count it as 1 CARB CHOICE. If less than that, they can be eaten freely.

*Green peas:* Fresh peas have a very short season, and most of the ones we eat are sold frozen. It's best to quickly steam or microwave peas. They are a good source of protein and vitamin C. Frozen green peas retain their colour, flavour and nutrients better than canned, and are low in sodium.

**Parsnips:** Considered a cold-weather root vegetable and a cousin to the carrot, they are easy to prepare. Vitamin C and folic acid are the most prominent nutrients. Steaming is the best way to cook them. But parsnips are also delicious dry-roasted alone or with other vegetables as in our **Oven-Roasted Winter Vegetables** (page 123).

**Winter squash:** An excellent source of beta-carotene, these are hard shelled and keep for a long time. A very versatile vegetable, squash can be baked, boiled, microwaved, or steamed as in **Butternut Squash Casserole** (page 124).

### Fresh, frozen or canned?

Vegetables, fresh from the field and used as soon as possible, have the best flavour, texture and the most nutritional value. However, if they're wilted, pale or stored improperly, you're better off with frozen or even canned. Vegetables, flash-frozen soon after picking, retain most of their nutrients. Canned vegetables lose some vitamin C and often have large amounts of sodium and sometimes sugar added during processing.

### What is the best way to cook vegetables?

We have developed the "rule of least" for cooking vegetables: least peeling, least amount of cooking water, least time to cook and least waiting time after cooking.

Vegetable skins contain nutrients and fibre, so peeling should be done only when absolutely necessary. Completely submerging vegetables in water, then boiling and draining them removes most, if not all, of the water-soluble vitamins, such as vitamin C, thiamine, niacin, B6, B12 and folic acid. The longer vegetables are cooked, the more vitamin C is destroyed. Vegetables are at their flavour peak when cooked tender-crisp. When vegetables are not served immediately after cooking, they lose flavour as well as nutrients.

Microwave cooking is perfect for vegetables. More nutrients are retained, next to no water is required, and it's fast. Cover vegetables while microwaving to reduce cooking time and nutrient loss. Cook quickly on High (100%). Stir-frying is also excellent for the same reasons. Steaming uses a minimum of water and is almost as good as the other two methods.

### Are some vegetables better for me than others?

The most nutritious vegetables are broccoli, spinach, Brussels sprouts, lima beans, peas, asparagus, artichokes, cauliflower and carrots, rated on their content of vitamin A, thiamin, niacin, riboflavin, vitamin C, potassium, iron and calcium.

## GRAINS & STARCHES

Carbohydrate stored as starch in plants is the single most important source of food energy in the world and our body's principal source of energy. Since the carbohydrate we eat also has a major impact on blood glucose, this food group is very important for people with diabetes. It needs to be part of every meal, but in limited amounts. Our dinner menus and recipes use a variety of GRAINS & STARCHES, with emphasis on slowly digested ones like pasta and parboiled rice, as well as sweet and white potatoes.

### Potatoes

The potato is a tuber, a swollen underground stem that stores surplus starch in order to feed the above-ground plant. Few foods are as wholesome as a potato. Carbohydrate, vitamins (particularly C) and minerals—the potato has them all in ample amounts and some protein as well. Many consider potatoes fattening. Not so; the only fat is what you add in cooking or at the table. Properly prepared, we feel potatoes taste so good they really don't need much of anything.

The best way to prepare potatoes is to cook them in their skins. The skin is an excellent source of fibre, with many nutrients just below it. So simply scrub unpeeled potatoes under cold water before cooking. Try to eat potatoes with their skin, which is where most of the iron and fibre are found. If you must peel them, use a vegetable peeler to remove the thinnest layer possible.

Potatoes are superb no matter how you cook them; boiled, grilled on the barbecue, or baked in the oven as in **Light Scalloped Potatoes** (page 128). Sweet potatoes are among the most nutritious foods in the vegetable kingdom. Sweet potato is sensational baked or mashed, or in **Sweet Potato Frites** (page 129). They have slightly more calories and carbohydrate than white potatoes but a lower glycemic index. With their dense, creamy texture, sweet potatoes cook well in the microwave.

## Rice and pasta

Rice and pasta are high in starchy carbohydrate. Both parboiled brown and white rice and whole grain pasta provide higher vitamin, mineral and fibre levels, and have a lower glycemic index. Both come in sufficient variety to delight the most adventurous cook. They are economical food choices. Preparation of both is fast and easy. Just follow the directions on the package.

## Rice or pasta "on call"

We think having rice "on call" in the freezer is the ultimate home convenience food. You may well ask, What's that? It is simply cooking extra rice, then measuring it into small freezer bags in appropriate serving sizes. Seal, label the bags and pop them into the freezer. Rice will keep frozen for up to six months. Keep pasta "on call" in the same manner as rice.

To reheat rice, transfer it from its bag to a small dish. Add 1 tbsp (15 mL) water, cover with waxed paper and reheat in a microwave oven on High (100%) for about 1 minute or until hot. Reheated rice makes a snap of Dinner Menus 4, 6 and 21.

To reheat pasta, remove it from its bag and lower it into a small saucepan of boiling water. Return to a boil and cook for 1 minute; drain. It is so convenient.

## MEAT & ALTERNATIVES

We have focused on a wide variety of protein foods in our dinner menus. Some are vegetarian, some have chicken or meat, some fish or seafood. But they all provide about 21 grams of protein in each dinner or 3 MEAT & ALTERNATIVES CHOICES.

Protein is the basic building material of life and should be part of every meal. It provides us with the amino acid building blocks we need for growth and repair. Nine of these amino acids are called essential. They must come from our daily diet because our bodies cannot make them. All animal sources of protein are *complete* proteins because they contain all nine essential amino acids. We get animal protein from meat, poultry, fish, eggs and dairy products. But you don't always need these foods to get the protein you require. It's possible to get all the necessary nutrients from a vegetarian diet and manage your diabetes effectively at the same time (see Meat Alternatives on pages 86–87).

### Meat

The saturated fat in meat is its one downside, but choosing leaner cuts of beef and trimming them well reduces the problem. So when cooking beef, choose cuts with the word *round* (top round, ground round) or *loin* (tenderloin, sirloin) in the name. These are among the leanest cuts. As with beef, the guidelines for pork and lamb are to choose lean cuts (tenderloin, centre loin or extra-lean). Trim all visible fat before cooking.

Lean cooking methods include roasting, broiling, grilling, stir-frying, braising and stewing. Less tender cuts benefit from braising or stewing, as in **Oven Beef Stew** (page 105). More tender cuts can be roasted, broiled or barbecued, as in **Balsamic Strip Loin Steak** (page 106).

### Poultry

Chicken and turkey breasts are extremely lean and low in calories. When cooking, be sure to remove the skin where most of the fat is. Use cooking methods similar to those for meat. See recipes for **Rosemary Lemon Chicken** (page 98) and **Chicken and Asparagus Stir-Fry** (page 96).

### Fish

Fast and easy to prepare, fish is a great substitute for higher-fat meats. Fish is delicate; if overcooked, it will be dry and tough. So use the "10-Minute Rule," also called the "Canadian Cooking Theory," devised by the Canadian Fisheries and Marine Service: measure the fish at its thickest point and cook at high heat (about 425°F/220°C) for 10 minutes for every inch (2.5 cm) of thickness. Fish can be baked, poached, grilled or microwaved. **Broiled Rainbow Trout with Fresh Tomato** (page 114) and **Oriental Salmon with Onions** (page 113) are two tantalizing and easy-to-prepare recipes.

### Meat alternatives

The term "meat alternatives," according to *Canada's Food Guide*, refers to eggs, dairy products, legumes, grains, nuts and seeds. Soy protein is the only *complete* plant-based protein. Other plant-based proteins are *incomplete*, because they lack one or more of the nine essential amino acids.

Lacto-ovo and lacto vegetarians add dairy products to meals in order to complete proteins, as we have in **Vegetarian Lasagna** (page 119). Strict vegetarians or vegans who eat only plant-based foods must balance grains with legumes and seeds to obtain adequate protein. A general guide is to combine grains or nuts and seeds with legumes, as in pasta with **Lentil Vegetable Spaghetti Sauce** (page 118). And you don't have to combine complementary proteins at the same meal as long as you eat a variety over the day. A dietitian can help you plan a healthy vegetarian diet, adequate in all nutrients, that is also suitable for diabetes.

## SUPERMARKET MEALS

In a hurry or want a break from cooking? Your local supermarket offers many frozen chicken, meat, fish or pasta entrées in single serving sizes. Although many are high in sodium, they are fine for occasional use. They can be conveniently heated and combined with vegetables and a salad for a satisfying meal. Just remember when shopping for frozen entrées to read labels carefully and compare. Look first at the amount of protein in one serving and then the amount of fat and calories. Choose the frozen entrée with the least fat and calories and the most protein. Compare them to our dinner menus, which contain about 35 grams of protein, 15 grams of fat, 60 grams of carbohydrate with around 500 calories for an *entire meal*, not just one course.

## DESSERTS

*Canada's Food Guide* recommends including more fruits in a greater variety in our meals. Our menus do just that. Fruit makes an excellent dessert. It tastes sweet, is relatively low in calories and is a major source of fibre, minerals and vitamins. Strawberries, pears and apples contain soluble fibre. Cantaloupe, oranges and bananas are rich in potassium. Most fruits are available all year long and can be purchased in small amounts. And if you don't happen to have the fruit suggested in a menu, check Appendix III, page 188, for other fruit choices.

We use fruit in some great-tasting and easy dessert recipes. Consider **Apple Bavarian Torte** (page 132), **Springtime Rhubarb Jelly Dessert** (page 138) with **Light Custard Sauce** (page 139) and **Granola Apple or Blueberry Crisp** (page 133).

In our dinner menus, we've tried to include many of your favourite comfort foods, updated so they're lower in fat and calories. An occasional higher-fat dessert has been balanced against a low-fat main course.

## Favourite Caesar Salad

**Dinner Menu 13, 20**

. . . . . . . . . . . . . . . . . . . . . . . . . . . . . . .

**SALAD:**
**Prep** · 15 minutes
**Yield** · 6 servings

**Each Serving** · ⅙ of recipe
| | |
|---|---|
| Carb choice | ½ |
| Fats choices | 1½ |

**Carbohydrate** 8 g
   Fibre 2 g
**Protein** 3 g
**Fat** 7 g
   Saturated 1 g
**Sodium** 117 mg
**Calories** 100

. . . . . . . . . . . . . . . . . . . . . . . . . . . . . . .

**DRESSING:**
**Prep** · 10 minutes
**Refrigerate** · up to 1 week
**Yield** · ¾ cup (175 mL) dressing

**Each Serving** · 1 tbsp (15 mL)
| | |
|---|---|
| Fats choices | 1½ |

**Carbohydrate** 1 g
   Fibre 0 g
**Protein** 0 g
**Fat** 7 g
   Saturated 1 g
**Sodium** 47 mg
**Calories** 64

In 1924, Caesar Cardini, an Italian restaurateur in Tijuana, Mexico, invented the famous Caesar salad. The original, which included raw eggs, has undergone some changes over the years. Ours, which eliminates the raw eggs, is far lighter and just as good as the popular full-fat version. You will have dressing left over for another meal.

| | | |
|---|---|---|
| 8 cups | torn romaine lettuce leaves (about 1 head) | 2 L |
| 1½ cups | toasted bread croutons | 375 mL |
| 1 tbsp | freshly grated Parmesan cheese | 15 mL |
| ⅓ cup | *Caesar Salad Dressing* | 75 mL |

In large salad bowl, combine torn lettuce, croutons and cheese.
Toss with salad dressing. Refrigerate remaining dressing for a second salad.

### CAESAR SALAD DRESSING:

| | | |
|---|---|---|
| 3 tbsp | light mayonnaise | 45 mL |
| 2 tbsp | red wine vinegar | 25 mL |
| 1 tbsp | Dijon mustard | 15 mL |
| 1 tbsp | fresh lemon juice | 15 mL |
| 1 | clove garlic, minced | 1 |
| ¼ cup | olive oil | 50 mL |
| 2 tbsp | water | 25 mL |
| Dash | hot pepper sauce | Dash |
| Dash | Worcestershire sauce | Dash |

In glass measure, whisk together mayonnaise, vinegar, mustard, lemon juice, garlic, hot pepper sauce and Worcestershire sauce.
Gradually whisk in olive oil and water until blended and smooth. Cover and refrigerate.

◉ *For single-serve salad, use about 1½ cups (325 mL) torn romaine lettuce leaves, ¼ cup (50 mL) toasted bread croutons, 1 tbsp (15 mL) salad dressing and ½ tsp (2 mL) freshly grated Parmesan cheese.*

# KATHRYN'S TABBOULEH SALAD

This Middle Eastern dish is made with bulgur, a processed form of wheat kernels available in coarse, medium or fine grind. Tabbouleh, always served cold, is a refreshing recipe for summertime dining. Marjorie's daughter-in-law makes this recipe for family gatherings.

| ¾ cup | bulgur | 175 mL |
|---|---|---|
| ¾ cup | water | 175 mL |
| 2 | tomatoes, seeded and chopped | 2 |
| ¼ cup | minced onion | 50 mL |
| 2 cups | loosely packed fresh parsley, minced | 500 mL |
| ¼ cup | chopped fresh mint | 50 mL |
| 3 tbsp | fresh lemon juice | 45 mL |
| 2 tbsp | olive oil | 25 mL |
| ½ tsp | salt | 2 mL |

In shallow covered bowl, soak bulgur in ¾ cup (175 mL) boiling water for 30 minutes or until all liquid is absorbed. Fluff with fork.

In large bowl, combine bulgur, tomatoes, onion, parsley, mint, lemon juice, oil and salt; toss lightly. Cover and refrigerate until ready to serve.

**Dinner Menu 10**

..........................................

**Prep** · 20 minutes
**Refrigerate** · at least 1 hour
before serving
**Yield** · 4 cups (1 L)

..........................................

**Each Serving** · 1 cup (250 mL)
Carb choice                     1
Fats choice                     1

..........................................

**Carbohydrate** 18 g
  Fibre 3 g
**Protein** 3 g
**Fat** 5 g
  Saturated 1 g
**Sodium** 114 mg
**Calories** 119

## Baby Greens with Oranges and Strawberries

**Dinner Menu 21**

We love the flavours of the lemon vinaigrette in this green salad with fruit. You can use the extra dressing over cooked vegetables—asparagus, green beans or broccoli. It's also great to drizzle over fish fillets before baking or grilling. You won't miss dessert with all these fruits!

### Salad:

**Prep** · 15 minutes
**Yield** · 4 servings

| 4 cups | mixed greens | 1 L |
|---|---|---|
| 1 | can (213 mL) mandarin oranges, drained | 1 |
| 2 cups | thinly sliced strawberries | 500 mL |
| ¼ cup | *Lemon Vinaigrette* | 50 mL |
| 2 tbsp | chopped toasted walnuts (see Tip) | 25 mL |

**Each Serving** · ¼ of recipe

| | |
|---|---|
| Carb choice | ½ |
| Fats choices | 2 |

**Carbohydrate** 14 g
  Fibre 4 g
**Protein** 4 g
**Fat** 10 g
  Saturated 1 g
**Sodium** 120 mg
**Calories** 147

In large salad bowl, combine greens, drained oranges and strawberries. Cover and refrigerate until ready to serve.

Just before serving, toss salad with vinaigrette. Divide evenly among 4 serving plates. Top each with walnuts to serve.

### Lemon Vinaigrette:

| ¼ cup | extra-virgin olive oil | 50 mL |
|---|---|---|
| 3 tbsp | fresh lemon juice | 45 mL |
| 2 tbsp | chopped chives, green onions or fresh dill | 25 mL |
| ½ tsp | sweetener (optional) | 2 mL |
| ¼ tsp | each salt and freshly ground pepper | 1 mL |

### Vinaigrette:

**Prep** · 10 minutes
**Refrigerate** · up to 2 weeks
**Yield** · about ½ cup (125 mL) dressing

In tightly sealed container, combine oil, lemon juice, chives, sweetener (if using), salt and pepper; shake well. Refrigerate until ready to use.

**Each Serving** · 1 tbsp (15 mL)

| | |
|---|---|
| Fats choices | 1½ |

⊕ *To toast walnuts (or other nuts), place them in a microwave-safe container and cook on High (100%) for 1 to 2 minutes, depending on how many you are toasting. Watch them, as some nuts will toast faster than others.*

**Carbohydrate** 1 g
  Fibre 0 g
**Protein** 0 g
**Fat** 7 g
  Saturated 1 g
**Sodium** 72 mg
**Calories** 61

## Herb Vinaigrette

Here's a zesty dressing to serve with leafy green salads or to drizzle over sliced cucumbers and tomatoes. And it doubles as a flavourful and tenderizing marinade for meat you plan to barbecue. Truly versatile!

| | | |
|---|---|---|
| ¼ cup | red wine vinegar | 50 mL |
| ¼ cup | chicken broth | 50 mL |
| 2 tbsp | fresh lemon or lime juice | 25 mL |
| 1 | clove garlic, minced | 1 |
| 1 tsp | dried tarragon (or 1 tbsp/15 mL chopped fresh) | 5 mL |
| ½ tsp | each dry mustard and paprika | 2 mL |
| ¼ tsp | freshly ground pepper | 1 mL |
| ¼ tsp | hot pepper sauce | 1 mL |
| 2 tbsp | olive or canola oil | 25 mL |

In container with tight-fitting lid, combine vinegar, chicken broth, lemon juice, garlic, tarragon, mustard, paprika, pepper and hot pepper sauce; shake well. Add oil and shake again. Refrigerate for up to 2 weeks.

◉ Use this vinaigrette as a marinade for chicken, beef and pork, as well as for grilled vegetable kebabs (Dinner Menu 4). Use about ⅓ cup (75 mL) to marinate each 1 lb (500 g) of meat.
◉ Marinating meat in a sealed plastic bag improves flavour—and there's no washing up!
◉ If desired, you can replace chicken broth with beef broth when marinating beef.

**Dinner Menu 4, 19**

**Prep** · 10 minutes
**Refrigerate** · up to 2 weeks
**Yield** · ¾ cup (175 mL)

**Each Serving** · 1 tbsp (15 mL)
Fats choice                    ½

**Carbohydrate** 1 g
  Fibre 0 g
**Protein** 0 g
**Fat** 2 g
  Saturated 0 g
**Sodium** 35 mg
**Calories** 24

# Light Parmesan Hollandaise

..........................................

**Prep** · 5 minutes
**Cook** · about 5 minutes
**Yield** · 4 servings,
         1 cup (250 mL)

..........................................

**Each Serving** · ¼ cup (50 mL)
Meat & Alternatives choice    1

..........................................

**Carbohydrate** 4 g
   Fibre 0 g
**Protein** 5 g
**Fat** 2 g
   Saturated 1 g
**Sodium** 246 mg
**Calories** 59

Replace rich, high-calorie sauces with this tangy, quickly prepared version of the classic sauce.

| | | |
|---|---|---|
| ¾ cup | low-fat plain yogurt | 175 mL |
| 1 | egg, lightly beaten | 1 |
| 1 tsp | cornstarch | 5 mL |
| ¼ tsp | prepared mustard | 1 mL |
| ¼ tsp | salt | 1 mL |
| Pinch | paprika | Pinch |
| Dash | hot pepper sauce | Dash |
| 2 tbsp | freshly grated Parmesan cheese | 25 mL |

In saucepan over medium heat, whisk together yogurt, egg, cornstarch, mustard, salt, paprika and hot pepper sauce; cook, stirring constantly, for about 5 minutes or until thickened. Stir in Parmesan cheese until melted.

## VARIATIONS
Use these sauce variations over cooked vegetables or for poached eggs on toasted English muffin halves.

***Light Classic Hollandaise:*** Omit cheese.
***Light Lemon Hollandaise:*** Omit cheese. Add ½ tsp grated lemon rind and 1 tsp (5 mL) fresh lemon juice.
***Light Herbed Hollandaise:*** Omit cheese. Add ¼ tsp (1 mL) each dried tarragon and thyme.

# Baked Chicken 'n' Mushroom Loaf

Meatloaf is traditionally made with ground beef, but one day we decided to make one with lean ground chicken. Wow, a real winner! All the vegetables add lots of extra flavour and moisture. You can also make chicken burgers with this mixture.

| | | |
|---|---|---|
| 1 lb | lean ground chicken | 500 g |
| 1 cup | finely chopped mushrooms (5 to 6 large) | 250 mL |
| ½ cup | large-flake rolled oats | 125 mL |
| ½ cup | each finely chopped onion, carrots and celery | 125 mL |
| ¼ cup | chopped fresh parsley | 50 mL |
| 1 | clove garlic, minced | 1 |
| 1 | egg, lightly beaten | 1 |
| 1 tsp | each dried tarragon and thyme | 5 mL |
| ¼ tsp | each salt and freshly ground pepper | 1 mL |

Spray 9- x 5-inch (2 L) loaf pan with non-stick cooking spray.

In large bowl, combine chicken, mushrooms, oats, onion, carrots, celery, parsley, garlic, egg, tarragon, thyme, salt and pepper; gently stir together just until mixed. Spoon into prepared loaf pan. Cover with foil.

Bake in 350°F (180°C) oven for 45 minutes. Uncover and bake for 15 minutes longer or until cooked through. Let stand for 5 minutes before cutting into 6 slices.

⊛ *Always cook poultry until well done, not medium or rare. When poultry is cooked properly, all juices from the meat should be clear, not pink.*

## Variation

**Baked Beef 'n' Mushroom Loaf:** Lean ground beef can be substituted for the ground chicken.

---

**Dinner Menu 12**

........................................

**Prep** • 20 minutes
**Cook** • about 60 minutes
**Yield** • 6 servings

........................................

**Each Serving** • ⅙ of recipe
Carb choice                    ½
Meat & Alternatives choices   2
Fats choices                  1½

........................................

**Carbohydrate** 9 g
  Fibre 2 g
**Protein** 17 g
**Fat** 13 g
  Saturated 0 g
**Sodium** 161 mg
**Calories** 222

# CHICKEN AND VEGETABLE BUNDLES

What an easy and clean way to cook an entire meal in individual packages! The technique, which originated in France, is called "en papillote." Food for each serving is baked inside a wrapping of greased parchment paper. At the table, the paper is slit and peeled back to reveal the contents. Foil rather than parchment is recommended for barbecuing to protect against setting fire to dinner.

| | | |
|---|---|---|
| 4 | boneless, skinless chicken breast halves (about 1 lb/500 g) | 4 |
| Pinch | paprika | Pinch |
| 1⅓ cups | thinly sliced carrots | 325 mL |
| 2 cups | sliced zucchini | 500 mL |
| 2 cups | halved small mushrooms | 500 mL |
| ½ cup | chopped onion | 125 mL |
| ⅓ cup | white wine or chicken broth | 75 mL |
| 1 tbsp | soft margarine or butter, melted | 15 mL |
| 1 tsp | dried tarragon leaves (or 1 tbsp/15 mL chopped fresh) | 5 mL |
| ¼ tsp | freshly ground pepper | 1 mL |

Cut 4 sheets of parchment paper or heavy-duty foil into squares twice as large as chicken breast. Spray with non-stick cooking spray. Place chicken breast in centre of paper. Sprinkle lightly with paprika. Distribute carrots, zucchini, mushrooms and onion evenly over chicken.

Combine wine, margarine, tarragon and pepper; drizzle over vegetables. Tightly enclose chicken by folding long ends of parchment paper twice; lift short ends, bring together and fold twice.

Bake in 350°F (180°C) oven for 45 minutes or until chicken is no longer pink inside and vegetables are tender. Or grill bundles in foil 5 inches (12 cm) from barbecue coals for 45 minutes, turning occasionally.

**Prep** · 15 minutes
**Cook** · 45 minutes
**Yield** · 4 servings

**Each Serving** · ¼ of recipe (1 bundle)
Carb choice ½
Meat & Alternatives choices 4

**Carbohydrate** 12 g
　Fibre 4 g
**Protein** 28 g
**Fat** 3 g
　Saturated 1 g
**Sodium** 94 mg
**Calories** 201

# CHICKEN AND ASPARAGUS STIR-FRY

**Dinner Menu 17**

........................................

**Prep** • 20 minutes
**Cook** • under 10 minutes
**Yield** • 4 servings, 5 cups (1.25 L)

........................................

**Each Serving** • ¼ of recipe,
      1¼ cups (300 mL)
Carb choice           ½
Meat & Alternatives choices   2

........................................

**Carbohydrate** 8 g
  Fibre 2 g
**Protein** 17 g
**Fat** 4 g
  Saturated 0 g
**Sodium** 242 mg
**Calories** 128

Stir-fry your dinner. The fast, high heat used in stir-frying helps preserve food's nutrients, flavour and crunch. Think spring with this recipe! Although asparagus is available for much of the year, locally grown always tastes the best.

| | | |
|---|---|---:|
| 3 | boneless, skinless chicken breast halves (about 3/4 lb/375 g) | 3 |
| 1 tbsp | light soy sauce | 15 mL |
| 2 tsp | cornstarch | 10 mL |
| ¼ tsp | freshly ground pepper | 1 mL |
| 2 cups | diagonally cut asparagus | 500 mL |
| 1½ cups | diagonally sliced celery | 375 mL |
| 4 | green onions, diagonally sliced | 4 |
| 1 | small sweet red pepper, thinly sliced | 1 |
| 2 tsp | canola oil | 10 mL |
| 1 tbsp | minced fresh gingerroot (see Tip) | 15 mL |
| 2 | cloves garlic, minced | 2 |
| ¼ cup | salt-reduced chicken broth | 50 mL |

Cut chicken into strips. In small bowl, combine soy sauce, cornstarch and pepper; stir in chicken and set aside.

In microwave-safe casserole, cover and cook asparagus, celery, onions and red pepper with 1 tsp (5 mL) water on High (100%) for 3 minutes or until vegetables are barely tender. Set aside.

In wok or large non-stick skillet, heat oil over medium-high heat; stir-fry gingerroot and garlic for 30 seconds. Add chicken and cook for 5 minutes or until no longer pink inside.

Add vegetable mixture and broth to wok; cook, stirring, for 3 minutes or until hot.

⊕ *Fresh gingerroot is a knobby brown spice with a hot and spicy flavour. Look for it in the produce section. When choosing a piece, look for one that is not shrivelled. To prepare, peel with a vegetable peeler and dice or shred. Store any leftovers in a small bottle and cover with vinegar or dry sherry. Or freeze and shred frozen as you need it.*

# Mediterranean Chicken

A full-flavoured vegetable stew covers chicken thighs in this one-dish recipe—rustic Mediterranean home cooking at its best.

| | | |
|---|---|---|
| 5 | skinless chicken thighs or drumsticks (1¼ lb/625 g) | 5 |
| ½ tsp | paprika | 2 mL |
| ¼ tsp | freshly ground pepper | 1 mL |
| 1 tsp | olive oil | 5 mL |
| ½ cup | chopped onion | 125 mL |
| ½ cup | chopped sweet green or red pepper | 125 mL |
| ½ cup | water | 125 mL |
| 1 | can (28 oz/796 mL) diced tomatoes, undrained | 1 |
| ¾ cup | parboiled brown or white rice | 175 mL |
| 2 | cloves garlic, sliced | 2 |
| | chopped fresh parsley and black olives (optional) | |

Sprinkle chicken thighs with paprika and pepper. In large non-stick skillet, heat oil over medium heat; brown thighs all over. Transfer to deep 6-cup (1.5 L) casserole.

In same skillet, cook onion and green pepper in water for 5 minutes. Add tomatoes with juice, rice and garlic; spoon over meat in casserole.

Cover and bake in 325°F (160°C) oven for 1¼ hours or until liquid is absorbed and rice is cooked.

Place 1 thigh and 1 cup (250 mL) vegetable-rice mixture on each plate. Garnish with parsley, and black olives (if using).

⊕ *Here is an opportunity to check labels—if you use regular brown rice, it will require a longer cooking time than if you use the faster-cooking parboiled whole grain one that we used in this recipe.*

---

**Dinner Menu 25**

..............................

**Prep** · 20 minutes
**Cook** · 1¼ hours
**Yield** · 5 servings

..............................

**Each Serving** · 1 chicken thigh and 1 cup (250 mL) vegetable-rice mixture
Carb choices     2
Meat & Alternatives choices   3

..............................

**Carbohydrate** 31 g
  Fibre 3 g
**Protein** 28 g
**Fat** 9 g
  Saturated 2 g
**Sodium** 337 mg
**Calories** 318

# Rosemary Lemon Chicken

**Dinner Menu 28**

..........................................................

**Prep** · 15 minutes
**Cook** · 60 minutes
**Yield** · 6 servings

..........................................................

**Each Serving** · ⅙ of recipe
        (1 thigh with pan juices)
Meat & Alternatives choices   3
Fats choice                          ½

..........................................................

**Carbohydrate** 2 g
   Fibre 0 g
**Protein** 22 g
**Fat** 11 g
   Saturated 2 g
**Sodium** 145 mg
**Calories** 198

After several hours in this marinade, the chicken acquires the zesty flavours of rosemary and lemon. Moist and extremely tasty, it is enjoyed by all ages.

| | | |
|---|---|---:|
| ⅓ cup | fresh lemon juice | 75 mL |
| 2 tbsp | olive oil | 25 mL |
| 2 tbsp | Dijon mustard | 25 mL |
| 1 tbsp | fresh rosemary (or 1 tsp/5 mL dried) | 15 mL |
| 2 | cloves garlic, minced | 2 |
| ½ tsp | freshly ground pepper | 2 mL |
| ½ tsp | hot pepper sauce | 2 mL |
| ¼ tsp | hot pepper flakes | 1 mL |
| 6 | boneless, skinless chicken thighs (about 1½ lb/750 g) | 6 |

In glass measure, combine lemon juice, oil, mustard, rosemary, garlic, pepper, hot pepper sauce and hot pepper flakes.

Place chicken in resealable plastic bag; pour in marinade, seal and refrigerate for up to 24 hours.

Transfer chicken and marinade to baking dish. Cover and bake in 375°F (190°C) oven for 60 minutes or until juices run clear when chicken is pierced.

⊕ *If you prefer to use chicken breasts, reduce cooking time to about 40 minutes.*

# Skewered Beef with Yogurt Feta Dip

Cooking thin pieces of marinated sirloin steak on wooden skewers is a quick way to a flavourful beef dinner.

## Skewered Beef:

| | | |
|---|---|---|
| 1 lb | lean sirloin steak, trimmed | 500 g |
| ¼ cup | fresh lemon juice | 50 mL |
| 1 tbsp | liquid honey | 15 mL |
| 3 | cloves garlic, crushed | 3 |
| 1½ tsp | dried marjoram or oregano | 7 mL |
| ½ tsp | dried mint (optional) | 2 mL |
| | *Yogurt Feta Dip* (page 100) | |

Slice meat across the grain into long, thin strips. In small bowl, whisk lemon juice, honey, garlic, marjoram and mint (if using). Toss beef strips with marinade and let stand at room temperature for 30 minutes (see Tip).

Thread beef onto soaked wooden skewers (see Tip). Lightly grease broiler or barbecue grill and preheat to medium-high. Place skewers on broiler or grill rack; cook, turning once, for 4 to 5 minutes or until meat reaches desired doneness. Serve with *Yogurt Feta Dip* (page 100).

⊚ *If not using beef right away, combine with marinade, then freeze in serving-size packages until ready to use. Using honey in the marinade gives the meat more colour when grilled. As well, the marinade will have a better consistency, which helps it adhere to the meat.*

⊚ *Always soak wooden skewers in cold water for about 30 minutes. This prevents them from burning during cooking. In fact, we have found that freezing soaked skewers is a great way to have them on hand, ready to use.*

**HIGH FIBRE**

**Dinner Menu 8**

.............................................

**Prep** · 20 minutes
**Cook** · about 5 minutes
**Yield** · 8 skewers (4 servings)

.............................................

**Each Serving** · 2 skewers
Carb choice ½
Meat & Alternatives choices 3½

.............................................

**Carbohydrate** 7 g
  Fibre 0 g
**Protein** 25 g
**Fat** 5 g
  Saturated 2 g
**Sodium** 52 mg
**Calories** 173

# Yogurt Feta Dip

**Dinner Menu 8**
**Snack Menu 4**

.........................................

**Yield** · 1⅓ cups (325 mL) dip

.........................................

**Each Serving** · ⅓ cup
(75 mL) dip
Carb choice                    ½
Meat & Alternatives choice   ½

.........................................

**Carbohydrate** 6 g
   Fibre 0 g
**Protein** 5 g
**Fat** 3 g
   Saturated 2 g
**Sodium** 179 mg
**Calories** 68

This delicious creamy dip is an ideal pairing for **Skewered Beef** (page 99) or great as a dip for fresh veggies.

| | | |
|---|---|---|
| 1 cup | low-fat plain yogurt | 250 mL |
| ⅓ cup | finely crumbled feta cheese | 75 mL |
| 2 tsp | fresh lemon juice | 10 mL |
| 2 | cloves garlic, minced | 2 |
| Pinch | each freshly ground pepper, cayenne pepper and dried mint | Pinch |

In small bowl, stir together yogurt, feta cheese, lemon juice, garlic, pepper, cayenne and mint. Let stand for 15 minutes to blend flavours. Refrigerate until ready to serve.

# Garlic Lovers' Pot Roast

Slow roasting is a low-fat method of cooking less tender cuts of beef. Garlic adds its own hearty aroma and taste to this simple but very delicious pot roast.

| | | |
|---|---|---|
| 1 | boneless beef chuck roast (about 3 lb/2.5 kg) | 1 |
| 10 | cloves garlic, peeled and cut in half lengthwise | 10 |
| 1 tsp | salt | 5 mL |
| ½ tsp | freshly ground pepper | 2 mL |
| 1 tbsp | canola oil | 15 mL |
| | water | |

Using the tip of a sharp paring knife, make 20 small, evenly spaced slits about 1½ inches (3.5 cm) deep all over surface of pot roast. Insert garlic cloves as deep into meat slits as possible. Season meat on all sides with salt and pepper.

In heavy saucepan or Dutch oven, heat oil over medium-high heat; evenly brown roast on all sides for about 8 minutes. Pour in a small amount of water (see Tip).

Reduce heat to medium-low, cover and roast, turning 2 or 3 times, for 3 hours or until very tender. Check occasionally to make sure there is always a little liquid in the bottom of the pan; if necessary, add more water.

Transfer to serving platter and cover with foil; let stand for about 10 minutes before slicing.

Meanwhile, make **Light Beef Gravy** (see page 173).

⊕ *The secret to producing a flavourful, tender roast is to not add too much liquid at any one time. Allow the meat to cook very slowly for a long time.*

**Dinner Menu 22**

.............................

**Prep** · 15 minutes
**Cook** · about 3 hours
**Yield** · 8 to 12 servings

.............................

**Each Serving** · 3 slices (90 g)
Meat & Alternatives choices   4

.............................

**Carbohydrate** 1 g
   Fibre 0 g
**Protein** 28 g
**Fat** 12 g
   Saturated 4 g
**Sodium** 244 mg
**Calories** 235

# CHILI CON CARNE

Chili tucked away in the freezer is always helpful on busy days. This recipe makes a large amount thanks to the addition of "extra" vegetables.

| | | |
|---|---|---|
| 1 lb | lean ground beef | 500 g |
| 1 cup | chopped onion | 250 mL |
| 1 | clove garlic, crushed | 1 |
| 3 cups | finely shredded cabbage | 750 mL |
| 2 cups | thinly sliced celery | 500 mL |
| ½ cup | chopped sweet green pepper | 125 mL |
| 1 | can (28 oz/796 mL) diced tomatoes, undrained | 1 |
| 1 | can (7.5 oz/213 mL) tomato sauce | 1 |
| 1 | can (19 oz/540 mL) kidney beans, drained and rinsed | 1 |
| 1 tbsp | chili powder | 15 mL |
| 1 tsp | dried oregano | 5 mL |
| ¼ tsp | hot pepper sauce | 1 mL |

In large non-stick skillet over medium-high heat, cook beef until brown and crumbly. Drain fat and discard. Add onion and garlic; cook for 5 minutes.

Add cabbage, celery, green pepper, tomatoes with juice, tomato sauce, kidney beans, chili powder, oregano and hot pepper sauce. Reduce heat to medium-low, cover and simmer, stirring occasionally, for 45 minutes or until vegetables are tender.

◉ *To freeze extra chili, portion it into single-serving plastic containers— a good use for all those yogurt or margarine containers everyone saves.*

**Lunch Menu 7**
**Dinner Menu 15**

..................................................

**Prep** · 20 minutes
**Cook** · about 45 minutes
**Yield** · about 8 servings,
    9 cups (2.25 L)

..................................................

**Each Serving** · 1¼ cups (300 mL)
Carb choice                          1
Meat & Alternatives choices   2

..................................................

**Carbohydrate** 19 g
  Fibre 6 g
**Protein** 16 g
**Fat** 7 g
  Saturated 2 g
**Sodium** 496 mg
**Calories** 191

**Dinner Menu 19**

..................................

**Prep** · 20 minutes
**Cook** · about 10 minutes
**Yield** · 4 servings

..................................

**Each Serving** · ¼ of recipe
Carb choices                              3
Meat & Alternatives choices 2½

..................................

**Carbohydrate** 47 g
    Fibre 7 g
**Protein** 25 g
**Fat** 9 g
    Saturated 3 g
**Sodium** 331 mg
**Calories** 374

## Italian Beef and Vegetables

This dish, which fuses Italian flavours and a Chinese stir-fry technique, is served over cooked fettuccine with a sprinkle of Parmesan cheese.

| | | |
|---|---|---|
| 2 tsp | canola oil | 10 mL |
| ½ lb | boneless top sirloin steak, cut into thin 2-inch (5 cm) long strips | 250 g |
| 2 | large cloves garlic, minced | 2 |
| 3 cups | broccoli florets | 750 mL |
| 1½ cups | cubed sweet yellow pepper | 375 mL |
| 1 cup | thinly sliced onion | 250 mL |
| ½ cup | dry red wine or beef broth | 125 mL |
| ½ cup | each tomato paste and water | 125 mL |
| 1 tsp | each dried thyme and rosemary | 5 mL |
| ¼ tsp | salt | 1 mL |
| Pinch | freshly ground pepper | Pinch |
| 4 cups | cooked fettucine (about 225 g) (see Tip) | 1 L |
| ¼ cup | freshly grated Parmesan cheese | 50 mL |

In large non-stick skillet, heat oil over high heat; stir-fry beef and garlic for 5 minutes or until browned. Remove and keep warm.

Add broccoli, yellow pepper, onion, wine, tomato paste, water, thyme, rosemary, salt and pepper. Reduce heat to medium-low, cover and cook for about 4 minutes or until vegetables are tender-crisp. Stir in beef and heat through.

Place 1 cup (250 mL) cooked fettuccine on each of 4 plates. Top each with one-quarter of the beef mixture. Sprinkle each with 1 tbsp (15 mL) of the cheese.

⊕ *To cook fettucine: Bring large pot of water to a boil; add fettuccine and cook according to package directions or until al dente (tender but firm), about 10 minutes. Drain well; return to pot to keep warm.*

⊕ *Most pasta packages vary somewhat in size. Check weight of package to determine how much to cook.*

## Oven Beef Stew

Beef stew is best made in large amounts, as in this recipe. Flavours are better that way, plus you'll have several meals ready as a result. Freeze the leftovers or invite friends over for a hearty winter meal. The recipe's lean beef fits a lower-fat diet. And the lean beef is kept lean by using low-fat cooking methods.

| | | |
|---|---|---|
| ¼ cup | all-purpose flour | 50 mL |
| ½ tsp | each paprika and dried thyme | 2 mL |
| ¼ tsp | freshly ground pepper | 1 mL |
| 1¼ lb | lean stewing beef | 625 g |
| 1 tbsp | canola oil | 15 mL |
| 1¼ cups | water | 300 mL |
| 1 | pkg (36 g) onion soup mix | 1 |
| 1 | bay leaf | 1 |
| 6 | small potatoes, peeled, cut in half | 6 |
| 3 | small onions, peeled, cut into wedges | 3 |
| 1 | medium carrot, peeled and sliced | 1 |
| 2 cups | sliced mushrooms | 500 mL |
| ½ cup | frozen peas | 125 mL |

Combine flour, paprika and thyme in plastic bag. Trim and discard all visible fat from beef. Cut beef into 1-inch (5 cm) cubes. Lightly toss in flour mixture; reserve excess flour.

Add oil to 6-cup (1.5 L) ovenproof casserole; add floured meat. Roast, uncovered and stirring once, in 450°F (230°C) oven for 30 minutes.

Reduce oven temperature to 350°F (180°C). Stir together water, onion soup mix, reserved flour and bay leaf; pour over meat.

Roast, covered and stirring once, for 1 hour. Add potatoes, onions, carrot, mushrooms and ¼ cup (50 mL) water if necessary. Roast, covered, for about 45 minutes or until meat and vegetables are tender, adding peas during last 10 minutes. Discard bay leaf before serving.

**Dinner Menu 24**

....................................................

**Prep** · 20 minutes
**Cook** · 2¼ hours
**Yield** · 6 servings

....................................................

**Each Serving** · ⅙ of recipe
         (1⅓ cups/325 mL)
Carb choices                2
Meat & Alternatives choices  3

....................................................

**Carbohydrate** 31 g
   Fibre 4 g
**Protein** 26 g
**Fat** 10 g
   Saturated 3 g
**Sodium** 592 mg
**Calories** 313

# BALSAMIC STRIP LOIN STEAK

.............................................

**Prep** · 10 minutes
**Cook** · about 4 minutes
      per side
**Yield** · 4 servings

.............................................

**Each Serving** · ¼ of recipe
Meat & Alternatives choices 3½

.............................................

**Carbohydrate** 2 g
  Fibre 0 g
**Protein** 25 g
**Fat** 8 g
  Saturated 2 g
**Sodium** 52 mg
**Calories** 185

Loin steaks are a tender cut you can grill right away, but they're even more tender and flavourful if marinated for 12 to 24 hours (see Tips below).

| 2 tbsp | finely chopped fresh oregano | 25 mL |
|---|---|---|
|  | (or 1 tsp/5 mL dried) |  |
| 2 tbsp | balsamic vinegar | 25 mL |
| 1 tbsp | extra-virgin olive oil | 15 mL |
| 6 | cloves garlic, smashed | 6 |
| ¼ tsp | freshly ground pepper | 1 mL |
| 4 | top sirloin steaks (each 4 oz/125 g) | 4 |

In large resealable plastic bag, combine oregano, vinegar, oil, garlic and pepper; add steaks, turning to coat. Seal and refrigerate, turning once, for 30 minutes, or for up to 24 hours.

Remove meat from marinade; reserve marinade. Place marinade in small saucepan and bring to a boil. Reduce heat and cook, covered, for 5 minutes; keep warm (see Tip).

Place steaks on greased grill over medium-high heat; brush generously with marinade. Close lid and grill until desired doneness, about 4 minutes per side for medium-rare (see Tip). Transfer to warm platter; tent with foil and let stand for 5 minutes before serving.

⊕ *When buying beef for grilling, ask your butcher if he carries Grilling or Marinating Beef Medallions. These thick-cut steaks make it easier to cook to the desired stage of doneness—rare, medium or well done—as they are cut about 1 inch (2.5 cm) thick. The cut of beef is either rib eye, cross rib or top sirloin.*

⊕ *When using leftover marinade to brush on meat, be sure to boil it for 5 minutes to kill any harmful bacteria left from marinating raw food.*

⊕ *To check meat for doneness, use your finger, rather than a knife: if the steak is soft through to the centre, it is rare; if it feels slightly firm but still spongy, it is medium; if it is firm to the touch, it is well done.*

⊕ *Always marinate meat, fish and poultry in the refrigerator.*

# Hearty Lamb Scotch Broth

Every cookbook needs at least one "meal-in-a-bowl" recipe. This Scottish soup is always made with lamb, barley and assorted vegetables. Make it when there isn't time to prepare a full meat-and-vegetable meal—or just because you like it. The soup freezes well for enjoying another day.

| | | |
|---|---|---|
| 1 lb | cubed trimmed lean lamb (see Tip) | 500 g |
| 1 cup | chopped onion | 250 mL |
| 3 | cloves garlic, thinly sliced | 3 |
| 6 cups | salt-reduced beef broth (see Tip) | 1.5 L |
| ½ cup | pot barley | 125 mL |
| ¼ cup | minced fresh dill | 50 mL |
| | (or 1 tbsp/15 mL dried dillweed) | |
| 2 tbsp | tomato paste | 25 mL |
| 2 | bay leaves | 2 |
| 1 tsp | dried thyme (or 1 tbsp/15 mL fresh) | 5 mL |
| ¼ tsp | freshly ground pepper | 1 mL |
| 1 cup | sliced carrots | 250 mL |
| 1 cup | diced turnip | 250 mL |

In large non-stick saucepan over medium-high heat, brown lamb with onion and garlic for 10 minutes, stirring often. Add beef broth, barley, dill, tomato paste, bay leaves, thyme and pepper; bring to a boil.

Reduce heat, cover and simmer for 45 minutes. Add carrots and turnip; cook for 15 minutes or until vegetables and lamb are tender. Discard bay leaves.

⊕ *The amount of lamb stated is weight after trimming. You'll need to buy extra since there will be some trimming of fat and fell to discard.*

⊕ *Chill the soup to remove any surface fat, then reheat before eating.*

⊕ ***Homemade Light Beef Broth*** *(page 57) is a good replacement.*

## HIGH FIBRE

**Dinner Menu 11**

....................................

**Prep ·** 30 minutes
**Cook ·** about 1 hour
**Yield ·** 6 servings, 8 cups (2 L)

....................................

**Each Serving ·** ⅙ of recipe
(1⅓ cups/325 mL)
Carb choice                          1
Meat & Alternatives choices   3

....................................

**Carbohydrate** 23 g
  Fibre 5 g
**Protein** 21 g
**Fat** 5 g
  Saturated 2 g
**Sodium** 649 mg
**Calories** 217

## Butterflied Leg of Lamb with Red Wine Sauce

**Dinner Menu 27**

......................................

**Prep** · 15 minutes
**Cook** · about 1 hour
**Refrigerate** · about 3 hours

......................................

**Yield** · 8 to 10 servings

......................................

**Each Serving** · 3 slices lamb
          (90 g) with 3 tbsp
          (45 mL) sauce
Meat & Alternatives choices   3

......................................

**Carbohydrate** 3 g
   Fibre 0 g
**Protein** 21 g
**Fat** 8 g
   Saturated 2 g
**Sodium** 159 mg
**Calories** 164

When roasting lamb, avoid overcooking. Rather, just cook it until there is some pink colour still remaining in the meat.

| | | |
|---|---|---:|
| 1 | boneless (butterflied) leg of lamb (3 lb/1.5 kg) | 1 |
| 2 tbsp | olive oil | 25 mL |
| 2 tbsp | dry mustard | 25 mL |
| 2 | cloves garlic, crushed | 2 |
| ¼ cup | cider vinegar | 50 mL |
| 2 tbsp | light soy sauce (see Tip) | 25 mL |
| 2 tbsp | fresh lemon juice | 25 mL |
| ¼ cup | each finely chopped fresh parsley and mint | 50 mL |
| | *Red Wine Sauce* (recipe follows) | |

Trim fat from lamb, leaving enough to hold leg in one piece; discard fat. If meat is not of uniform thickness, slash thickest part and open up like a book. Place meat in dish large enough that it can lie flat.

In small bowl, stir together oil, mustard and garlic until fairly smooth. Spread both sides of meat with mixture. Cover and refrigerate for at least 1 hour.

In bowl, stir together vinegar, soy sauce, lemon juice, parsley and mint. Pour over meat; cover and refrigerate for at least 2 hours or overnight.

Remove meat from marinade; place fat side up on rack in shallow roasting pan. Discard any remaining marinade.

Bake in 325°F (160°C) oven for about 20 minutes per pound (500 g) or until meat thermometer reaches 140°F (60°C) for rare or 155°F (70°C) for medium.

Remove lamb from oven. Let stand for 10 minutes before carving across the grain. Serve with warm *Red Wine Sauce*.

◉ *Light soy sauce, sometimes called "lite," refers to a sauce that contains 50 per cent less salt than the regular version.*

## Red Wine Sauce:

| ½ cup | dry red wine | 125 mL |
|-------|--------------|--------|
| 1 tbsp | cider vinegar | 15 mL |
| ¼ tsp | granulated sugar | 1 mL |
| 1 cup | salt-reduced chicken broth | 250 mL |
| 1 tbsp | cornstarch | 15 mL |
| 1 tbsp | chopped fresh parsley | 15 mL |

In small saucepan over medium heat, simmer wine, vinegar and sugar for 5 minutes. Whisk together broth and cornstarch; whisk into wine mixture and simmer, stirring frequently, until slightly thickened. Stir in parsley to serve.

**Prep** • 5 minutes
**Cook** • about 5 minutes
**Yield** • 1½ cups (375 mL)

# STUFFED PORK TENDERLOIN

Caramelized onions in the stuffing and a mustard-honey glaze on the pork both contribute to this dazzling entrée.

| 2 | pork tenderloins (¾ lb/375 g each) | 2 |

### STUFFING:

| 1 tbsp | olive oil | 15 mL |
| 2 | medium onions, thinly sliced | 2 |
| 1 tbsp | balsamic vinegar | 15 mL |
| ¼ tsp | each salt and freshly ground pepper | 1 mL |
| ⅓ cup | fresh bread crumbs | 75 mL |
| 3 tbsp | chopped fresh parsley | 45 mL |
| | grated rind of 1 orange | |

### GLAZE:

| 2 tbsp | Dijon mustard | 25 mL |
| 2 tbsp | liquid honey | 25 mL |
| ¼ tsp | freshly ground pepper | 1 mL |

With sharp knife, cut each tenderloin lengthwise from end to end, being careful not to cut through to other side. Set aside.

*Stuffing:* In non-stick skillet, heat oil over medium heat; sauté onions, stirring frequently, for about 20 minutes or until deep golden brown. Stir in vinegar, salt and pepper; cook for 5 minutes. Remove from heat. Stir in bread crumbs, parsley and orange rind. Set aside.

Place filling along length of one tenderloin. Top with second tenderloin and tie with string. Place meat on rack set over a foil-lined roasting pan.

*Glaze:* In small bowl, combine mustard, honey and pepper; brush over pork. Roast in 375°F (190°C) oven for 40 minutes or until cooked through and juices run clear (internal temperature will be about 160°F/70°C). Cover and let stand for 10 minutes before carving into ½-inch (1 cm) thick slices.

**Dinner Menu 29**

.....................................

**Prep** · 30 minutes
**Cook** · about 40 minutes
**Yield** · 6 servings

.....................................

**Each Serving** · 2 slices with stuffing (90 g)
Carb choice 1
Meat & Alternatives choices 3

.....................................

**Carbohydrate** 13 g
  Fibre 1 g
**Protein** 26 g
**Fat** 7 g
  Saturated 2 g
**Sodium** 219 mg
**Calories** 215

# Herbed Citrus Pork Chop

**Dinner Menu 16**

....................................

**Prep** · 10 minutes
**Cook** · about 10 minutes
**Yield** · 4 servings

....................................

**Each Serving** · ¼ of recipe
Meat & Alternatives choices 3

....................................

**Carbohydrate** 4 g
   Fibre 0 g
**Protein** 23 g
**Fat** 4 g
   Saturated 1 g
**Sodium** 80 mg

**Calories** 149

Citrus and pork complement each other in this very easy-to-make recipe.

| 4 | boneless loin pork chops (each 100 g) | 4 |
|---|---|---|
| ¼ cup | orange juice | 50 mL |
| 1 tsp | Dijon mustard | 5 mL |
| 1 tsp | liquid honey | 5 mL |
| ½ tsp | each dried thyme and tarragon | 2 mL |
| ½ tsp | freshly ground pepper | 2 mL |

Trim fat from chops and discard. In non-stick skillet over medium heat, brown chops, turning once, for 5 minutes.

In small bowl, combine orange juice, mustard, honey, thyme, tarragon and pepper; pour over chops. Cover and cook for 5 minutes or until just a hint of pink remains inside chops.

# Oriental Salmon with Onions

Salmon has so much flavour that the simplest of cooking methods is often the best. In this recipe, the fish is cooked with caramelized onion sauce.

| | | |
|---|---|---|
| 2 tsp | olive oil | 10 mL |
| 2 cups | chopped onion | 500 mL |
| 4 | salmon fillets (each 100 g) | 4 |
| ¼ cup | light soy sauce | 50 mL |
| ¼ cup | water or white wine | 50 mL |
| | finely chopped green onion or chives for garnish | |

In large non-stick skillet, heat oil over medium-high heat; cook onion, stirring frequently, for 5 minutes or until golden brown.

Place salmon over onions; drizzle with soy sauce and water. Cover and cook over medium-low heat for 8 minutes or until fish flakes easily with fork. Garnish with green onion to serve.

**Dinner Menu 14**

..........................................

**Prep ·** 10 minutes
**Cook ·** about 13 minutes
**Yield ·** 4 servings

..........................................

**Each Serving ·** ¼ of recipe
Carb choice                                    ½
Meat & Alternatives choices   3

..........................................

**Carbohydrate** 8 g
  Fibre 1 g
**Protein** 22 g
**Fat** 9 g
  Saturated 1 g
**Sodium** 586 mg
**Calories** 203

## Broiled Rainbow Trout with Fresh Tomato

### Dinner Menu 9

..................................

**Prep** · 10 minutes
**Cook** · 5 minutes
**Yield** · 4 servings

..................................

**Each Serving** · ½ fillet with
        ¼ of tomato mixture
Meat & Alternatives choices   4
Extra

..................................

**Carbohydrate** 6 g
   Fibre 1 g
**Protein** 27 g
**Fat** 8 g
   Saturated 2 g
**Sodium** 111 mg
**Calories** 211

The delicate texture of trout requires broiling or baking in a hot oven rather than grilling on a barbecue. Tomatoes and lime juice give this low-fat fish recipe extra moistness and flavour.

| | | |
|---|---|---|
| 1 lb | rainbow trout fillets (2 medium or 4 small) | 500 g |
| ½ cup | finely chopped fresh coriander (see Tip) | 125 mL |
| ½ tsp | grated lime rind | 2 mL |
| 2 tbsp | fresh lime juice | 25 mL |
| 1 tsp | olive oil | 5 mL |
| Pinch | each salt and freshly ground pepper | Pinch |
| 2 cups | chopped tomatoes | 500 mL |

Wipe fish with paper towels; split medium fillets lengthwise. Spray shallow baking dish with non-stick cooking spray; arrange fillets in dish in single layer.

Stir together coriander, lime rind, lime juice, oil, salt and pepper. Combine 2 tbsp (25 mL) of the lime mixture with chopped tomatoes; set aside. Spread remainder over fish; let stand for 10 minutes.

Broil fish 4 inches (10 cm) from heat for 5 minutes or until fish flakes easily with fork. Serve with reserved tomato mixture.

⊕ *Coriander, also called cilantro or Chinese parsley, has a lively, pungent fragrance. It is widely used in Asian, Caribbean and Latin American cooking.*

# Salmon with Roasted Cherry Tomatoes

Tomatoes, thyme and garlic cooked with the salmon create a wonderful combination of flavours. We like to serve it with couscous or rice.

| | | |
|---|---|---|
| 4 cups | cherry tomatoes | 1 L |
| 2 tsp | chopped fresh thyme or dill | 10 mL |
| | (or ½ tsp/2 mL dried) | |
| 3 | cloves garlic, minced | 3 |
| 2 tsp | olive or canola oil | 10 mL |
| ¼ tsp | freshly ground pepper | 1 mL |
| 4 | salmon fillets (each 100 g) | 4 |
| 3 tbsp | fresh lemon juice | 45 mL |

In bowl, combine tomatoes, thyme, garlic, oil and pepper. Spray baking dish with non-stick cooking spray. Spread tomato mixture in dish. Bake in 400°F (200°C) oven for 10 minutes.

Add fish; bake for 10 minutes longer or until fish flakes easily with fork.

Serve fish topped with tomato mixture. Drizzle with lemon juice.

**Dinner Menu 26**

**Prep** · 15 minutes
**Cook** · about 20 minutes
**Yield** · 4 servings

**Each Serving** · 1 fillet and ½ cup (125 mL) tomato mixture

| | |
|---|---|
| Carb choice | ½ |
| Meat & Alternatives choices | 3 |
| Fats choice | 1 |

**Carbohydrate** 8 g
  Fibre 2 g
**Protein** 21 g
**Fat** 14 g
  Saturated 3 g
**Sodium** 64 mg
**Calories** 239

# Salmon Loaf with Tartar Sauce

**Dinner Menu 23**

........................................

**Loaf:**
**Prep** · 25 minutes
**Cook** · 1 hour
**Yield** · 4 servings

**Each Serving** · ¼ of loaf
Meat & Alternatives choices   3

**Carbohydrate** 5 g
    Fibre 1 g
**Protein** 20 g
**Fat** 10 g
    Saturated 2 g
**Sodium** 544 mg
**Calories** 192

........................................

**Sauce:**
**Refrigerate** · 30 minutes for
                sauce
**Yield** · ½ cup (125 mL) sauce

**Each Serving** · 2 tbsp (25 mL)
                sauce
Fats choice                    ½

**Carbohydrate** 4 g
    Fibre 0 g
**Protein** 2 g
**Fat** 2 g
    Saturated 0 g
**Sodium** 121 mg
**Calories** 43

A tangy tartar sauce does great things for salmon loaf. Omega-3 fatty acids found in salmon make this a "heart-healthy" recipe. Mashing salmon bones in with the fish provides a source of calcium.

| 2 | cans (7.5 oz/213 g each) salmon, undrained | 2 |
|---|---|---|
| ¾ cup | fresh whole wheat bread crumbs | 175 mL |
| ¼ cup | minced green onion | 50 mL |
| 1 | egg | 1 |
| ½ tsp | dry mustard | 2 mL |
| ½ tsp | Worcestershire sauce | 2 mL |
| ¼ tsp | freshly ground pepper | 1 mL |

Lightly spray 9- x 5-inch (2 L) loaf pan with non-stick cooking spray.

In bowl, flake salmon. Add bread crumbs, onion, egg, mustard, Worcestershire sauce and pepper; spoon into prepared pan. Place in larger pan half filled with hot water.

Cover and bake in 350°F (180°C) oven for 1 hour or until firm. Let stand for 10 minutes before slicing.

## Tartar Sauce:

| ½ cup | low-fat plain yogurt | 125 mL |
|---|---|---|
| 2 tbsp | light mayonnaise | 25 mL |
| 1 tbsp | pickle relish | 15 mL |
| 1 tbsp | chopped drained capers (optional) | 15 mL |
| 1 tsp | Dijon mustard | 5 mL |

In small bowl, stir together yogurt, mayonnaise, relish, capers (if using) and mustard. Refrigerate for 30 minutes or longer to allow flavours to develop. Serve with Salmon Loaf.

# CURRIED SHRIMP AND MUSHROOMS

A close friend who lives in Calgary gave us this recipe. We love its superb flavours as well as its simplicity. Served with rice and a salad, it makes a great dinner for guests. Brief cooking time keeps shrimp from getting tough.

| | | |
|---|---|---|
| 2 tsp | olive oil | 10 mL |
| 3 | green onions, sliced | 3 |
| 2 | cloves garlic, minced | 2 |
| ½ lb | whole mushrooms, sliced | 250 g |
| 1 | pkg (454 g) frozen raw shrimp, thawed | 1 |
| ¾ cup | light sour cream | 175 mL |
| 2 tbsp | mango chutney | 25 mL |
| 2 tbsp | dry sherry | 25 mL |
| 1 tbsp | curry powder | 15 mL |

In non-stick skillet, heat oil over medium-high heat; sauté onions and garlic for 2 minutes. Add mushrooms; sauté for 2 minutes or until golden.

Add shrimp; cook for 3 minutes or until pink and opaque. Do not overcook.

Meanwhile, in small bowl, stir together sour cream, chutney, sherry and curry powder. Stir into shrimp just before serving.

**Dinner Menu 21**

**Prep** · 15 minutes
**Cook** · about 10 minutes
**Yield** · 4 servings

**Each Serving** · ¼ of recipe
Carb choice                    1
Meat & Alternatives choices   3

**Carbohydrate** 14 g
  Fibre 1 g
**Protein** 27 g
**Fat** 7 g
  Saturated 2 g
**Sodium** 270 mg
**Calories** 240

## LENTIL VEGETABLE SPAGHETTI SAUCE

**Dinner Menus 13, 20**

....................................

**Prep** · 20 minutes
**Cook** · 2 hours
**Yield** · 9 servings,
　　　　9 cups (2.25 L) sauce

....................................

**Each Serving** · 1 cup (250 mL)
Carb choice　　　　　　　　1
Meat & Alternatives choice　½

....................................

**Carbohydrate** 19 g
　Fibre 5 g
**Protein** 6 g
**Fat** 2 g
　Saturated 0 g
**Sodium** 358 mg
**Calories** 107

How do you boost your veggie intake? Try adding veggies to spaghetti sauce. Use this one for **Vegetarian Lasagna** (page 119) or as a sauce for pasta. Freeze leftovers for future use.

| | | |
|---|---|---:|
| 1 tbsp | canola oil | 15 mL |
| 3 cups | finely chopped zucchini (3 medium) | 750 mL |
| 1 cup | chopped onion (1 medium) | 250 mL |
| ½ cup | finely chopped carrot (1 medium) | 125 mL |
| 2 | cloves garlic, minced | 2 |
| 1 | can (28 oz/796 mL) diced tomatoes, undrained | 1 |
| 1 | can (3.5 oz/198 mL) tomato paste | 1 |
| 1 | can (10 oz/284 mL) mushroom stems and pieces, undrained | 1 |
| 1 | can (19 oz/540 mL) lentils, drained and rinsed | 1 |
| 2 tsp | dried oregano | 10 mL |
| 1½ tsp | dried basil | 7 mL |
| ¼ tsp | freshly ground pepper | 1 mL |

In large saucepan, heat oil over medium-high heat; cook zucchini, onion, carrot and garlic, stirring frequently, for 10 minutes or until onions are tender.

Add tomatoes, tomato paste, ½ cup (125 mL) water, mushrooms, lentils, oregano, basil and pepper. Cover and simmer, stirring occasionally, for 2 hours or until sauce is thickened. Add more water if required. Taste and adjust seasonings, if necessary.

# Vegetarian Lasagna

This recipe converts *Lentil Vegetable Spaghetti Sauce* (page 118) and frozen spinach into a crowd-pleasing vegetarian lasagna.

| | | |
|---|---|---|
| 8 | whole wheat lasagna noodles | 8 |
| 2 | pkg (300 g) frozen chopped spinach, thawed and well drained | 2 |
| 1 | tub (500 g) low-fat cottage cheese | 1 |
| 1 | egg | 1 |
| ¼ tsp | each freshly ground pepper & ground nutmeg | 1 mL |
| 4 cups | *Lentil Vegetable Spaghetti Sauce* (page 118) | 1 L |
| 1½ cups | shredded light mozzarella cheese | 375 mL |
| 2 tbsp | freshly grated Parmesan cheese | 25 mL |

In large pot of boiling water, cook lasagna noodles according to package directions or until al dente (tender but firm). Drain well and set aside.

In bowl, combine drained spinach, cottage cheese, egg, pepper and nutmeg.

Spread 1 cup (250 mL) of the spaghetti sauce in bottom of 13- x 9-inch (3.5 L) baking dish. Place 4 noodles, overlapping, over sauce; add half of the spinach mixture and half of the remaining spaghetti sauce; repeat layers. Sprinkle evenly with mozzarella and Parmesan cheeses.

Bake in 350°F (180°C) oven for about 1 hour or until hot and bubbly. Let stand for 10 minutes before cutting into 6 servings.

**HIGH FIBRE**

**Dinner Menu 20**

....................................................

**Prep** · 20 minutes if *Lentil Vegetable Spaghetti Sauce* is already prepared
**Cook** · 60 minutes
**Yield** · 6 servings

....................................................

**Each Serving** · ⅙ of recipe
Carb choice                    1
Meat & Alternatives choices 3½

....................................................

**Carbohydrate** 26 g
  Fibre 7 g
**Protein** 27 g
**Fat** 8 g
  Saturated 4 g
**Sodium** 791 mg
**Calories** 277

## MINTED COUSCOUS

**Dinner Menu 7**

....................................

**Prep** · 10 minutes
**Cook** · about 10 minutes
**Yield** · 6 servings,
    about 4 cups (1 L)

....................................

**Each Serving** · ⅔ cup (150 mL)
Carb choices            1½

....................................

**Carbohydrate** 27 g
    Fibre 2 g
**Protein** 5 g
**Fat** 1 g
    Saturated 0 g
**Sodium** 349 mg
**Calories** 140

Mint and couscous are staples of North African cuisine. Couscous is durum wheat more coarsely ground than normal wheat flours. It takes only minutes to cook.

| | | |
|---|---|---|
| 1 tsp | olive oil | 5 mL |
| 1 cup | sliced leek (white part only) | 250 mL |
| 1 | clove garlic, minced | 1 |
| 1½ cups | salt-reduced chicken broth (see Tip) | 375 mL |
| 1 cup | whole wheat couscous | 250 mL |
| 1 tbsp | chopped fresh mint | 15 mL |
| Pinch | white pepper | Pinch |

In saucepan, heat oil over medium heat; cook leek and garlic, covered, for 5 minutes or until softened.

Add broth; bring to a boil and stir in couscous. Remove from heat and let stand, covered, for 5 minutes or until grains are tender and liquid is absorbed. Fluff with fork. Stir in mint and pepper.

⊕ *Of course, an excellent replacement for salt-reduced chicken broth is our* **Homemade Light Chicken Broth** *(page 58).*

# GRILLED POLENTA

Polenta, a staple of northern Italy, is made by boiling cornmeal in water with a little olive oil. It is considered the Italian "comfort food." Polenta packaged in rolls is finding its way into the deli section of our supermarkets. Using one of these rolls makes preparation of this crisp, tasty dish fast and easy.

| 1 | roll (1 lb/500 g) polenta | 1 |
| 2 tsp | olive oil | 10 mL |
| 1 tbsp | each chopped fresh parsley and basil | 15 mL |

Slice polenta into 12 even slices.

In non-stick skillet, heat oil over medium-high heat; sauté sliced polenta for 5 minutes per side or until golden. Sprinkle with parsley and basil to serve.

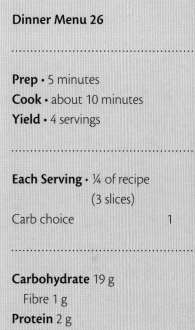

**Dinner Menu 26**

...................................................

**Prep** • 5 minutes
**Cook** • about 10 minutes
**Yield** • 4 servings

...................................................

**Each Serving** • ¼ of recipe
(3 slices)
Carb choice                1

...................................................

**Carbohydrate** 19 g
  Fibre 1 g
**Protein** 2 g
**Fat** 1 g
  Saturated 0 g
**Sodium** 361 mg
**Calories** 99

## Barley Pilaf

Barley, a whole grain rich in soluble fibre, gives the pilaf a nut-like flavour. Make this dish ahead of time and reheat it in the oven or microwave just before serving.

| | | |
|---|---|---|
| 2 tsp | olive oil | 10 mL |
| 1½ cups | sliced mushrooms | 375 mL |
| ⅓ cup | chopped onion | 75 mL |
| 2½ cups | salt-reduced chicken broth (see Tip) | 625 mL |
| 1 cup | pearl barley | 250 mL |
| ¼ cup | chopped fresh parsley | 50 mL |

In saucepan, heat oil over medium-high heat; sauté mushrooms and onion for 3 to 4 minutes.

Add chicken broth and barley; cover and cook for about 30 minutes or until barley is tender. Stir in parsley to serve (see Tip).

◉ *If you have it available, this is a great use for* **Homemade Light Chicken Broth** *(page 58).*

◉ *Extra may be frozen in ½-cup (125 mL) serving sizes to reheat at a later time.*

---

**Dinner Menu 18**

**Prep** · 15 minutes
**Cook** · 30 minutes
**Yield** · 8 servings, 4 cups (1 L)

**Each Serving** · ½ cup (125 mL)
Carb choice 1
Fats choice ½

**Carbohydrate** 22 g
  Fibre 2 g
**Protein** 4 g
**Fat** 2 g
  Saturated 0 g
**Sodium** 457 mg
**Calories** 112

# Oven-Roasted Winter Vegetables

Canadian cooks are challenged to develop superb-tasting root vegetable dishes during our long winters, when imported vegetables are expensive. This recipe is a favourite in our homes.

| | | |
|---|---|---|
| 1 | medium parsnip, peeled and cut into 8 chunks (1½ cups/375 mL) | 1 |
| 8 | peeled turnip chunks (1½ cups/375 mL) | 8 |
| 2 | medium carrots, cut into 12 chunks (1½ cups/375 mL) | 2 |
| 2 | medium onions, quartered (see Tip) | 2 |
| 2 tbsp | dark rum or 1 tsp (5 mL) rum extract | 25 mL |
| 1 tbsp | olive oil | 15 mL |
| ½ tsp | ground nutmeg | 2 mL |
| Pinch | each salt and freshly ground pepper | Pinch |

In shallow casserole, combine parsnip, turnip, carrots and onions. In small bowl, combine rum, oil, nutmeg, salt and pepper; drizzle over vegetables.

Cover and bake in 350°F (180°C) oven for 1 hour or until vegetables are tender.

⊛ *These root vegetables all cook in about the same amount of time. Cut all the vegetable pieces in a similar size for even baking.*

**Dinner Menu 27**

...............................................

**Prep** · 15 minutes
**Cook** · 1 hour
**Yield** · 4 servings

...............................................

**Each Serving** · ¼ of recipe
Carb choices                    1½
Fats choice                      1

...............................................

**Carbohydrate** 26 g
  Fibre 4 g
**Protein** 3 g
**Fat** 4 g
  Saturated 1 g
**Sodium** 103 mg
**Calories** 158

## BUTTERNUT SQUASH CASSEROLE

**Dinner Menu 29**

....................................................

**Prep** · 20 minutes
**Cook** · 20 minutes in oven
**Yield** · 8 servings, 4 cups (1 L)

....................................................

**Each Serving** · ½ cup (125 mL)
Carb choice        ½
Fats choice        ½

....................................................

**Carbohydrate** 11 g
   Fibre 2 g
**Protein** 2 g
**Fat** 3 g
   Saturated 0 g
**Sodium** 37 mg
**Calories** 71

Calling all squash lovers! Squash, one of the all-time favourite fall and winter vegetables, responds well to simple, no-fuss roasting or baking. The microwave makes their preparation simpler than ever.

| | | |
|---|---|---:|
| 7 cups | peeled cubed butternut squash (1 large) | 1.75 L |
| ½ cup | fresh bread crumbs | 125 mL |
| ¼ cup | chopped fresh parsley | 50 mL |
| 2 tbsp | coarsely chopped walnuts | 25 mL |
| 1 tbsp | melted soft margarine or butter | 15 mL |
| ¼ tsp | ground nutmeg | 1 mL |

Steam squash over saucepan of boiling water or microwave in very small amount of water on High (100%) for 10 minutes or until tender. Drain well and mash.

Lightly spray shallow casserole with non-stick cooking spray; spoon in squash.

Combine bread crumbs, parsley, walnuts, margarine and nutmeg; sprinkle over squash. Bake in 350°F (180°C) oven for 20 minutes or until hot.

⊕ *For those who like to purchase squash peeled and cut up, you'll need about two 500-g packages.*

# Baked Orange Squash

Citrus provides a delightful zest to the full flavour of butternut squash. Squash is a versatile vegetable, a good accompaniment for many meat dishes.

| | | |
|---|---|---|
| 4 cups | cubed butternut squash | 1 L |
| ½ | medium orange | ½ |
| 1 tsp | orange zest | 5 mL |
| 1 tsp | each ground ginger and nutmeg | 5 mL |
| 1 tsp | vanilla extract | 5 mL |
| ½ tsp | salt | 2 mL |

In boiling water, cook squash for 15 minutes or until tender; drain. Cool slightly before mashing. (There will be about 2 cups/500 mL mashed squash).

Grate orange rind and squeeze out juice from orange ; stir both into squash along with ginger, nutmeg, vanilla and salt. Spoon into 4-cup (1 L) baking dish. Bake for 20 minutes in 350°F (180°C) oven or until hot.

**Dinner Menu 12**

**Prep ·** 15 minutes
**Cook ·** about 35 minutes
**Yield ·** 4 servings,
2 cups (500 mL)

**Each Serving ·** ½ cup (125 mL)
Carb choice 1

**Carbohydrate** 16 g
Fibre 3 g
**Protein** 2 g
**Fat** 1 g
Saturated 0 g
**Sodium** 280 mg
**Calories** 69

# Snow Peas with Ginger

**Prep** · 10 minutes
**Cook** · about 3 minutes
**Yield** · 4 servings

**Each Serving** · ¼ of recipe
Carb choice      ½
Fats choice      ½

**Carbohydrate** 8 g
  Fibre 2 g
**Protein** 3 g
**Fat** 2 g
  Saturated 0 g
**Sodium** 4 mg
**Calories** 61

This simple yet delightful side dish spiked with fresh ginger and sesame oil comes together in minutes, adding a colourful note to the dinner table. Snow peas, referred to by the French as *mange tout* ("eat all"), are sweet and crisp, pods and all.

| | | |
|---|---|---|
| 1½ tsp | dark sesame or canola oil (see Tip) | 7 mL |
| 3 cups | snow peas, trimmed (about 1 lb/500 g) | 750 mL |
| 1 tsp | minced fresh gingerroot | 5 mL |
| | freshly ground pepper | |

In large non-stick skillet, heat oil over medium-high heat; sauté snow peas and gingerroot, stirring frequently, for 3 minutes. Remove from heat; sprinkle with pepper and serve.

◉ *Sesame oil has a wonderful nutty taste that's excellent for everything from salad dressings to sautéing. Once opened, store in the refrigerator.*

# Minted Carrots and Snow Peas

Mint gives a refreshing herb zest to carrots and peas. Keep fresh mint (and other fresh herbs) refrigerated in a glass of water covered with a plastic bag.

| | | |
|---|---|---|
| 2 cups | sliced carrots (see Tip) | 500 mL |
| 3 cups | trimmed snow peas (about ½ lb/250 g) | 750 mL |
| 1 tbsp | fresh lemon juice | 15 mL |
| 1 tbsp | chopped fresh mint leaves (or 1 tsp/5 mL dried) | 15 mL |
| 1 tsp | soft margarine or butter | 5 mL |

In saucepan, cook carrots in small amount of boiling water for about 10 minutes or until tender, adding peas during last 5 minutes of cooking (do not overcook). Drain well.

Stir in lemon juice, mint and margarine.

◉ *Reserve all cooking water to add to soups or gravies.*

**Dinner Menu 30**

...................................................

**Prep** · 10 minutes
**Cook** · 10 minutes
**Yield** · 4 servings

...................................................

**Each Serving** · ⅔ cup (150 mL)
Carb choice                     ½

...................................................

**Carbohydrate** 11 g
  Fibre 2 g
**Protein** 2 g
**Fat** 1 g
  Saturated 0 g
**Sodium** 35 mg
**Calories** 58

# Light Scalloped Potatoes

A lighter version of a traditional favourite! We think scalloped potatoes are one of the most comforting hot vegetable dishes.

**Prep** · 10 minutes
**Cook** · 1 hour
**Yield** · 4 servings,
about 3 cups (750 mL)

**Each Serving** · ¼ of recipe
(¾ cup/175 mL)
Carb choice                                    1

**Carbohydrate** 19 g
Fibre 2 g
**Protein** 3 g
**Fat** 0 g
**Sodium** 149 mg
**Calories** 88

| | | |
|---|---|---|
| 2½ cups | thinly sliced peeled potatoes (3 medium) | 625 mL |
| ⅓ cup | thinly sliced onion (1 medium) | 75 mL |
| ½ cup | low-fat milk | 125 mL |
| ¼ tsp | each celery seed and freshly ground pepper | 1 mL |
| 1 | sachet (4.5 g) salt-reduced chicken bouillon | 1 |

Spray 8-cup (2 L) baking dish or casserole with non-stick cooking spray. Alternately layer potato and onion slices in dish.

In small saucepan, heat milk, celery seed, pepper and bouillon, stirring to dissolve bouillon; pour over vegetables. Cover and bake in 350°F (180°C) oven for 1 hour or until liquid is absorbed and vegetables are tender.

# SWEET POTATO FRITES

Low-fat frites with the taste of sweet potatoes are a different and delightful treat.

| 2 | large sweet potatoes, peeled and cut into thin strips | 2 |
| 1 tbsp | olive or canola oil | 15 mL |
| ¼ tsp | salt | 1 mL |
| Pinch | paprika | Pinch |

Place potatoes in bowl of ice water and let stand for 20 minutes. Drain and pat dry.

Transfer potatoes to bowl; add oil, salt and paprika and toss to coat.

Spray baking sheet with non-stick cooking spray. Place strips on pan in single layer. Bake in 450°F (230°C) oven, stirring occasionally, for 15 minutes or until golden brown and tender.

---

**Dinner Menu 30**

..................................................

**Prep** · 20 minutes
**Cook** · about 15 minutes
**Yield** · 4 servings

..................................................

**Each Serving** · ¼ of recipe

| | |
|---|---|
| Carb choice | 1 |
| Fats choice | 1 |

..................................................

**Carbohydrate** 17 g
  Fibre 2 g
**Protein** 1 g
**Fat** 4 g
  Saturated 1 g
**Sodium** 146 mg

**Calories** 102

# APPLE CRANBERRY CLAFOUTI DESSERT

Clafouti originated in central France. A layer of fresh fruit is topped with a thick egg-and-milk batter, then baked and served warm. This peasant dessert is sheer heaven! In France, it's sometimes served with thick cream.

| | | |
|---|---|---:|
| 2 tsp | soft margarine or butter, melted | 10 mL |
| 3 cups | sliced peeled apples | 750 mL |
| ⅓ cup | fresh or frozen cranberries | 75 mL |
| ½ cup | low-fat milk | 125 mL |
| 3 tbsp | all-purpose flour | 45 mL |
| 3 tbsp | granular low-calorie sweetener with sucralose | 45 mL |
| 3 | eggs | 3 |
| 1 tsp | rum or brandy extract | 5 mL |
| | or 2 tsp (10 mL) rum or brandy | |
| ½ tsp | baking powder | 2 mL |
| 1 tbsp | granulated sugar | 15 mL |
| ½ tsp | cinnamon | 2 mL |

Place melted margarine in 4-cup (1 L) shallow casserole; add apples and cranberries.

In small bowl, whisk together milk, flour, sweetener, eggs, rum extract and baking powder; pour over fruit.

Combine sugar and cinnamon; sprinkle over batter. Bake in 350°F (180°C) oven for 35 minutes or until apples are tender and dessert is puffed and set. Cut into 6 servings and serve warm.

**Dinner Menu 23**

**Prep** · 20 minutes
**Cook** · about 35 minutes
**Yield** · 6 servings

**Each Serving** · ⅙ of recipe
| | |
|---|---:|
| Carb choice | 1 |
| Fats choice | 1 |

**Carbohydrate** 17 g
  Fibre 2 g
**Protein** 4 g
**Fat** 4 g
  Saturated 1 g
**Sodium** 85 mg
**Calories** 121

# Apple Bavarian Torte

**Dinner Menu 9**

................................

**Prep** · 30 minutes
**Cook** · about 40 minutes
**Yield** · 8 servings

................................

**Each Serving** · ⅛ recipe
Carb choices                1½
Fats choices                3

................................

**Carbohydrate** 25 g
    Fibre 2 g
**Protein** 5 g
**Fat** 15 g
    Saturated 5 g
**Sodium** 306 mg
**Calories** 246

This lower-fat wafer crumb crust replaces the dessert's traditional rich shortbread base. Warm from the oven, it's a marvellous dessert to enjoy with family or guests.

## CRUST:

| | | |
|---|---|---|
| 1 cup | graham cracker crumbs | 250 mL |
| 2 tbsp | melted soft margarine or butter | 25 mL |
| ½ tsp | cinnamon | 2 mL |

Spray 9-inch (23 cm) springform pan with non-stick cooking spray. Blend together crumbs, melted margarine and cinnamon. Press into bottom of pan.

Bake in 350°F (180°C) oven for 8 minutes or until lightly browned.

## FILLING:

| | | |
|---|---|---|
| 1 | pkg (250 g) light cream cheese | 1 |
| 2 | egg whites | 2 |
| ¼ cup | granular low-calorie sweetener with sucralose | 50 mL |
| 1 tsp | vanilla extract | 5 mL |
| 2¼ cups | thinly sliced peeled apples | 550 mL |
| 3 tbsp | packed brown sugar | 45 mL |
| 2 tbsp | all-purpose flour | 25 mL |
| 2 tbsp | soft margarine or butter | 25 mL |
| ½ tsp | cinnamon | 2 mL |
| ¼ cup | slivered almonds | 50 mL |

In food processor or with electric mixer, beat cream cheese, egg whites, sweetener and vanilla until very smooth; spoon over crust. Arrange apple slices in circles in single layer over cheese layer.

In bowl, combine sugar, flour, margarine and cinnamon until in coarse crumbs; sprinkle over apples. Top with almonds.

Bake in 350°F (180°C) oven for 45 minutes or until set and apples are tender. Cool and cut into 8 wedges.

⊕ *Refrigerate leftovers to reheat in the microwave oven or to serve cold.*

# Granola Apple Crisp

Oatmeal fruit crisps, whether apple or blueberry, are truly year-round comfort desserts. Unlike traditional crisps, this one is low in the sugar and saturated fat that typically top this sweet treat.

| | | |
|---|---|---|
| 2 | medium apples, peeled and sliced (about 2 cups/500 mL) | 2 |
| ½ cup | *Multi-Grain Morning Granola* (page 26) | 125 mL |
| 2 tbsp | granular low-calorie sweetener with sucralose | 25 mL |
| 1 tbsp | soft margarine or butter | 15 mL |
| ½ tsp | cinnamon | 2 mL |

Layer apple slices evenly in 4-cup (1 L) casserole.

In small bowl, combine granola, sweetener, margarine and cinnamon; sprinkle over apples. Bake in 350°F (180°C) oven for 30 minutes or until apples are tender and topping is golden brown.

## Variation

*Granola Blueberry Crisp:* Replace apples with 2 cups (500 mL) fresh or frozen blueberries; substitute ground ginger for cinnamon.

◉ *The crisp can also be microwaved, uncovered, on High (100%) for 5 minutes or until the fruit is cooked.*

**Dinner Menus 16, 22**

**Prep** · 10 minutes if *Multi-Grain Morning Granola* is already prepared.
**Cook** · about 30 minutes
**Yield** · 4 servings

**Each Serving** · ¼ of recipe
Carb choice                    1
Fats choice                    1

**Carbohydrate** 17 g
  Fibre 2 g
**Protein** 2 g
**Fat** 6 g
  Saturated 1 g
**Sodium** 50 mg

**Calories** 120

**Granola Blueberry Crisp:**
**Each Serving** · ¼ of recipe
Carb choice                    1
Fats choice                    1

**Carbohydrate** 19 g
  Fibre 3 g
**Protein** 2 g
**Fat** 6 g
  Saturated 1 g
**Sodium** 54 mg

**Calories** 127

## MOCHACCINO DESSERT CAKE

All the flavours of a mochaccino—cappuccino's chocolate-flavoured cousin—come together in this chilled dessert. Prepare it ahead of time and refrigerate overnight for best flavour.

| | | |
|---|---|---|
| 1 cup | low-fat cottage cheese | 250 mL |
| 1 cup | light sour cream | 250 mL |
| ½ | pkg (250 g) light cream cheese | ½ |
| ⅓ cup | granular low-calorie sweetener with sucralose | 75 mL |
| 3 tbsp | coffee liqueur or strong coffee | 45 mL |
| 2 tbsp | granulated sugar | 25 mL |
| ⅓ cup | very strong coffee | 75 mL |
| 24 | crisp ladyfinger cookies (125 g pkg) (see Tip) | 24 |
| ½ tsp | unsweetened cocoa powder | 2 mL |
| 1 cup | raspberries | 250 mL |

In food processor, combine cottage cheese, sour cream, cream cheese, sweetener, liqueur and sugar; process until smooth. Set aside.

Pour strong coffee into shallow bowl. Quickly dip each cookie into coffee just long enough to slightly soften it.

Arrange 12 cookies in bottom of 8-inch (20 cm) serving bowl or square pan, preferably not overlapping. Spread half of the cheese mixture over top (about 1½ cups/375 mL). Repeat layers. Cover and refrigerate for at least 3 hours or overnight.

Just before serving, sprinkle lightly with cocoa powder and garnish with raspberries.

◉ *Look for these ladyfingers in the Italian section of your grocery store.*

**Dinner Menu 17**

.............................................

**Prep** · 20 minutes
**Refrigerate** · 3 hours or
overnight
**Yield** · 8 servings

.............................................

**Each Serving** · ⅛ of recipe
and 2 tbsp (25 mL)
raspberries
Carb choices                 1½
Meat & Alternatives choice   ½
Fats choice                   1

.............................................

**Carbohydrate** 23 g
Fibre 1 g
**Protein** 8 g
**Fat** 7 g
Saturated 4 g
**Sodium** 237 mg
**Calories** 195

# Coffee Flan

**Dinner Menu 27**

........................................

**Prep** · 10 minutes
**Cook** · about 3 minutes for
    each batch of 4 flans
**Yield** · 8 servings

........................................

**Each Serving** · ⅛ of recipe
Carb choice            1
Meat & Alternatives choice  ½

........................................

**Carbohydrate** 14 g
  Fibre 0 g
**Protein** 6 g
**Fat** 2 g
  Saturated 1 g
**Sodium** 82 mg
**Calories** 100

The traditional Spanish flan is a custard that's coated with caramel. Our easy microwave version has a distinctive coffee flavour but no caramel.

| | | |
|---|---|---:|
| ½ cup | strong brewed coffee | 125 mL |
| 1 | can (385 mL) low-fat evaporated milk | 1 |
| 3 tbsp | packed brown sugar | 45 mL |
| ½ cup | granular low-calorie sweetener with sucralose | 125 mL |
| 3 | eggs | 3 |
| 1 tsp | rum extract | 5 mL |
| 8 | strawberries | 8 |

In glass measure, combine coffee and milk. Microwave on High (100%) for 5 minutes or until hot. Meanwhile, divide brown sugar evenly among 8 custard cups.

In large bowl, combine sweetener, eggs and rum extract. Whisk in coffee mixture. Divide evenly among prepared custard cups.

Arrange 4 cups in circle in microwave oven; cook on Medium (70%) for 3 minutes or until bubbling. Remove each cup when it shows signs of bubbling. (Do not overcook; custards will still be slightly liquid but will firm up on standing.) Repeat with remaining 4 cups.

Just before serving, turn cups upside down onto individual plates. Garnish with a sliced strawberry. Serve warm or chilled.

# Frozen Mango Dessert

Not only are mangoes a delicious tropical fruit with lush texture and beautiful colour, but they are also rich in nutrients. Make this easy tropical dessert when mangoes are ripe and delicious.

| | | |
|---|---|---|
| 1 cup | light vanilla ice cream | 250 mL |
| 1 cup | mashed ripe mango (2 medium) (see Tip) | 250 mL |
| ¼ tsp | ground nutmeg (optional) | 1 mL |

Soften ice cream for about 20 minutes in refrigerator. Blend with mango and nutmeg (if using) until well combined. Scoop into 4 small serving dishes, cover and freeze until ready to serve.

◉ *Unsweetened frozen peeled mango is available in the frozen food section of many supermarkets.*

**Dinner Menu 8**

..............................................

**Prep** · 15 minutes
**Yield** · 4 servings,
   2 cups (500 mL)

..............................................

**Each Serving** · ½ cup
      (125 mL) each
Carb choice                1
Fats choice                ½

..............................................

**Carbohydrate** 16 g
   Fibre 1 g
**Protein** 1 g
**Fat** 2 g
   Saturated 2 g
**Sodium** 38 mg
**Calories** 83

## SPRINGTIME RHUBARB JELLY DESSERT

**Dinner Menu 5**

··········································

**RHUBARB JELLY DESSERT:**
 **Prep** · 10 minutes
**Refrigerate** · 3 hours
**Yield** · 6 servings,
      3 cups (750 mL)
**Each Serving** · ½ cup (125 mL)
Carb choice                    ½

Carbohydrate 8 g
 Fibre 2 g
**Protein** 1 g
**Fat** 0 g
 Sodium 37 mg
**Calories** 37

Ginger dances with rhubarb in this light jellied dessert. Keep rhubarb in your freezer and experience this springtime delight year-round. Serve it with **Light Custard Sauce** (page 139) for an extra special treat.

| | | |
|---|---|---|
| 4 cups | fresh rhubarb, cut into ½-inch (2 cm) slices | 1 L |
| 1 cup | water | 250 mL |
| ½ cup | granular low-calorie sweetener with sucralose | 125 mL |
| 1 tbsp | finely chopped candied ginger | 15 mL |
| 1 | pkg (10.1 g) light strawberry or other fruit flavour jelly powder | 1 |

In large saucepan over medium heat, bring rhubarb, water, sweetener and ginger to a boil, stirring constantly. Continue boiling for 2 minutes. Remove from heat.

Stir in jelly powder until completely dissolved. Pour evenly into 6 dessert cups.

Refrigerate for 3 hours or until set.

## RHUBARB FOOL

**Dinner Menu 18**

··········································

**RHUBARB FOOL:**
 **Prep** · 5 minutes if sauce is
      already prepared
**Yield** · 6 servings
**Each Serving** · ⅙ of recipe
Carb choice                    1
Fats choice                    1

Carbohydrate 22 g
 Fibre 2 g
**Protein** 3 g
**Fat** 4 g
 Saturated 2 g
**Sodium** 42 mg
**Calories** 130

Here's a very refreshing dessert to prepare year-round, providing you have rhubarb in the freezer.

| | | |
|---|---|---|
| 2 cups | frozen vanilla yogurt | 500 mL |
| 2½ cups | *Spring Rhubarb Sauce* (page 74) | 625 mL |
| ¼ cup | toasted sliced almonds | 50 mL |

Divide half of the yogurt among 6 parfait dishes. Top each with ⅓ cup (75 mL) of the rhubarb sauce. Repeat layers. Sprinkle with almonds.

# LIGHT CUSTARD SAUCE

Turn simple fresh fruit into a delectable dessert with a custard sauce. Our mothers and grandmothers made it, but their high-fat, high-sugar recipes could not have a place in this book. Our recipe uses low-fat milk and sweetener instead of cream and sugar. We believe our mothers and grandmothers would still find it delectable.

| ¼ cup | granular low-calorie sweetener with sucralose | 50 mL |
| 1 tbsp | cornstarch | 15 mL |
| Pinch | salt | Pinch |
| ½ cup | low-fat evaporated milk | 125 mL |
| ½ cup | low-fat milk | 125 mL |
| 1 | egg, beaten | 1 |
| 1 tsp | soft margarine or butter | 5 mL |
| 1 tsp | rum extract or 1 tbsp (15 mL) rum | 5 mL |
| ½ tsp | vanilla extract | 2 mL |

In small saucepan over medium-low heat, combine sweetener, cornstarch and salt. Slowly whisk in evaporated and low-fat milk; cook, stirring constantly, for 5 minutes or until mixture comes to a boil. Remove from heat.

Stir small amount of hot mixture into beaten egg. Return pan to stove and whisk in egg mixture. Stir constantly for 3 minutes or until mixture returns to a boil. Remove from heat; stir in margarine and rum and vanilla extracts. Sauce can be covered and refrigerated for up to 3 days.

*Microwave:* Combine sweetener, cornstarch, salt and evaporated and skim milk in 2-cup (500 mL) glass measure. Cook on High (100%) for 2 to 3 minutes or until boiling; stir small amount into beaten egg. Return egg mixture to measure and cook at Medium-Low (30%) for 1 minute or until thickened. Stir in margarine and rum and vanilla extracts.

**Dinner Menu 5, 19**

..................................................

**Prep** · 5 minutes
**Cook** · about 8 minutes
**Yield** · 6 servings, about
　　　1½ cups (375 mL)

..................................................

**Each Serving** · ¼ cup (50 mL)
Carb choice　　　　　　½

..................................................

**Carbohydrate** 6 g
　Fibre 0 g
**Protein** 3 g
**Fat** 2 g
　Saturated 0 g
**Sodium** 89 mg
**Calories** 54

# LEMON CURD WITH STRAWBERRY SAUCE

This ethereal citrus dessert, traditionally made of lemon juice, sugar, butter and egg yolks, has been adjusted for the low-fat, low-carbohydrate profile. With a little strawberry sauce poured over top, it's a light, refreshing dessert fit for the gods!

## LEMON CURD:

**Prep** • 15 minutes
**Cook** • about 7 minutes
**Refrigerate** • 1½ hours
**Yield** • 2 cups (500 mL)

**Each Serving** • ⅙ of recipe
⅓ cup (75 mL)

| | |
|---|---:|
| Carb choice | 1 |
| Fats choice | ½ |

**Carbohydrate** 12 g
  Fibre 0 g
**Protein** 3 g
**Fat** 2 g
  Saturated 1 g
**Sodium** 24 mg
**Calories** 73

### LEMON CURD:

| | | |
|---|---|---:|
| 1⅓ cups | cold water | 325 mL |
| ⅔ cup | fresh lemon juice | 150 mL |
| ¼ cup | granulated sugar | 50 mL |
| ¼ cup | granular low-calorie sweetener with sucralose | 50 mL |
| 2 | eggs, lightly beaten | 2 |
| 2 tbsp | grated lemon rind, divided | 25 mL |
| 2 tsp | unflavoured gelatin | 10 mL |

In small saucepan, combine water, lemon juice, sugar, sweetener, eggs, lemon rind and gelatin over medium heat; cook, stirring, for 7 minutes or until gelatin is dissolved and mixture comes to a boil.

Remove from heat; transfer to bowl and refrigerate, stirring occasionally, for about 1½ hours or until mixture is consistency of unbeaten egg whites. Alternatively, place in freezer, stirring occasionally, for 30 minutes.

## STRAWBERRY SAUCE:

**Prep** • 5 minutes
**Refrigerate** • up to 5 days
**Yield** • 2 cups (500 mL)

**Each Serving** • ⅓ cup (75 mL)

| | |
|---|---:|
| Carb choice | ½ |

**Carbohydrate** 7 g
  Fibre 2 g
**Protein** 1 g
**Fat** 0 g
**Sodium** 1 mg
**Calories** 30

### STRAWBERRY SAUCE:

| | | |
|---|---|---:|
| 3 cups | fresh strawberries or 1 pkg (300 g) frozen unsweetened strawberries, thawed | 750 mL |
| 3 tbsp | granular low-calorie sweetener with sucralose | 45 mL |

In bowl, mash berries; stir in sweetener. Cover and refrigerate until ready to serve over lemon curd.

### VARIATION

*Raspberry Sauce:* Replace strawberries with 3 cups (750 mL) fresh or frozen unsweetened raspberries, thawed.

## Honey Almond Dip

Enjoy this simple but tasty dip with fresh fruits as they come into sseason. Great to have on hand, fast to make!

| | | |
|---|---|---|
| 1 cup | low-fat cottage cheese | 250 mL |
| ½ cup | low-fat plain yogurt | 125 mL |
| 2 tbsp | liquid honey | 25 mL |
| ¼ tsp | almond extract | 1 mL |

In food processor or blender, process cottage cheese until very smooth. Transfer to bowl; stir in yogurt, honey and almond extract. Cover and refrigerate for up to 5 days.

**Dinner Menu 4**

..................................................

**Prep** · 10 minutes
**Refrigerate** · up to 5 days
**Yield** · 1½ cups (325 mL)
    8 servings

..................................................

**Each Serving** · 3 tbsp (45 mL)
Carb choice                                    ½
Meats & alternatives choice  ½

..................................................

**Carbohydrate** 7 g
    Fibre 0 g
**Protein** 5 g
**Fat** 0 g
**Sodium** 142 mg
**Calories** 50

# SNACKS

## TO SNACK OR NOT TO SNACK?

### WHY DO WE SNACK?

Perhaps because we're hungry, bored, anxious or just need a boost in energy. But if you have diabetes, there's an even better reason. Studies have shown that spreading the food you need over several small meals a day improves diabetes control by smoothing out blood glucose highs and lows. And if you want to lose some weight, a planned snack can keep you satisfied between meals and discourage overeating at the next meal.

### ARE SNACKS A GOOD IDEA?

Most people need more food energy and nutrients than three meals can provide. To begin with, choosing any three menus of breakfast, lunch and dinner from *Choice Menus* gives you about 1,300 calories of food energy per day. This is a significant weight loss path for most people, and you may need more calories. How many more? Your dietitian can recommend an energy intake based on your age, activity level and weight goal (see How to Use This Book, page 15). You then plan whatever snacks are required to make up any difference between the basic 1,300 calories and your prescribed calorie intake.

The snack menus in the split-pages section come in three different sizes: 75 calories, for when you want just a bite; 150 calories, for mid-morning, mid-afternoon or bedtime; and 300 calories (essentially small meals), for active days or for shift workers. If you're counting carbohydrate, each snack menu is marked in the upper right-hand corner with the number of carbs it contains. Our motto is "a planned snack is better than an unplanned snack."

### WHEN SHOULD YOU SNACK?

Planning a snack when you have a long stretch between meals, usually more than four hours, keeps your appetite under control, at the same time making sure your blood glucose doesn't dip uncomfortably low before your next meal. This may mean planning to have mid-morning, mid-afternoon or bedtime snacks that fit within the total calories of your meal plan. Those taking insulin or pills for their diabetes may find that a mid-afternoon snack or a bedtime snack helps protect against hypoglycemia (low blood sugar). Doing blood

SNACKS · 145

glucose tests can help you and your health professional decide whether to add a snack or to reduce medication.

Our snacks are planned to be suitable for the usual snacking times. You'll find snacks to go with tea or coffee or a glass of milk (**Cranberry Raisin Oatmeal Cookies**, page 155, or **Cornmeal Cheddar Muffins**, page 153), or to carry with you when you're away from home (**Popcorn Munch**, page 152). A delayed meal, perhaps on a social occasion, is another time for a planned snack. **Bruschetta Appetizer** (page 150), or **Hummus Dip** (page 151) or **Veggie 'n' Hummus Layered Spread** (page 149) served with **Tortilla Crisps** (page 151) or pita bread, are all healthy choices that both you and your guests will enjoy.

### WHAT FOODS MAKE HEALTHY SNACK CHOICES?

Fresh fruits and vegetables are always healthy choices rich in vitamins and fibre, and you'll find them in many of our Snack Menus. Whole grain crackers and cereals provide fibre as well as B vitamins. And snacks are a great opportunity to work in more calcium-rich milk, whether it be a refreshing glass of cold milk or a warming latte or café au lait, or a cup of light hot chocolate.

Now that all food products require nutritional information on their labels, it's easier to make an informed choice among packaged snack foods as well. The key words to look for are whole grain, low fat and zero trans fat. Then check Nutrition Facts for size of serving and available carbohydrate (total carbohydrate minus fibre) to see how it might fit into your meal plan. See pages 6 and 24 for more advice on how to read labels.

# Ham 'n' Cheddar Cheese Spread

Ham and Cheddar cheese are conveniently combined in this recipe to make a flavour-packed spread. Enjoy it on whole wheat crackers or in a sandwich.

| ½ lb | sliced ham | 250 g |
|---|---|---|
| ½ cup | shredded light medium Cheddar cheese | 125 mL |
| ¼ cup | light mayonnaise | 50 mL |
| 1 tbsp | Dijon mustard | 15 mL |
| 1 tbsp | drained horseradish | 15 mL |
| | chopped fresh parsley | |

In food processor, pulse ham until finely chopped. Add cheese, mayonnaise, mustard and horseradish; pulse again until almost smooth.

Spoon into tightly covered container and refrigerate for up to 2 days. To serve, spoon into an attractive serving dish and garnish with parsley.

**Snack Menu 6, 20**

.....................................

**Prep** · 10 minutes
**Refrigerate** · up to 2 days
**Yield** · 1¾ cups (425 mL)

.....................................

**Each Serving** · 2 tbsp (25 mL)
Meat & Alternatives choice    1

.....................................

**Carbohydrate** 1 g
  Fibre 0 g
**Protein** 5 g
**Fat** 3 g
  Saturated 1 g
**Sodium** 340 mg
**Calories** 53

# Zesty Sardine Spread

**Snack Menu 8, 30**

**Prep** · 10 minutes
**Refrigerate** · up to 3 days
**Yield** · ¾ cup (175 mL)

**Each Serving** · ¼ cup (50 mL)
Meat & Alternatives choice    1

**Carbohydrate** 1 g
   Fibre 0 g
**Protein** 6 g
**Fat** 2 g
   Saturated 0 g
**Sodium** 91 mg
**Calories** 50

This lively spread is strictly for sardine lovers. It's high in omega-3 fats and adds great taste to whole wheat Melba toasts.

| | | |
|---|---|---:|
| 1 | can (92 g) sardines, packed in water, drained | 1 |
| ¼ cup | light mayonnaise | 50 mL |
| 1 tbsp | each finely chopped onion and chopped fresh parsley | 15 mL |
| 2 tsp | drained capers, chopped (optional) | 10 mL |
| 1 tsp | finely grated lemon rind | 5 mL |
| 2 tsp | fresh lemon juice | 10 mL |

In small bowl, mash sardines with mayonnaise, onion, parsley, capers (if using), lemon rind and juice.

Spoon into tightly covered container and refrigerate for up to 3 days.

◉ *About 20 small capers will give you 2 tsp (10 mL) chopped.*

# Veggie 'n' Hummus Layered Spread

Remember how wonderful hummus is served with warm pita bread? Well, consider serving this same hummus in layers with a base of *Yogurt Cheese*, topped with red pepper, cucumber, green onion, crumbled feta cheese and chopped fresh parsley.

| | | |
|---|---|---|
| ⅔ cup | *Yogurt Cheese* | 150 mL |
| ¾ cup | *Hummus Dip* (page 151) | 175 mL |
| 2 tbsp | each diced sweet red pepper and cucumber | 25 mL |
| 1 | green onion, finely chopped | 1 |
| ¼ cup | crumbled feta cheese | 50 mL |
| 2 tbsp | chopped fresh parsley | 25 mL |

Spoon hummus into shallow glass serving bowl. Spread *Yogurt Cheese* over hummus. Just before serving, sprinkle with red pepper, cucumber, green onion, feta cheese and parsley.

Serve with warm pita bread, *Tortilla Crisps* (page 151) or low-fat crackers.

## Yogurt Cheese:

| | | |
|---|---|---|
| 1 cup | low-fat plain yogurt (see Tip) | 250 mL |

Line sieve with cheesecloth or coffee filter paper set over a bowl. Place yogurt in sieve. Cover and refrigerate for several hours or until reduced to ⅔ cup (150 mL). Gather edges of cheesecloth together and gently squeeze out any remaining whey. Transfer yogurt cheese to a bowl. Set liquid aside (see Tip). Cover and refrigerate yogurt cheese for up to 1 week.

◉ *When making yogurt cheese, be sure to choose a plain yogurt without gelatin, starch or gums as they will not drain. Whole milk yogurt makes a richer-tasting, smoother and milder-flavoured cheese than lower-fat yogurt. Low- and non-fat yogurt makes a more tart, tangy-tasting cheese.*

◉ *The remaining whey from the yogurt can be added to soups, as it contains B vitamins and minerals. To store yogurt cheese, cover and refrigerate for up to one week. Yogurt cheese can also be used for spreads, salad dressings, on baked potatoes and for a cream cheese replacement.*

**Snack Menu 12**

..............................................

**Prep** • 20 minutes if *Hummus Dip* is already prepared
**Refrigerate** • several hours
**Yield** • about 1½ cups (375 mL)

..............................................

**Each Serving** • ¼ cup (50 mL)
Carb choice                     ½
Meat & Alternatives choice   ½

..............................................

**Carbohydrate** 10 g
  Fibre 2 g
**Protein** 5 g
**Fat** 2 g
  Saturated 1 g
**Sodium** 133 mg
**Calories** 77

# Bruschetta Appetizer

**Snack Menu 13**
**Dinner Menu 30**

..........................................

**Prep** · 10 minutes
**Cook** · about 5 minutes
**Yield** · 4 servings

..........................................

**Each Serving** · 1 slice

| | |
|---|---|
| Carb choice | 1 |
| Fats choice | ½ |

..........................................

**Carbohydrate** 18 g
   Fibre 2 g
**Protein** 4 g
**Fat** 3 g
   Saturated 1 g
**Sodium** 210 mg
**Calories** 112

Top thick slices of toasted Italian bread with ruby cubes of tomatoes flavoured with garlic, basil and Parmesan cheese. It's the quintessential Italian appetizer and can be eaten as a snack or as part of dinner.

| | | |
|---|---|---|
| 4 | slices Italian bread, cut ¾ inch (2 cm) thick (120 g in total) | 4 |
| 1 cup | finely chopped fresh tomato (1 medium tomato) | 250 mL |
| 1 tbsp | freshly grated Parmesan cheese | 15 mL |
| 1 tsp | olive oil | 5 mL |
| 1 tsp | dried basil (or 1 tbsp/15 mL chopped fresh) | 5 mL |
| 1 | small clove garlic, minced | 1 |

Broil or toast bread on each side until golden brown.

In small bowl, mix together tomato, cheese, oil, basil and garlic. Spoon ¼ cup (50 mL) onto each slice of toast.

Return to broiler for 2 to 3 minutes to warm slightly.

# Hummus Dip with Tortilla Crisps

Hummus is a high-fibre vegetarian dip of Middle Eastern origin. "East meets West" when we serve hummus with tortillas, the bread of Mexico! There's a range of garlic for those who may like more.

## Hummus:

| | | |
|---|---|---|
| 1 | can (19 oz/540 mL) chickpeas, drained and rinsed | 1 |
| 1 or 2 | cloves garlic, minced | 1 or 2 |
| ½ cup | low-fat plain yogurt | 125 mL |
| 3 tbsp | fresh lemon juice | 45 mL |
| ½ tsp | ground cumin | 2 mL |
| Dash | hot pepper sauce | Dash |
| | freshly ground pepper | |

In food processor or blender, purée chickpeas with garlic until coarsely chopped. Add yogurt, lemon juice, cumin, hot pepper sauce, and pepper to taste; blend to smooth paste.

Transfer to covered container and refrigerate for at least 2 hours so flavours develop or freeze for up to 6 months.

## Tortilla Crisps:

| | | |
|---|---|---|
| 4 | 8-inch (20 cm) whole wheat flour tortillas | 4 |

With scissors, cut each tortilla into 12 triangles. Place in single layer on baking sheet.

Bake in 300°F (150°C) oven for 15 minutes or until crisp and golden. Cool before storing in tightly sealed container.

⊕ *Freeze hummus in small amounts for future use.*
⊕ *Since flour tortillas come in packages of 10 or 12, it's worth baking lots since they keep well in a tightly sealed container.*

# POPCORN MUNCH

Snack Menus 4, 15, 21

**Prep** · 10 minutes
**Cook** · about 35 minutes
**Yield** · 11 cups (2.75 L)

**Each Serving** · 1 cup (250 mL)
Carb choice          1
Fats choice          1

**Carbohydrate** 17 g
  Fibre 2 g
**Protein** 3 g
**Fat** 4 g
  Saturated 1 g
**Sodium** 207 mg
**Calories** 113

This yummy snack is much lower in fat than either potato or tortilla chips.

| | | |
|---|---|---:|
| 8 cups | air-popped popcorn (see Tip) | 2 L |
| 2 cups | small shredded wheat cereal squares | 500 mL |
| 1¼ cups | broken slim pretzels | 300 mL |
| 3 tbsp | melted soft margarine or butter | 45 mL |
| 2 tbsp | freshly grated Parmesan cheese | 25 mL |
| 1 tsp | chili powder | 5 mL |
| ½ tsp | garlic powder | 2 mL |

In plastic bag, combine cooled air-popped popcorn, cereal squares and pretzels.

In small bowl, combine margarine, cheese, chili powder and garlic powder; pour over popped corn mixture and shake well to distribute.

Spread on large baking sheet. Bake in 275°F (140°C) oven for 35 minutes or until golden brown and crispy. Cool before storing in airtight container or small sandwich bags.

⊛ *To air-pop popcorn, use an automatic corn popper. Or heat a large non-stick skillet over medium-high heat for several minutes; add about ½ cup (125 mL) unpopped kernels and shake pan until all kernels are popped. Cool, then measure the required 8 cups (2 L).*

## VARIATIONS
Try these interesting flavour variations in place of the chili and garlic powders:
*Italian:* dried oregano, basil and garlic powder
*Sweet seasonings:* cinnamon, ground nutmeg and ground cloves
*Hot 'n' spicy:* dry mustard, hot pepper sauce and paprika

# Cornmeal Cheddar Muffins

Cheddar cheese accents give a comforting lift to cornmeal muffins. Add dried herbs for a savoury muffin or orange rind for a tea-time treat.

| | | |
|---|---|---|
| 1¼ cups | low-fat milk | 300 mL |
| ¾ cup | cornmeal | 175 mL |
| ¼ cup | olive or canola oil | 50 mL |
| 1 | egg, beaten (or 2 egg whites) | 1 |
| ½ cup | shredded light medium Cheddar cheese | 125 mL |
| 1 cup | all-purpose flour | 250 mL |
| 3 tbsp | granular low-calorie sweetener with sucralose | 45 mL |
| 1 tbsp | baking powder | 15 mL |
| ½ tsp | each dried oregano and basil | 2 mL |
| ¼ tsp | salt | 1 mL |

In bowl, stir together milk and cornmeal; let stand for 5 minutes. Stir in oil, egg and cheese.

In separate bowl, combine flour, sweetener, baking powder, oregano, basil and salt. Add cornmeal mixture; stir just until combined.

Spoon batter into 12 non-stick or paper-lined medium muffin cups. Bake in 375°F (190°C) oven for about 18 minutes or until tops are golden brown and firm to the touch.

---

**Snack Menus 11, 22**
**Lunch Menu 17**

........................................

**Prep** · 10 minutes
**Cook** · about 18 minutes
**Yield** · 12 medium muffins

........................................

**Each Serving** · 1 muffin

| | |
|---|---|
| Carb choice | 1 |
| Fats choice | 1 |

........................................

**Carbohydrate** 16 g
  Fibre 1 g
**Protein** 4 g
**Fat** 6 g
  Saturated 1 g
**Sodium** 167 mg

**Calories** 135

# PEANUT BUTTER COOKIES

**Snack Menu 8**

........................................

**Prep** • 15 minutes
**Cook** • about 10 minutes
**Yield** • about 4 dozen

........................................

**Each Serving** • 2 cookies
Carb choice                     ½
Fats choice                      1

........................................

**Carbohydrate** 10 g
  Fibre 2 g
**Protein** 3 g
**Fat** 4 g
  Saturated 1 g
**Sodium** 60 mg
**Calories** 87

Peanut butter cookies are a fond childhood memory for many of us. These cookies are as full of great peanut flavour as the ones your mother made. But unless she used whole wheat flour, these are healthier.

| | | |
|---|---|---:|
| 1½ cups | whole wheat flour | 375 mL |
| ½ tsp | each baking powder and baking soda | 2 mL |
| ¼ tsp | salt | 1 mL |
| ¾ cup | crunchy peanut butter | 175 mL |
| ⅓ cup | soft margarine or butter | 75 mL |
| ½ cup | granular low-calorie sweetener with sucralose | 125 mL |
| ¼ cup | lightly packed brown sugar | 50 mL |
| 1 | egg | 1 |

In bowl, combine flour, baking powder, baking soda and salt; set aside.

In large bowl, cream peanut butter and margarine until smooth. Add sweetener, sugar and egg; beat until well combined. Add flour mixture; stir until well mixed.

Drop by teaspoonfuls onto ungreased baking sheet and flatten with fork.

Bake in 350°F (180°C) oven for 10 minutes or until edges are browned. Transfer to rack to cool.

# CRANBERRY RAISIN OATMEAL COOKIES

Making whole grain cookies from scratch is a snap. They also taste better and are better for you than commercial ones. Freeze them in a tightly closed container.

| 1 cup | whole wheat flour | 250 mL |
|---|---|---|
| 1 tsp | baking soda | 5 mL |
| ½ tsp | each ground nutmeg and cinnamon | 2 mL |
| ½ cup | soft margarine or butter | 125 mL |
| ½ cup | granular low-calorie sweetener with sucralose | 125 mL |
| ½ cup | lightly packed brown sugar | 125 mL |
| 1 | egg | 1 |
| 1 | egg white | 1 |
| 1 tsp | vanilla extract | 5 mL |
| 2 cups | large-flake rolled oats | 500 mL |
| ½ cup | raisins | 125 mL |
| ⅓ cup | dried sweetened cranberries | 75 mL |

In bowl, combine flour, baking soda, nutmeg and cinnamon. Set aside.

In large bowl, beat together margarine, sweetener, sugar, egg, egg white and vanilla until well blended. Add flour mixture and beat again until well mixed. Stir in oats, raisins and cranberries.

Spray baking sheet with non-stick cooking spray. Drop dough by spoonfuls onto pan. Bake in 350°F (180°C) oven for 10 minutes or until cookies are golden brown. Transfer to rack to cool.

**Snack Menu 13**

................................................

**Prep** • 20 minutes
**Cook** • about 10 minutes
**Yield** • 4 dozen cookies

................................................

**Each Serving** • 2 cookies

| Carb choice | 1 |
|---|---|
| Fats choice | 1 |

................................................

**Carbohydrate** 17 g
  Fibre 2 g
**Protein** 2 g
**Fat** 5 g
  Saturated 1 g
**Sodium** 105 mg
**Calories** 118

# SPECIAL MEALS FOR SPECIAL OCCASIONS

Anniversaries, birthdays, retirements, reunions and gatherings of friends are all reasons for celebration and often centre around a meal. Our four special-occasion menus anticipate such a celebration at home. Be it barbecue fare, a crown roast of pork, a roast turkey or a Greek dinner, there is a celebratory dinner here for most occasions. The menus are for six to eight persons, but they can all be doubled.

Naturally, these meals require more preparation time than our regular day-to-day menus, but they are, after all, for special occasions. However, they're still based on the dinner meal plan (page 79). Several dinners are a little higher in fat and calories, but carbohydrate content and number of carb choices remain the same. After all, it's what you eat most of the time, not what you eat occasionally, that really matters. All menus meet healthy eating goals and provide suggested serving sizes for people watching portions.

### EATING OUT

Invited to someone's home for dinner? Not being in control of the menu doesn't have to be a challenge for the person with diabetes. Just stay with your usual portions and leave food that doesn't fit your meal plan. Dining out at a restaurant? Not a problem! You can make choices from the menu.

### BEVERAGES AND SPECIAL OCCASIONS

Special occasions often include an alcoholic drink before or with a meal. As a general rule, there is no need to avoid alcohol because you have diabetes. Current guidelines for everyone, not just those with diabetes, advise "moderation," meaning no more than one drink per day for women, two per day for men. If you have other problems, such as elevated cholesterol or triglycerides, hypertension, or are taking insulin or diabetes pills or other medications, discuss the use of alcoholic beverages with your diabetes health care team first.

Of course, substituting a low-calorie non-alcoholic beverage is another solution. Some choices are mineral or soda water with lime, diet soft drinks, lemonade and tea or coffee.

Here are some tips to remember when drinking alcoholic beverages.

- Always eat carbohydrate foods when drinking alcohol. Never drink on an empty stomach. Do not take extra insulin to offset the carbohydrate content of alcoholic drinks.
- If you are on insulin or certain diabetes medications, alcohol can cause hypoglycemia or low blood sugar (see page 191). Learn how to recognize symptoms (cold, sweating, shaking, very hungry), how to treat it (glucose tablets or juice) and, better still, how to prevent it (don't skip your usual meals and snacks during the day to make up for the meal out, and have an extra snack if your meal is going to be much later than usual).
- When going out, take your glucose meter and wear diabetes identification.
- Be aware of the amount of alcohol in the beverage you are drinking. Pour your own drinks whenever possible and drink slowly. Drink less alcohol, and stretch your drinks with sugar-free mixes.
- If you are watching your weight, remember that alcohol adds extra calories.

| BEVERAGE | STANDARD SERVING SIZE | CARBOHYDRATE CONTENT (g) | ENERGY VALUE (CALORIES) |
|---|---|---|---|
| **Beer** | | | |
| regular | 360 mL (12 fl oz) | 10 | 140 |
| light | 360 mL (12 fl oz) | 5 | 100 |
| non-alcoholic | 360 mL (12 fl oz) | 11–15 | 50–75 |
| low-carb | 360 mL (12 fl oz) | 2.5 | 90–97 |
| **Wine** | | | |
| red or white | 150 mL (5 oz) | 1–2.5 | 102–108 |
| dessert | 150 mL (5 oz) | 17–21 | 231–243 |
| non-alcoholic | 150 mL (5 oz) | 2 | 9 |
| **Spirits/hard liquor** | 45 mL (1.5 fl oz) | 0 | 98 |
| **Liqueurs and cordials** | 45 mL (1.5 fl oz) | 17–21 | 163–190 |
| **Mixes** | | | |
| Sugar-free pop | 240 mL (8 fl oz) | 0.2 | 2 |
| Regular pop | 240 mL (8 fl oz) | 22–31 | 84–120 |
| Club soda | 240 mL (8 fl oz) | 0 | 0 |
| Tonic water | 240 mL (8 fl oz) | 22 | 84 |
| Tomato juice | 240 mL (8 fl oz) | 9 | 41 |
| Clamato juice | 240 mL (8 fl oz) | 26 | 116 |
| Orange juice | 240 mL (8 fl oz) | 25 | 110 |

Source: *Alcohol + Diabetes* (2006), published by the Canadian Diabetes Association. Used with permission.

......................................

**Prep** · 5 minutes
**Refrigerate** · up to 5 days
**Yield** · ¾ cup (175 mL),
       6 servings

......................................

**Each Serving** · 2 tbsp (25 mL)
Carb choice                    ½

......................................

**Carbohydrate** 8 g
   Fibre 1 g
**Protein** 1 g
**Fat** 0 g
**Sodium** 351 mg
**Calories** 32

## SEAFOOD COCKTAIL DIP

This is the classic seafood dip, but with an upgrade of sun-dried tomatoes. Make it ahead—the flavours improve.

| | | |
|---|---|---|
| ⅔ cup | ketchup or chili sauce | 150 mL |
| 2 tbsp | prepared horseradish | 25 mL |
| 2 | sun-dried tomatoes (not oil-packed), finely chopped | 2 |
| 2 tsp | Worcestershire sauce | 10 mL |

In small bowl, combine ketchup, horseradish, sun-dried tomatoes and Worcestershire sauce; stir well.

Cover and refrigerate for up to 5 days.

# Herb-Rubbed Grilled Chicken

Rubs add great flavour and no calories to meat. This herb rub produces a lightly seasoned meat for summertime grilling. And it can be used with other meats.

| 6 | boneless, skinless chicken breast halves (100 g each) | 6 |
|---|---|---|

Trim excess fat from chicken and discard.

## Rub:

| 2 tbsp | fresh lemon juice | 25 mL |
|---|---|---|
| 2 tbsp | Dijon mustard | 25 mL |
| 1 tsp | each paprika and freshly ground pepper | 5 mL |
| 1 tsp | brown sugar | 5 mL |
| ½ tsp | each ground cumin and garlic powder | 2 mL |
| Pinch | cayenne pepper | Pinch |
|  | chopped fresh chives or parsley |  |

In small bowl, combine lemon juice, mustard, paprika, pepper, sugar, cumin, garlic powder and cayenne; press mixture over both sides of chicken. Place in shallow non-reactive container. Cover and refrigerate for 30 minutes or longer.

Preheat grill on high for 5 minutes. Place chicken on greased grill; close lid and cook, turning once, for 12 to 15 minutes or until tender and no longer pink inside.

To serve, slice each chicken breast crosswise into slices and fan slices over plate. Garnish with chives.

**Grill Time & The Cookin' Is Easy**

**Special Occasion Menu 1**

........................................

**Prep** · 10 minutes
**Cook** · about 15 minutes
**Yield** · 6 servings

........................................

**Each Serving** · ⅙ of recipe
Meat & Alternatives choices   3

........................................

**Carbohydrate** 2 g
   Fibre 0 g
**Protein** 20 g
**Fat** 2 g
   Saturated 1 g
**Sodium** 109 mg
**Calories** 110

.................................................

**Prep** · 30 minutes
**Refrigerate** · 30 minutes or
     longer
**Yield** · 6 servings,
     3 cups (750 mL) salad

.................................................

**Each Serving** · ½ cup (125 mL)
Carb choice          1
Fats choice          1

.................................................

**Carbohydrate** 18 g
  Fibre 2 g
**Protein** 5 g
**Fat** 5 g
  Saturated 1 g
**Sodium** 110 mg
**Calories** 133

# SUMMERTIME POTATO SALAD

When the weather outside is steamy, carefree cool meals are important. Prepare this chilled salad ahead of time. It will come in very handy for last-minute meals.

| | | |
|---|---|---:|
| 2 cups | cubed peeled potatoes | 500 mL |
| 2 | eggs | 2 |
| ⅔ cup | sliced celery | 150 mL |
| ¼ cup | sliced green onion | 50 mL |
| ¼ cup | chopped fresh parsley | 50 mL |
| ¼ cup | light mayonnaise | 50 mL |
| ¼ cup | low-fat plain yogurt (see Tip) | 50 mL |
| 1 tbsp | malt vinegar | 15 mL |
| ½ tsp | dried tarragon | 2 mL |
| ¼ tsp | each dry mustard and freshly ground pepper | 1 mL |
| | leaf lettuce | |

In saucepan of boiling water, cook potatoes for 10 minutes or until just tender; drain and cool. Simmer eggs in separate saucepan of water for about 20 minutes. Drain well and cool. Peel and cut eggs into quarters; set aside.

In large bowl, combine potatoes, celery, onion and parsley.

In small bowl, whisk together mayonnaise, yogurt, vinegar, tarragon, mustard and pepper; stir gently into potato mixture. Place in bowl lined with lettuce leaves and garnish with egg quarters. Cover and refrigerate for at least 30 minutes before serving.

◉ *If you have* **Handy Mayo Dip** *(page 52) already prepared, ½ cup (125 mL) is a perfect replacement for the mayonnaise and yogurt in this recipe.*

## Spinach Orange Salad with Raspberry Vinaigrette

Nothing says summer more than a bowlful of garden-fresh greens. Add orange sections, some red onion and toss with a flavourful raspberry vinaigrette. It will refresh on a hot summer day or provide a light counterpoint to a hearty midwinter dinner.

| | | |
|---|---|---|
| 6 cups | baby spinach leaves, loosely packed | 1.5 L |
| 1 cup | orange sections | 250 mL |
| ½ | red onion, thinly sliced | ½ |
| 2 tbsp | *Raspberry Vinaigrette* | 25 mL |

Wash and dry spinach. Remove stems and tear leaves into bite-size pieces.

In large salad bowl, combine spinach, oranges and red onion. Cover and refrigerate for at least 30 minutes. Just before serving, toss salad with dressing.

### Raspberry Vinaigrette:

| | | |
|---|---|---|
| ⅓ cup | raspberry vinegar (see Tip) | 75 mL |
| ¼ cup | olive oil | 50 mL |
| 1 tbsp | granular low-calorie sweetener with sucralose | 15 mL |
| 1 tsp | poppy seeds | 5 mL |
| ¼ tsp | salt | 1 mL |
| | freshly ground pepper | |

In container with tight-fitting lid, combine vinegar, oil, sweetener, poppy seeds, salt, and pepper to taste; shake well and refrigerate until ready to use.

◉ *Raspberry vinegar is quite expensive. To make your own, add 3 cups (750 mL) fresh or frozen raspberries to 1½ cups (375 mL) white wine vinegar. Cover and let stand at room temperature for several days. Strain and pour into clean sealed bottles. Makes about 2 cups (500 mL) vinegar. Keeps well refrigerated.*

---

**Grill Time & The Cookin' Is Easy**

**Special Occasions Menu 1**
**Dinner Menu 24**

........................................

**Salad:**
**Prep** · 15 minutes
**Refrigerate** · about 30 minutes or longer
**Yield** · 6 servings, 6 cups (1.5 L)

**Each Serving** · ⅙ of recipe
Fats choice                    1

**Carbohydrate** 6 g
  Fibre 2 g
**Protein** 2 g
**Fat** 3 g
  Saturated 0 g
**Sodium** 70 mg
**Calories** 48

........................................

**Vinaigrette:**
**Prep** · 5 minutes
**Refrigerate** · up to 1 week
**Yield** · ½ cup (125 mL)

**Each Serving** · 1 tbsp (15 mL)
Fats choices                    1½

**Carbohydrate** 1 g
  Fibre 0 g
**Protein** 0 g
**Fat** 7 g
  Saturated 0 g
**Sodium** 72 mg
**Calories** 64

..................................................

**Prep** · 15 minutes
**Freeze** · about 1 hour
**Yield** · about 3 cups (750 mL)

..................................................

**Each Serving** · ⅙ of recipe
          ½ cup (125 mL)
Carb choice                    1

..................................................

**Carbohydrate** 17 g
   Fibre 1 g
**Protein** 1 g
**Fat** 0 g
**Sodium** 4 mg
**Calories** 65

# WATERMELON ICE

If you enjoy the refreshing flavours of frozen fruits, this ice will be a wonderful light dessert after a meal. Watermelon, low in calories and rich in sweetness, is an all-ages favourite.

| | | |
|---|---|---:|
| 2 cups | cubed seeded watermelon | 500 mL |
| 1 cup | water | 250 mL |
| 3 tbsp | liquid honey | 45 mL |
| 3 tbsp | granular low-calorie sweetener with sucralose | 45 mL |
| 1 tbsp | grated lemon rind | 15 mL |
| 2 tbsp | fresh lemon juice | 25 mL |
| | fresh mint leaves | |

In blender or food processor, purée watermelon, water, honey, sweetener, lemon rind and lemon juice until smooth.

Pour into metal pan and freeze for 1 hour or until frozen around outside, or freeze in ice cream maker according to manufacturer's directions.

Store in tightly sealed container in freezer until ready to serve. Transfer to refrigerator 15 minutes before serving. Garnish with mint to serve.

**VARIATION**
You can substitute other melons for watermelon.

# Spicy Tomato Wine Bouillon

This light soup excites the taste buds in anticipation of the elegant meal to follow, yet adds few calories.

| | | |
|---|---|---|
| 4 cups | salt-reduced vegetable juice cocktail | 1 L |
| 3 cups | salt-reduced beef broth (see Tip) | 750 mL |
| ½ cup | chopped onion | 125 mL |
| 3 | sprigs fresh parsley | 3 |
| 1 tbsp | granular low-calorie sweetener with sucralose | 15 mL |
| ¼ tsp | freshly ground pepper | 1 mL |
| 2 | whole cloves | 2 |
| 1 cup | dry white or red wine (see Tip) | 250 mL |
| ¼ cup | dry sherry | 50 mL |
| 1 | lemon, thinly sliced | 1 |
| | paprika | |

In large saucepan, combine tomato juice, broth, onion, parsley, sweetener, pepper and cloves; bring to a boil. Reduce heat and add wine and sherry; cover and simmer for 30 minutes.

Strain, return to saucepan and heat to serving temperature. Serve with lemon slices sprinkled with paprika.

- *Using vegetable juice cocktail and beef broth that are reduced in salt lowers sodium content considerably. If you prefer to make your own broth, see page 57 for our **Homemade Light Beef Broth**.*
- *When cooking with wine, always add it halfway through the cooking time so the flavours are not boiled away. Alcohol evaporates when wine is simmered—all you are left with is the superb taste. If you wish to omit the wine and sherry, replace them with extra broth.*

## The Crowning Moment

**Special Occasion Menu 2**

**Prep** · 10 minutes
**Cook** · about 30 minutes
**Yield** · 8 servings, 8 cups (2 L)

**Each Serving** · 1 cup (250 mL)
Carb choice                    ½

**Carbohydrate** 8 g
  Fibre 2 g
**Protein** 2 g
**Fat** 0 g
**Sodium** 270 mg
**Calories** 61

**Special Occasion Menu 2**

..................................................

**Prep** · 15 minutes
**Cook** · about 3½ hours
**Yield** · 14 to 16 chops and
     about 9 cups (2.25 L)
     dressing

..................................................

**Each Serving** · 1 chop and
     ½ cup (125 mL) dressing
Carb choice            ½
Meat & Alternatives choices  3

..................................................

**Carbohydrate** 13 g
  Fibre 2 g
**Protein** 23 g
**Fat** 7 g
  Saturated 2 g
**Sodium** 155 mg
**Calories** 208

# CROWN ROAST OF PORK WITH WILD RICE ALMOND DRESSING

For that "ritzy" special occasion, what's more spectacular than a lean, gourmet crown roast of pork with a wild rice dressing? Have your butcher partially cut the rib bones to make carving easier. Any leftovers will be divine served cold.

| 7 lb | lean crown roast of pork (14 to 16 chops) | 3 kg |
|---|---|---|

## DRESSING:

| | | |
|---|---|---|
| 1 cup | wild rice | 250 mL |
| 2 | bay leaves | 2 |
| 2 tsp | soft margarine or butter | 10 mL |
| 2 cups | sliced mushrooms (about 12 small) | 500 mL |
| 1 cup | chopped onion (about 1 large) | 250 mL |
| 1 cup | thinly sliced celery | 250 mL |
| 6 | slices whole wheat bread | 6 |
| ⅓ cup | slivered almonds, toasted | 75 mL |
| ¼ cup | chopped fresh parsley | 50 mL |
| 1 tsp | dried thyme (or 1 tbsp/15 mL chopped fresh) | 5 mL |
| ½ tsp | each salt, freshly ground pepper and dried summer savory | 2 mL |

Place meat on rack in shallow pan. Wrap rib bones with foil. Stuff ball of foil in middle to keep cavity open. Roast, uncovered, in 325°F (160°C) oven for 2 hours.

*Dressing:* Meanwhile, wash wild rice thoroughly under cold running water. In saucepan, bring 3 cups (750 mL) water to a boil. Add rice and bay leaves; reduce heat, cover and simmer for 45 minutes or until rice is tender. Drain and discard bay leaves.

In large non-stick skillet over medium-high heat, melt margarine; cook mushrooms, onion and celery for about 6 minutes or until tender. Stir into rice.

Crumble bread into crumbs. Stir bread crumbs, almonds, parsley, thyme, salt, pepper and savory into onion mixture.

Remove roast from oven; remove foil and fill centre with some of the dressing. Cover dressing with small piece of foil. Place remaining dressing in casserole (see Tip for cooking directions).

Place meat thermometer in thickest part of meat, not touching bone. Roast for 45 to 90 minutes or until thermometer registers 160°F (70°C). Place meat on carving platter; tent with foil and let stand for 10 minutes before carving. Remove foil from dressing. Slice between ribs to serve.

- *There will not be enough room for all the dressing in the centre of the roast. Place the extra in a casserole lightly sprayed with non-stick cooking spray. Cook alongside roast for about 1 hour or until heated and golden.*
- *The tasty dressing is also perfect for stuffing a medium turkey (about 10 lb/4.5 kg) or a large roasting chicken (8 lb/3.5 kg).*

...................................

**Prep** · 10 minutes
**Cook** · 15 minutes
**Yield** · about 6 cups (1.5 L),
8 servings

...................................

**Each Serving** · ⅛ of recipe
(¾ cup/175 mL)
Fats choice                    ½

...................................

**Carbohydrate** 7 g
Fibre 2 g
**Protein** 3 g
**Fat** 2 g
Saturated 0 g
**Sodium** 74 mg
**Calories** 52

# Balsamic Baked Mushrooms

This wonderful, unique low-fat vegetable recipe is an excellent accompaniment to roast pork, chicken or turkey. The mushrooms also barbecue well placed on the rack above grilling meats.

| | | |
|---|---|---|
| 9 cups | thickly sliced mushrooms (2 lb/1 kg) | 2.25 L |
| ¾ cup | thinly sliced onions | 175 mL |
| 2 tbsp | balsamic vinegar | 25 mL |
| 1 tbsp | olive oil | 15 mL |
| 1 | clove garlic, minced | 1 |
| ¼ tsp | each salt and freshly ground pepper | 1 mL |

In shallow baking dish, evenly arrange mushrooms and onions, overlapping.

In small bowl, whisk vinegar, oil, garlic, salt and pepper; drizzle over vegetables and toss to mix.

Bake, uncovered, in 375°F (190°C) oven for 20 minutes or until mushrooms are cooked and lightly browned.

# Chocolate Fondue

Many believe the perfect finish for a meal is chocolate. Satisfy this craving with some luscious fondue sauce served over fresh fruit. We used cocoa powder instead of higher-fat chocolate.

| ¼ cup | soft margarine or butter | 50 mL |
| ½ cup | unsweetened cocoa powder | 125 mL |
| 1 | can (385 mL) low-fat evaporated milk | 1 |
| ⅓ cup | corn syrup | 75 mL |
| 1½ tbsp | cornstarch | 22 mL |
| ½ cup | granular low-calorie sweetener with sucralose | 125 mL |
| 2 tsp | vanilla or rum extract | 10 mL |

In small saucepan, melt margarine over medium-low heat. Whisk in cocoa powder until smooth.

In small bowl, whisk evaporated milk, corn syrup, cornstarch and sweetener; whisk into cocoa mixture. Cook gently, stirring occasionally, over low heat for 5 minutes or until bubbly and smooth. Stir in vanilla.

Cool before storing in covered container in refrigerator. Serve cold or warm.

## THE CROWNING MOMENT

**Special Occasion Menu 2**
**Dinner Menu 7**

......................................................

**Prep** • about 5 minutes
**Cook** • about 5 minutes
**Refrigerate** • up to 1 week
**Yield** • 2 cups (500 mL)

......................................................

**Each Serving** • ¼ cup (50 mL)

| Carb choice | 1 |
| Fats choices | 1½ |

......................................................

**Carbohydrate** 22 g
  Fibre 2 g
**Protein** 5 g
**Fat** 7 g
  Saturated 1 g
**Sodium** 146 mg
**Calories** 157

# ROAST TURKEY WITH SAVOURY DRESSING

The best dressing is made with bread one or two days old. Stuff turkey (or chicken) just before you roast it. This recipe makes enough to stuff a 6-lb (3 kg) chicken; double the recipe for a 12-lb (6 kg) turkey.

### DRESSING:

| | | |
|---|---|---|
| 6 | slices bread (180 g), crusts included (See Tip) | 6 |
| 2 tbsp | soft margarine or butter | 25 mL |
| 1 cup | chopped mushrooms | 250 mL |
| ½ cup | each chopped celery and onion | 125 mL |
| ¼ cup | chopped fresh parsley | 50 mL |
| 1 tsp | dried tarragon | 5 mL |
| ½ tsp | paprika | 2 mL |
| Pinch | ground nutmeg and freshly ground pepper | Pinch |

Prepare bread crumbs in food processor or by hand. In non-stick skillet, melt margarine over medium-high heat; cook mushrooms, celery, onion and parsley for 5 minutes or until vegetables are softened. Cool. Stir in tarragon, paprika, nutmeg and pepper. Stir into bread crumbs.

◉ *If you have bread crumbs in the freezer, approximately 4 cups (1 L) fresh crumbs is the equivalent of 6 slices of bread.*

## To Stuff and Roast Poultry

Rinse and dry the cavity; stuff loosely with prepared dressing. Close opening by trussing with a large needle and string, or insert skewers and criss-cross the string. Cross legs and tie with string so legs are close to body. Turn wings back, tuck under bird and secure with skewers or string.

Place on rack in uncovered roasting pan, breast side up; insert meat thermometer in thigh. Roast in 325°F (160°C) oven until thermometer reaches 185°F (85°C) or juices run clear. If breast starts to brown too much, cover with foil.

## Roasting Chart

Since cooking times are approximate, using a meat thermometer is the most accurate way to gauge doneness. Roast until internal temperature of poultry reaches 180ºF (85°C). A general rule of thumb when roasting is to allow 18 to 20 minutes per pound (500 g) for both turkey and chicken.

| Whole Turkey | Total Cooking Time in Hours |
|---|---|
| 10 lb (4.5 kg) | 3 to 3½ |
| 15 lb (6.75 kg) | 4 to 4½ |
| 20 lb (9 kg) | about 6 |

| Whole Chicken | |
|---|---|
| 6 lb (3 kg) | 2¼ to 2¾ |

# LIGHT CRANBERRY SAUCE

Tradition says it's not roast turkey or chicken without cranberry sauce. We make this fast and easy "light" version with a very small amount of sugar plus sweetener.

**Prep** · 5 minutes
**Cook** · about 10 minutes
**Refrigerate** · up to 1 week
**Yield** · 2 cups (500 mL)

| | | |
|---|---|---|
| 1 | pkg (340 g) fresh or frozen cranberries (3 ½ cups/875 mL) | 1 |
| 1 cup | water | 250 mL |
| ¾ cup | granular low-calorie sweetener with sucralose | 175 mL |
| 1 tbsp | granulated sugar | 15 mL |

**Each Serving** · 2 tbsp (25 mL)
Extra

In saucepan over medium heat, combine cranberries, water, sweetener and sugar; bring to a boil. Reduce heat to low and cook, uncovered, for 10 minutes or until cranberries have popped and mixture is thickened. Cool slightly.
Cover and refrigerate for up to 1 week.

**Carbohydrate** 5 g
   Fibre 1 g
**Protein** 0 g
**Fat** 0 g
**Sodium** 1 mg
**Calories** 18

◉ *Fresh cranberries store well—for one month in the refrigerator and one year in the freezer. Freeze them unwashed in their bags, then wash just the amount you need before using.*

# LIGHT TURKEY GRAVY

The most flavourful low-fat gravy is made from the poultry pan drippings with all visible fat removed.

| | | |
|---|---|---|
| | pan juices | |
| | water or vegetable liquid | |
| 2 tbsp | cornstarch | 25 mL |
| | salt and freshly ground pepper | |

Pour pan juices through a sieve into 2-cup (500 mL) glass measuring cup. Skim fat with spoon or bulb baster, or drop ice cubes into the strained pan juices to chill fat layer, then remove hardened fat with ice.

Add enough water or vegetable liquid to pan juices to measure 1½ cups (375 mL). Return to roasting pan and bring to a boil.

Mix cornstarch with 2 tbsp (25 mL) cold water; gradually add to boiling liquid. Cook, stirring, for 5 minutes or until smooth and thickened. Season with salt and pepper to taste.

## VARIATION

*Light Beef Gravy:* Prepare as above recipe using beef pan juices instead.

**Special Occasion Menu 3**

..........................................

**Prep** • 10 minutes
**Cook** • about 8 minutes
**Yield** • 6 servings,
       1½ cups (300 mL)

..........................................

**Each Serving** • ¼ cup (50 mL)
Extra

..........................................

**Carbohydrate** 3 g
   Fibre 0 g
**Protein** 1 g
**Fat** 0 g
**Sodium** 29 mg
**Calories** 15

## BRAISED RED CABBAGE WITH CRANBERRIES

**Special Occasion Menu 3**

..............................................

**Prep** · 20 minutes
**Cook** · about 30 minutes
**Yield** · 6 servings, 4 cups (1 L)

..............................................

**Each Serving** · ⅔ cup (150 mL)
Carb choice ½

..............................................

**Carbohydrate** 10 g
Fibre 2 g
**Protein** 1 g
**Fat** 1 g
Saturated 0 g
**Sodium** 8 mg
**Calories** 53

The pleasing ruby colour and tart flavour of this unusual vegetable dish is a wonderful match with roast turkey.

| | | |
|---|---|---|
| 1 tsp | olive oil | 5 mL |
| 1 tbsp | brown sugar | 15 mL |
| 3 | large cloves garlic, crushed | 3 |
| 1 cup | fresh or frozen cranberries, divided | 250 mL |
| 3 tbsp | red wine vinegar | 45 mL |
| 5 cups | shredded red cabbage (¾ lb/375 g) (see Tip) | 1.25 L |
| ⅓ cup | dry red wine | 75 mL |
| Pinch | cayenne pepper | Pinch |
| | salt and freshly ground pepper | |

In large saucepan, heat oil, brown sugar and garlic over medium heat for 2 minutes.

Add ½ cup (125 mL) of the cranberries and vinegar; cover and cook for about 5 minutes or until cranberries pop their skins.

Add cabbage, wine and cayenne; reduce heat to low, cover and cook, stirring occasionally, for about 20 minutes or until cabbage is tender.

Stir in remaining cranberries and remove from heat. Cover and let stand for 5 minutes or until cranberries are just warm. Season with salt and pepper to taste. Serve hot or cold.

◉ *A food processor makes short work of shredding the cabbage.*

# Tzatziki

This light and refreshing *oretakia* (Greek for "appetizer") is best made with drained yogurt, often referred to as yogurt cheese. You can adjust the garlic hit to suit your personal taste—more or less.

| | | |
|---|---|---|
| 1 | small seedless cucumber, unpeeled, grated (about 2 cups/500 mL) | 1 |
| 2 | small cloves garlic, crushed | 2 |
| 2 tsp | each olive oil and white vinegar | 10 mL |
| 1 tbsp | chopped fresh dill | 15 mL |
| ¼ tsp | each salt and freshly ground pepper | 1 mL |
| | *Yogurt Cheese* | |

Drain and squeeze liquid from cucumber. Stir cucumber, garlic, oil, vinegar, dill, salt and pepper into yogurt cheese. Cover and refrigerate until ready to serve. Stir just before serving.

## YOGURT CHEESE:

| | | |
|---|---|---|
| 1 cup | low-fat plain yogurt (see Tip) | 250 mL |

Line sieve with cheesecloth or coffee filter paper set over a bowl. Place yogurt in sieve. Cover and refrigerate for several hours or until reduced to ⅔ cup (150 mL). Gather edges of cheesecloth together and gently squeeze out any remaining whey. Transfer yogurt cheese to a bowl. Set liquid aside (see Tip). Cover and refrigerate yogurt cheese for up to 1 week.

⊕ *When making yogurt cheese, be sure to choose a plain yogurt without gelatin, starch or gums as they will not drain. Whole milk yogurt makes a richer-tasting, smoother and milder-flavoured cheese than lower-fat yogurt. Low- and non-fat yogurt makes a more tart, tangy-tasting cheese.*

⊕ *The remaining whey from the yogurt can be added to soups, as it contains B vitamins and minerals. To store yogurt cheese, cover and refrigerate for up to one week. Yogurt cheese can also be used for spreads, salad dressings, on baked potatoes and for a cream cheese replacement.*

**A GREEK TAVERNA DINNER**

**Special Occasion Menu 4**

**Prep** · 10 minutes
        if yogurt is drained
**Refrigerate** · up to 4 days
**Yield** · 8 servings,
        2 cups (500 mL)

**Each Serving** · ¼ cup (50 mL)
Carb choice                ½

**Carbohydrate** 6 g
  Fibre 0 g
**Protein** 3 g
**Fat** 1 g
  Saturated 0 g
**Sodium** 117 mg
**Calories** 46

**Prep** • 30 minutes
**Cook** • 40 minutes
**Yield** • 6 servings

**Each Serving·** ⅙ of recipe
Carb choices                    1½
Meat & Alternatives choices   3

**Carbohydrate** 26 g
  Fibre 5 g
**Protein** 25 g
**Fat** 9 g
  Saturated 4 g
**Sodium** 461 mg
**Calories** 296

# MOUSSAKA

There are as many versions of moussaka as there are Greek cooks. One of the best-known classic Greek dishes, it remains a favourite everywhere. In traditional recipes, the eggplant is sautéed in olive oil. Our way of baking the eggplant slices reduces fat yet retains the flavours of the traditional recipe.

| | | |
|---|---|---|
| 2 | large eggplants (1 lb/500 g each) | 2 |
| 1 tsp | garlic powder | 5 mL |
| 1 lb | extra-lean ground beef or lamb | 500 g |
| ½ cup | chopped onion | 125 mL |
| 1 | can (7.5 oz/213 mL) tomato sauce | 1 |
| ½ cup | dry red or white wine, or chicken broth | 125 mL |
| ¼ tsp | each ground cloves, cinnamon, nutmeg and freshly ground pepper | 1 mL |
| | **White Sauce** (recipe follows) | |
| ¼ cup | freshly grated Parmesan cheese | 50 mL |

Slice eggplants into ¼-inch (5 mm) thick slices. Spray 2 large rimmed baking sheets with non-stick cooking spray. Place eggplant slices on pans without overlapping. Sprinkle with garlic powder. Bake in 425°F (220°C) oven for 15 minutes or until lightly browned. Set aside.

Meanwhile, in large non-stick skillet over medium heat, cook beef, stirring to break up, for 5 minutes or until no pink remains. Drain fat and discard.

Return meat to skillet; add onion and cook for 5 minutes or until onion is tender. Add tomato sauce, wine, cloves, cinnamon, nutmeg and pepper; simmer, stirring occasionally, for 15 minutes.

Lightly spray 11- x 7-inch (2 L) baking dish with non-stick cooking spray. Arrange half of the eggplant in overlapping slices in bottom of dish. Top with half of the meat mixture. Spread with half of the **White Sauce**. Repeat layers; sprinkle with Parmesan cheese.

Cover and bake in 350°F (180°C) oven for 30 minutes; remove cover and cook for 10 minutes longer or until thoroughly heated.

## White Sauce:

| | | |
|---|---|---|
| 1 | can (385 mL) low-fat evaporated milk | 1 |
| ½ cup | chicken broth | 125 mL |
| ¼ cup | all-purpose flour | 50 mL |
| Pinch | white pepper | Pinch |

In saucepan over medium heat, whisk together milk, broth, flour and pepper; cook, stirring frequently, for 10 minutes or until smooth and thickened.

··································

**Prep** · 10 minutes
**Yield** · 6 servings

··································

**Each Serving** · ⅙ of recipe

Fats choice                           1

··································

**Carbohydrate** 2 g
   Fibre 1 g
**Protein** 1 g
**Fat** 5 g
   Saturated 1 g
**Sodium** 44 mg

**Calories** 50

# MAROULI SALATA

*Salata* is the Greek word for "salad," and *marouli* means "romaine lettuce." Slicing the romaine lettuce as thinly as possible gives this very traditional salad its unique character. A serving is an excellent source of folic acid.

| | | |
|---|---|---|
| 1 | medium head romaine lettuce, trimmed and washed | 1 |
| 3 | green onions, sliced | 3 |
| 2 tbsp | chopped fresh dill | 25 mL |
| 2 tbsp | each olive oil and fresh lemon juice | 25 mL |
| Pinch | each salt and freshly ground pepper | Pinch |

Spin lettuce to dry. Roll 4 or 5 leaves tightly together; thinly slice with sharp knife. Repeat with remaining leaves until you have about 8 cups (2 L).

In large salad bowl, combine lettuce, onions and dill. Just before serving, pour oil and lemon juice over greens and toss well. Sprinkle with salt and pepper.

# APPENDICES

# 1 · BEYOND THE BASICS: MEAL PLANNING FOR HEALTHY EATING

*Beyond the Basics: Meal Planning for Healthy Eating, Diabetes Prevention and Management* (published by the Canadian Diabetes Association, 2006) has replaced the earlier *Good Health Eating Guide* system of meal planning used by many people with diabetes. As before, it is based on *Canada's Food Guide,* with some changes to meet the needs of people with diabetes. The goal of *Beyond the Basics* is to make it easy for you to include a variety of foods in meals and, at the same time, keep carbohydrate intake consistent, thus promoting good diabetes management.

Foods are divided into two categories, based on whether they contain carbohydrate or not. The food groups that contain carbohydrate and raise blood glucose are GRAINS & STARCHES, FRUITS, MILK & ALTERNATIVES and OTHER CHOICES. Any choice from any of these groups contains 15 grams of available carbohydrate and is called a Carbohydrate Choice or Carb Choice. Groups containing little or no carbohydrate are the VEGETABLES, MEAT & ALTERNATIVES, FATS and EXTRAS groups.

Within each of these eight groups, foods are divided into two categories: foods to "choose more often" and foods to "choose less often." Although all foods may be enjoyed in moderation, the foods in the first group are considered healthier since they are higher in fibre, higher in vitamins and minerals, or lower in fat.

A serving of a food is described as a "Choice," since it is your choice. By following a meal plan and choosing a variety of foods from each group, you're sure to get all the nutrients you need, as well as having a consistent amount of carbohydrate at each meal.

## CARBOHYDRATE-CONTAINING FOODS

### Grains & Starches
This group includes all types of breads and cereals, as well as rice, corn, pasta and potatoes. These foods contain the carbohydrate you need for energy and are also the ones that have the greatest impact on blood glucose. Most are low in fat and often high in fibre, especially whole grains, but the amount you eat at any one meal matters. The

amount of any food described as 1 GRAINS & STARCHES CHOICE (or 1 CARB CHOICE) contains 15 grams of available carbohydrate (total carbohydrate minus fibre).

**Breads and rolls:** You can choose any bread you like—they all fit into your meal plan. The trick is to know how much. One ounce (or 30 grams) of any fresh bread item is equal to 1 CARB CHOICE. Packaged breads, bagels, pita breads and so on clearly state the weight of one slice or one piece on the label. If your favourite bread or roll comes unpackaged, a small kitchen scale makes it easy to determine the weight (see pages 23–24).

**Crackers and breadsticks:** There are many healthy high-fibre, whole grain, low-fat, lower-salt varieties out there. Read labels. Look to see how many crackers the label says are in a serving, then compare the fat and fibre content (and sodium, if you're watching your salt intake). Because Melba toasts, breadsticks and crackers contain less moisture than breads, 20 grams of crackers is usually equal to 1 CARB CHOICE.

**Breakfast cereals:** When reading Nutrition Facts on labels, subtract fibre from total carbohydrate and get the actual amount of available carbohydrate. To make this simpler, we've included a list of popular ready-to-eat breakfast cereals in Appendix II (page 187), showing the amount of each that's equal to 1 CARB CHOICE.

**Rice, pasta and legumes:** A good rule of thumb is that ½ cup (125 mL) cooked pasta or ⅓ cup (75 mL) cooked rice is equal to 1 GRAINS & STARCHES or 1 CARB CHOICE. Use a ½-cup (125 mL) or ⅓-cup (75 mL) measure when serving these foods. With meat alternatives such as dried peas, beans or lentils, 1 cup (250 mL) cooked would count as 1 CARB CHOICE plus 1 MEAT & ALTERNATIVES CHOICE. See the *Beyond the Basics* resource for more detail.

**Starchy vegetables:** Potatoes and corn are classed as GRAINS & STARCHES (even though we may think of them as vegetables), and ½ cup (125 mL) of either one is 1 CARB CHOICE.

**Fruits**

We have used a wide variety of fruits in our menus and recipes. Each choice from this group contains 15 grams available carbohydrate and counts as 1 FRUITS CHOICE (or 1 CARB CHOICE). This could describe an orange or a small apple, half a medium mango or 2 cups (500 mL) strawberries. You'll find that the more moisture and fibre a fruit contains, the larger the serving. Each of these choices contains a variety of vitamins and minerals, as well as fibre.

For your convenience, we have included a list of the fruits we've used in menus, so if you don't have the one named, you can replace it with another and still get the same amount of carbohydrate (Appendix III, page 188).

**Milk & Alternatives**

*Milk and yogurt:* Low-fat or non-fat milk and yogurt are excellent sources of calcium and protein and good sources of riboflavin, phosphorus and vitamin B12. Our menus and recipes call for low-fat milk, which could be non-fat skim or 1%; we leave the choice up to you. The amount of milk sugar is the same; the only difference is in fat and calories. A cup (250 mL) of non-fat skim has 80 calories; the same amount of 1% has 100 calories. Both contain 8 grams of protein and 15 grams of carbohydrate. And both would be called 1 MILK & ALTERNATIVES or 1 CARB CHOICE. You may prefer to do as we do—drink skim and use it in cooking, and have 1% on hand to use on cereal and in tea or coffee.

*Lactose intolerance:* Some people have difficulty digesting the lactose (milk sugar) in regular milk because they lack the necessary digestive enzyme. However, low-fat lactose-reduced milk is available in the dairy section of most supermarkets. It has the same nutrients and the same amount of carbohydrate and protein as regular milk, so 1 cup (250 mL) still counts as 1 MILK & ALTERNATIVES or 1 CARB CHOICE.

*Soy beverage:* Some prefer a milk made from soybeans, and if unsweetened and enriched with calcium, 1 cup (250 mL) soy beverage counts as 1 MILK & ALTERNATIVES or 1 CARB CHOICE. If sweetened or fruit flavoured, the serving would be ½ cup (125 mL). Read labels for fat and sugar content.

***Cheese:*** Usually cheese is included in discussions of milk products. However, since cheese lacks the carbohydrate of milk but contains protein and fat, it is found in the MEAT & ALTERNATIVES group.

## Other Choices

This group includes a wide variety of snacks and sweet foods that add variety but tend to lack nutrients and are high in calories. However, used occasionally and in moderation, they will not upset diabetes control. The key is *how much* and *when*. Sugars should be spread throughout the day as part of slowly digested meals. The trick is to work it into a meal, not just add it on. Each choice from the OTHER CHOICES group contains 15 grams carbohydrate, so it could take the place of a Carb Choice in a regular meal or snack. We have included cookies and ice cream on occasion as part of our planned menus. For more details, see the *Beyond the Basics* resource.

## FOODS THAT CONTAIN LITTLE OR NO CARBOHYDRATE

### Vegetables

The majority of vegetables are low in carbohydrate, calories and fat. They are also an excellent source of vitamins, minerals and fibre. *Beyond the Basics* recommends eating these vegetables freely. A few of the sweeter vegetables count as a Carb Choice only when more than one cup (250 mL) is eaten at a meal (see pages 80–84 for lots more about vegetables).

### Meat & Alternatives

This group contains meat, poultry, fish, eggs and cheese. 1 CHOICE is equal to 1 ounce or 30 grams of cooked meat. Each choice contains about 7 grams of protein and 3 grams of fat, although some choices may have more (or less) fat than this.

***Meat*** is a good source of protein but can contain too much saturated fat for heart health. Choose smaller portions, leaner cuts and trim well. Since most of the fat in poultry is in or under the skin, remove either before or after cooking.

***Fish and shellfish*** are also excellent sources of protein and are relatively low in calories and fat, especially saturated fat. Eating even one or two servings of fish a week is associated with a lower risk of heart disease. And the higher the fat content of the fish, the greater the "heart-healthy" benefits since fatty fish have the most omega-3 fatty acids (see Appendix IV, page 191). Fish with a moderate to high fat content include bass, catfish, halibut, herring, mackerel, ocean perch, orange roughy, rainbow trout, salmon, sardines and smelt. Whitefish, cod, haddock and shellfish are very low in total fat.

*Eggs:* Since they are an inexpensive source of quality protein as well as vitamins B12 and E, eggs are listed as "choose more often." Eggs have been given an undeserved bad reputation as being high in fat and high in cholesterol. First of all, one egg yolk contains only 2 grams of saturated fat and 5 grams total fat. And second, it is the saturated and trans fats in food that are the main villain when it comes to increasing risk of heart disease, not the cholesterol in food. Egg whites contain no fat or cholesterol; two whites can replace one egg in many recipes.

*Cheese:* Like all dairy products, cheese is high in protein and calcium. It also tends to be high in saturated fat and sodium. However, some types of cheese are already low or moderate in fat (part-skim mozzarella, ricotta, low-fat cottage cheese, light cheeses). All cheese is marked with its fat content, so read labels and choose those with less fat (17% or less) as often as possible. Whenever we use cheese in a menu or recipe, we specify the weight in grams. Usually 30 grams of cheese equals 1 MEAT & ALTERNATIVES CHOICE.

*Meat alternatives:* Dried beans, peas and lentils are also excellent sources of protein as well as carbohydrate.

### Fats

Fats have little or no carbohydrate and therefore little effect on blood glucose. They are found in butter, margarine, oils, nuts and seeds, as well as in baked products and snack foods. We do need some fat in our diet to store energy, provide insulation and build hormones, but it is easy to go overboard. Choosing the right type and amount of dietary fat is important for people with diabetes, as some fats are more heart healthy than others (see Appendix IV, pages 189–190).

Since fat has twice the calories of carbohydrate or protein, how much fat you eat is an important factor in weight control. Each FATS

CHOICE (such as 1 tsp/5 mL margarine or butter or oil) contains 5 grams fat and has 45 calories. This group also contains foods such as nuts and seeds that are high in hidden fat. In a healthy diet, fats and oils should be used sparingly.

*Margarine:* A healthy margarine is soft, non-hydrogenated, trans fat–free, low in saturated fat, and made from vegetable oils rich in monounsaturated fat (such as canola or olive oil). Light or diet margarine has been diluted with water to reduce calories, so it's not recommended for cooking or baking.

*Butter:* Butter contains the same amount of calories and fat as margarine, so we give it as an alternative in our menus. If your diet is already low in fat, a little butter now and then won't hurt you.

*Vegetable oils:* Olive, canola and corn oils are all heart-healthy choices. The highest in monounsaturated oils are canola and olive (see page 13), so choose those often.

## EXTRAS

Last but not least are the things that add flavour to food. The term EXTRAS means that one serving of any item in this group contains less than 5 grams carbohydrate and no more than 20 calories per serving. This group includes "Extras" that can be used without limit: beverages such as herbal teas, coffee, mineral water and diet pop; and seasonings and flavours such as herbs and spices, lemon and lime juice, and non-nutritive sweeteners (see below).

Also in this group are condiments that contain more carbohydrate and are "extra" in *measured amounts* only. Examples are ketchup, reduced sugar fruit spreads (see pages 24–25), barbecue sauce and so on. See the *Beyond the Basics* resource for more information.

### Non-nutritive sweeteners

There are different kinds and forms of sweeteners with different tastes and different uses. Some come in packets as tabletop sweeteners, others in tablets, others as liquids. Health Canada has approved all the sweeteners listed below as safe for all Canadians. However, only Ace-K, aspartame and sucralose are permitted in packaged foods and beverages. Stevia has not been approved by Health Canada as a sweetener.

Generic names are listed first, followed by brand names.

*acesulfame potassium (Ace-K):* added to foods but not available as sweetener

*aspartame (Equal, Nutrasweet, Sweet'N Low):* available in packets, tablets, granulated

*cyclamate (Sucaryl, Sugar Twin, Sweet'N Low):* available in packets, tablets, liquid and granulated

*saccharin (Hermesetas):* available in tablets

*sucralose (Splenda):* available in packets or granulated

We have used a variety of sweeteners in our recipes and menus. Some sweeteners may lose sweetness or develop a bitter taste at high temperatures. However, in all recipes that are cooked or baked, we have used sucralose with excellent results. In recipes where cooking is not required, use the sweetener of your choice.

The *Beyond the Basics* resource contains more about sweeteners, reading labels, dining out, travel, and managing meals when you're feeling sick. It can be ordered at **www.diabetes.ca.**

# II · BREAKFAST CEREALS OF YOUR CHOICE

Most ready-to-eat cold cereals are sweetened, but remember that it is total carbohydrate that counts. *Beyond the Basics* defines the amount of cereal equal to 1 GRAINS & STARCHES CHOICE (or 1 CARB CHOICE) as the amount that contains 15 grams of carbohydrate (not including fibre). The Nutrition Facts panel sometimes describes a serving that is larger than this. To avoid having to do the math, refer to the list below when you want to exchange one cereal in our menus for another. All are healthy choices.

| | |
|---|---|
| ½ cup (125 mL) | All-Bran |
| ½ cup (125 mL) | All-Bran Buds |
| ½ cup (125 mL) | 100% Bran |
| ½ cup (125 mL) | Shreddies |
| ⅓ cup (75 mL) | wheat germ |
| ½ cup (125 mL) | bran flakes |
| ⅔ cup (150 mL) | plain Cheerios |
| ¼ cup (50 mL) | granola (low fat) |
| 3 tbsp (45 mL) | Grape-Nuts |
| ⅓ cup (75 mL) | Mueslix |
| 1½ cups (375 mL) | puffed wheat |
| 1 | shredded wheat biscuit |

# III · FRUITS OF YOUR CHOICE

We have used a wide variety of fruits in our menus. Each choice from this group contains 15 grams carbohydrate and is called 1 FRUITS or 1 CARB CHOICE.

For your convenience, we have included a list of the fruits we've used so that if you don't have the one named in the menu, you can replace it with another and still get the same amount of carbohydrate.

Each of the following is 1 FRUITS CHOICE (or 1 CARB CHOICE).

| | | |
|---|---|---|
| 1 | medium apple | (138 g) |
| ½ cup (125 mL) | applesauce | |
| 4 | apricots | (140 g) |
| 1 | small banana, without peel | (100 g) |
| 1 cup (250 mL) | blueberries | (150 g) |
| 1 cup (250 mL) | cantaloupe | (160 g) |
| 15 | cherries, with pits | (100 g) |
| 2 | clementine oranges | (150 g) |
| 1 | small grapefruit | (240 g) |
| 15 | red or green grapes | (80 g) |
| 1 cup (250 mL) | honeydew melon | (170 g) |
| 2 | medium kiwi fruit | (150 g) |
| ½ cup (125 mL) | mango | (85 g) |
| 1 | medium orange, with rind | (130 g) |
| 1 cup (250 mL) | papaya | (150 g) |
| 1 | large peach | (170 g) |
| 1 | medium pear, with skin and core | (165 g) |
| 2 | slices fresh pineapple | (120 g) |
| 2 | rings canned pineapple in juice | (100 g) |
| 2 | medium plums | (130 g) |
| 2 | stewed prunes in juice | (65 g) |
| 2 cups (500 mL) | raspberries | (245 g) |
| 2 cups (500 mL) | strawberries | (290 g) |
| 1 | wedge watermelon, with rind | (310 g) |
| ½ cup (125 mL) | canned fruit in light syrup or juice | |
| 1 cup (250 mL) | tomato juice | |
| ½ cup (125 mL) | orange, grapefruit or cranberry juice | |

From *Beyond the Basics*, published by the Canadian Diabetes Association (2006)

# IV · THE ABCs OF NUTRITION AND DIABETES

**A1C (glycosolated hemoglobin)** is a measure of your average blood glucose level over the past two to three months. The goal is an A1C of less than 7%.

**Antioxidants** are substances in food that repair cell damage and protect the body against disease. Vitamins A, C and E act as antioxidants.

**Beta-carotene** comes from dark green and yellow vegetables and fruits and is converted into vitamin A in the body. It is thought to act as an antioxidant.

**Carbohydrate** provides energy for the body in the form of glucose. It comes mainly from sugar (found naturally in fruits and vegetables or added to food) and starch (found in grains and legumes). Carbohydrate breaks down into glucose during digestion and raises blood glucose.

**Cholesterol** is a waxy substance found naturally in the bloodstream and body cells. It is needed by the body to build cells and certain hormones. Most is manufactured in the liver after eating saturated fat from animal products, as well as trans fats from baked goods and fried foods. Plant foods do not contain cholesterol. Too much cholesterol in the blood is linked to increased risk of heart disease.

**Diabetes** is a lifelong condition in which the body either cannot produce insulin or cannot use the insulin it produces effectively (see *Insulin, type 1* and *type 2 diabetes*).

**Fatty acids** are the building blocks that make up fats and oils. There are four different types of fatty acids: *saturated, monounsaturated, polyunsaturated* and *trans*. All fats in food are combinations of both *saturated* and *unsaturated* fatty acids.

- *Saturated fatty acids* are loaded (or saturated) with all the hydrogen they can carry. Fats containing a lot of saturated fat are usually solid at room temperature. Most come from animal fats, but both palm oil and coconut oil contain saturated fat. A diet high in saturated fat can raise LDL cholesterol levels and increase risk of heart disease or stroke.

- *Unsaturated fatty acids* still have room for more hydrogen and are either monounsaturated or polyunsaturated. Fats containing these fatty acids are usually liquid at room temperature and come from plants and fish.

- *Monounsaturated* fatty acids are highest in olive oil and canola oil.

- *Polyunsaturated* fats, made up of omega-3 and omega-6 fatty acids, are essential to good health. Omega-3 fatty acids are found in fish oils as well as canola and soybean oils. Omega-6 is highest in corn, sunflower and soybean oils.

- *Trans fatty acids* are formed when hydrogen is added to the liquid vegetable oils used in the making of shortening and margarine. This *hydrogenation* makes them harder and more stable. These fats are used in many commercial bakery products and fried foods. They are even more harmful than saturated fats since they not only raise the "bad" LDL cholesterol but also lower the "good" HDL cholesterol that protects against heart disease.

**Fibre** comes in two forms: *soluble* (found in oat bran, barley, legumes and pectin-rich fruit) and *insoluble* (found in wheat bran, whole grains and seeds, and fruit and vegetable skins). Both types of fibre are important (see pages 7–8).

**Glucose** is the simplest form of sugar, found in fruits and vegetables, and is the end result of starch digestion. Glucose circulates in the blood as the body's main source of energy. When too much glucose is present in the blood, as in uncontrolled diabetes, the condition is called *hyperglycemia*.

A **glucose monitor or meter** is a small hand-held electronic device that can estimate one's blood glucose level from a drop of blood placed on a sensor pad. The blood is obtained by pricking one's finger. Glucose monitoring at regular intervals makes improved diabetes control possible.

*Glycemic index (GI)* is a way of measuring how quickly a food is digested. This is influenced by many factors, such as amount of fibre and degree of processing. It compares the rise in blood glucose that occurs after different carbohydrate-containing foods are eaten with the rise in blood glucose that occurs when the same person eats the same amount of carbohydrate as white bread only. Slowly digested foods have a low glycemic index, while more rapidly digested foods have a higher glycemic index, closer to that of white bread. Foods with a low GI can help you manage your diabetes.

*Glycogen* is a form of starchy carbohydrate stored in our muscles and liver. Glycogen serves as a reserve of glucose energy that can be used during periods of fasting or increased exercise.

*Hypoglycemia* occurs when blood glucose levels are lower than usual, usually below 3.5 millimoles per litre of blood. Normal blood glucose values are between 4 and 6 mmol/L. Usually only those using insulin or certain diabetes pills are at risk. Symptoms of hypoglycemia may include sweating, trembling, hunger, dizziness, change of mood, confusion, blurred vision and nausea.

*Insulin* is a hormone produced by the beta cells of the pancreas in response to a rise in blood glucose. Insulin is the "key" that allows glucose to enter your body cells.

*Monounsaturated fatty acids* (see *Fatty acids*).

*Omega-3 fatty acids* are a type of polyunsaturated fatty acid found in cold-water fatty fish. They not only help lower blood triglyceride but also make blood platelets less "sticky" or likely to clot, thus reducing the risk of heart attack and stroke (see *Fatty acids*).

*Polyunsaturated fatty acids* (see *Fatty acids*).

*Protein*, the basic material of life, exists in many forms and is not intended to be an energy source (although an excess may end up as excess calories). Muscles, organs, antibodies, some hormones and all enzymes are mostly protein. Proteins consist of chains of 22 assorted amino acids in different combinations. Some of these amino acids (the 10 *essential* ones) can only be obtained from food. The rest can be manufactured in the body (so are *non-essential* in our diet).

**Proteinuria** is the abnormal loss of protein into the urine and is considered a measure of kidney function.

**Saturated fatty acids** (see *Fatty acids*).

**Sodium** is most familiar as part of sodium chloride, which we know as table salt. However, many processed foods may have other kinds of sodium added to preserve or flavour them, such as sodium citrate or nitrite. Baked goods often contain sodium bicarbonate as baking soda or baking powder. People with high blood pressure or hypertension find it easier to control their blood pressure if they restrict their salt and sodium intake.

**Sorbitol** is an alcohol form of sugar often used to sweeten dietetic candies and chocolate. It is more slowly digested than sugar but can end up as glucose in the blood. These foods are often high in fat and calories as well. Too much at one time can cause cramping and diarrhea.

**Trans fatty acids** (see *Fatty acids*).

**Triglyceride** is a kind of fat found in the blood, often measured at the same time as cholesterol. Too much (hypertriglyceridemia) is also considered a risk factor for heart disease, especially in diabetes.

**Type 1 diabetes** is the less common form of diabetes, usually but not always diagnosed before age 40. The pancreas either does not produce insulin or produces very, very little, making a person with type 1 diabetes dependent on daily injections of insulin for life.

**Type 2 diabetes** is the type affecting 90 per cent of those with diabetes. In this type, the pancreas can still make insulin, but the body doesn't use the insulin effectively. *Type* 2 diabetes can sometimes be treated with diet and physical activity alone, or in combination with diabetes pills and/or insulin injections.

# V · FOOD AND COOKING GLOSSARY

**Balsamic vinegar:** A dark, rich-flavoured, slightly sweet vinegar from Italy. Widely available in grocery stores.

**Blanch:** To plunge food (usually vegetables and fruit) into boiling water briefly, then into cold water to stop the cooking process.

**Braise:** A cooking method by which food (usually meat or vegetables) is first browned in a non-stick or heavy pan, then cooked, tightly covered, in a small amount of liquid at low heat for a lengthy period of time, thus tenderizing the foods.

**Bran:** The outer layer of grains (including bran from wheat and oats) that is removed during milling. Wheat and oat bran are both excellent sources of fibre. They are found in cereals and baked goods and can be purchased at health-food stores and supermarkets.

**Broil:** Food, generally meat, is cooked directly under the electric or gas heat source in an oven, or on a barbecue grill, either directly over charcoal or another heat source. Any fat in the meat drains away during cooking.

**Cruciferous vegetables:** This is the scientific name for a group of vegetables that may provide protection against certain cancers. Included in this group are broccoli, Brussels sprouts, cabbage, and cauliflower.

**Flaxseed:** These tiny seeds contain several essential nutrients, including calcium, iron, phosphorus and vitamin E, and are a source of omega-3 fatty acids. Flaxseed has a mild, nutty flavour. Since it has a high fat content, it is best stored in the refrigerator, where it will keep for up to six months (see Tip 2 on page 35 for ground flax).

**Hydroponics:** The science of growing plants in a liquid nutrient solution rather than soil, thus producing increased yields.

**Parboil:** To partially cook food by boiling it briefly in water.

**Rye flakes:** These resemble rolled oats and are made by the same process. They can be used in much the same way as oats.

**Sauté:** To cook food quickly in a small amount of oil or broth in a skillet over direct heat, thus creating intensely flavoured meats and sauces.

**Steaming:** A method of cooking vegetables, whereby they are placed in a steamer basket over a small amount of boiling water and covered, then cooked for a short time until tender-crisp. It is the preferred stove-top method for retaining flavour, shape, texture, and vitamin and mineral content.

**Stir-frying:** Food is cooked at a very high heat for a very short time. This cooking technique requires a minimum amount of fat and results in fresh-tasting, tender-crisp food.

**Tortillas:** Mexico's everyday bread, the tortilla resembles a flat pancake and can be made from corn or wheat flour. Both corn and wheat tortillas are sold pre-packaged in most supermarkets.

**Wheat flakes:** These are whole wheat berries that have been flattened between rollers and resemble rolled oats. They can be used in much the same way as rolled oats and rye flakes.

**Yogurt cheese:** Made by draining yogurt (see page 175 for procedure), it has a thick, creamy texture and is a substitute for higher-fat dairy products, such as sour cream and cream cheese, in spreads and dips.

## WHERE DO WE USE HERBS?

*Basil:* meats, poultry, eggs and cheese, vegetables and soups, stews and sauces

*Dill:* fish, eggs and cheese, vegetables, salad dressings and soups, stews and sauces

*Mint:* vegetables, salads and dressings, fruit, meats (especially lamb)

*Oregano:* fish, meats, poultry, vegetables, salad dressing, soups, stews and sauces

*Parsley:* fish, meats, poultry, eggs and cheese, vegetables, salad dressings, soups, stews and sauces

*Rosemary:* fish, meats, poultry, vegetables, salad dressings

*Sage:* meats, poultry, eggs and cheese

*Tarragon:* fish, poultry, eggs and cheese, vegetables, salad dressing, soups, stews and sauces

*Thyme:* fish, meats, eggs and cheese, vegetables, poultry, soups, stews and sauces

## WHERE DO WE USE SPICES?

*Allspice:* soups, stews and sauces, fish, meats, poultry, pastry, cookies and desserts

*Cinnamon:* soups, stews and sauces, meats, vegetables, pastry, cookies and desserts

*Cloves:* soups, stews and sauces, meats, poultry, pastry, cookies and desserts

*Cumin:* fish, meats, poultry, eggs and cheese

*Ginger:* soups, stews and sauces, fish, meats, poultry, vegetables, salad dressing, pastry, cookies and desserts

*Nutmeg:* vegetables, soups, stews and sauces, pastry, cookies and desserts

*Pepper:* soups, stews and sauces, fish, meats, poultry, eggs and cheese, vegetables, salad dressings

### FRESH VS DRIED

Nothing quite beats using fresh herbs, and today they are widely available in stores. Grow your favourites in the garden or keep a pot in the house on the windowsill. If using dried herbs, be sure they are stored in tightly closed containers in a dark cupboard away from heat, light and moisture. Replace them once a year.

# VII · NUTRIENT ANALYSIS OF RECIPES AND MENUS

Analysis of the recipes was based on Imperial measures and weights (except for foods packaged and labelled in metric amounts) and on the specified number of servings.

Actual cooked weights were used where applicable.

Whenever appropriate, menus were analyzed using portion sizes specified in *Beyond the Basics: Meal Planning for Healthy Eating, Diabetes Prevention and Management,* published by the Canadian Diabetes Association (2006).

Lower-fat dairy products were used in all recipes and menus. Low-fat milk used in recipes as ingredients and in menus as beverages was analyzed as skim unless otherwise indicated.

All menus can be assumed to include 2 tbsp (25 mL) 1% milk for tea or coffee whenever milk is not included as a beverage.

Food Choice Values were assigned according to Canadian Diabetes Association (CDA) guidelines (2006), with carbohydrate based on total carbohydrate minus dietary fibre. Total carbohydrate and dietary fibre are stated separately in recipe nutrition information, and nutrient values are rounded to the nearest whole number.

Menus were planned to reflect current CDA nutritional guidelines: carbohydrate provides 50% of total energy; fat provides 30% or less, with 10% or less from saturated fat and with monounsaturated fats and oils used wherever possible.

Recipes were tested and analyzed using canola or olive oils and soft non-hydrogenated margarines unless otherwise specified.

Optional ingredients were not included in analysis.

Menu items and recipe ingredients were chosen for their fibre content and glycemic effect whenever possible.

Menus and recipes were planned in accordance with *Canada's Guidelines for Healthy Eating* (2006), with an emphasis on variety, inclusion of whole grains as cereals, breads and other grain products, generous use of vegetables and fruit, and the use of leaner meats and food prepared with little or no fat.

Food Choice Values were determined using the values below:

| Food Group | Carbohydrate (g) | Protein (g) | Fat (g) | Calories |
|---|---|---|---|---|
| Grains & Starches | 15 | 3 | | 70 |
| Fruits | 15 | 1 | | 65 |
| Milk & Alternatives | 15 | 8 | variable | 90 |
| Other Choices | 15 | variable | variable | variable |
| Meat & Alternatives | 0 | 7 | 3 to 5 | 55 to 75 |
| Fats | 0 | 0 | 5 | 45 |
| Extras | fewer than 5 | | | fewer than 20 |

# ACKNOWLEDGEMENTS

With the completion of this revised edition of *Choice Menus*, we wish to recognize the support and guidance many people have given us. We offer our sincere thanks and appreciation to:

A very helpful team at Collins Canada, a division of HarperCollins Publishers Ltd: Brad Wilson, senior editor; Lloyd Kelly, vice president; designer Sharon Kish; managing editor Noelle Zitzer; and freelance copy editor Julia Armstrong.

The staff at the Canadian Diabetes Association: Donna Lillie, Vice-President, Research and Professional Education, for writing the foreword, and Sharon Zeiler, Senior Manager, Nutrition Initiatives and Strategies, for her counsel and guidance.

The dietitians and diabetes educators who volunteered to review the manuscript ensuring its accuracy: Beverley Harris, PDT, CDE; Linda Mailhot-Hall, RD, CDE; Rebecca Horsman, RD; Michelle Knezic, RD, CDE; Shari Segal, PDT, CDE; Wendy Levin, RD, CDE; and Sharon Zeiler, RD.

Marian Hebb for legal counsel; and Judy Thomson and John Howard for their editing skills.

Photographer Hal Roth and assistant Paolo Christante for making all the pictures so representative of the recipes in the book, and to food stylist Julie Zambonelli and prop stylist Maggie Jones, who made each dish look so enticing.

Graduates of TRIDEC (Tri-Hospital Diabetes Education Centre), Women's College Hospital, whose requests for "a month of menus" led to the writing of the first *Choice Menus*.

We gratefully acknowledge our families' support and critiques.

Finally, we're thankful for the happy coincidence that found the two of us in the same class at the University of Western Ontario, which led to a lifelong friendship and this edition of *Choice Menus*.

# RECIPE INDEX

# DIABETES AND NUTRITION INDEX